DIMENSIONS OF EVIL

"Terry Cooper has written an incisive study of the four-letter word we rarely use in the field of psychotherapy, psychology, counseling—*evil*. He has done it with rare depth of analysis of the darker side of human experience, wide reference to other thinkers, writers, and researchers, and keen insight into the malignant destructiveness we humans are capable of practicing against each other. He is descriptive where others cannot resist becoming prescriptive, masterful in offering analysis where it is tempting to moralize, and then surprisingly prophetic in pointing incisively toward the heart of the issue."

David W. Augsburger
Professor of Pastoral Care and Counseling
Fuller Theological Seminary

"Terry Cooper has gifted this century with a profound analysis of evil, rooted in the contributions of Darwin, Freud, and their scientific successors in the last century. Examining evil in its natural, social, and personal origins, he sympathetically reads liberation and feminist critics, but he gives the last constructive word to Reinhold Niebuhr supplemented by the University of Chicago thinkers: Paul Tillich, David Tracy, Paul Ricoeur, and Langdon Gilkey. The volume is in itself a significant contribution to the theoretical development of the method of correlation and is highly recommended for personal reading, but especiall·

Ronald H. Sto
John Witherspoon Professor o
Pittsburgh Theological

DIMENSIONS OF EVIL

CONTEMPORARY PERSPECTIVES

TERRY D. COOPER

FORTRESS PRESS · MINNEAPOLIS

For Bob, Dan, David, Marty, James, Rick, Hazel, and Mike

Excellent friends and conversation partners

DIMENSIONS OF EVIL
Contemporary Perspectives

Copyright © 2007 Fortress Press, an imprint of Augsburg Fortress. All rights reserved. Except for brief quotations in critical articles or reviews, no part of this book may be reproduced in any manner without prior written permission from the publisher. Visit http://www.augsburgfortress.org/copyrights/contact. asp or write to Permissions, Augsburg Fortress, Box 1209, Minneapolis, MN 55440.

Cover and text design: Danielle Carnito

Library of Congress Cataloging-in-Publication Data
Dimensions of evil : contemporary perspectives / Terry D. Cooper.
        p. cm.
Includes bibliographical references and index.
ISBN 978-0-8006-6217-2 (alk. paper)
1. Good and evil. 2. Human behavior. I. Cooper, Terry D.
BJ1406.D495 2007
170—dc22
            2007017017

The paper used in this publication meets the minimum requirements of American National Standard for Information Sciences—Permanence of Paper for Printed Library Materials, ANSI Z329.48-1984.

Manufactured in the U.S.A.

11 10 09 08 07 1 2 3 4 5 6 7 8 9 10

CONTENTS

INTRODUCTION

Writing a book on evil is an overwhelming task that can easily push an author into feelings of embarrassing grandiosity. On several occasions, I've been assaulted by questions such as, "Who do you think you are to write a book on one of the most perplexing, all-encompassing, mysterious, multidisciplinary topics imaginable?" A sheepish silence from me has been prevented only by a major qualifier: I'm not trying to write a definitive book on the entire problem of evil. I doubt that such a book is possible in today's world. Consulting one resource often means denying another. If I investigated everything that has been said about evil and human destruction, even in the past few decades, I would never put pen to paper. There is always a new angle, a slightly different perspective, a creative nuance of an old theme. There are thousands of ways to approach this topic. I make no pretensions whatsoever to write an all-inclusive tome on evil. Besides, as my friend and mentor Don Browning likes to say, the point is not to provide a final, definitive answer but to further the conversation.

I do, however, attempt to bring together in one volume a lively interaction of multiple perspectives. We will examine perspectives from evolutionary biology, evolutionary psychology, philosophical and systematic theology, ethics, psychology, psychoanalysis, social theory, feminist theory, liberation theology, and other sources. We will deal with pivotal thinkers such as Charles Darwin, Richard Dawkins, John Haught, Langdon Gilkey, Rosemary Radford Ruether, E. O. Wilson, David Buss, Stephen Jay Gould, Sigmund Freud, Erich Fromm, Ernest Becker, Aaron Beck, Carl Jung, Stanley Milgram, Philip Zimbardo, Roy Baumeister, Reinhold Niebuhr, Paul Tillich, Judith Plaskow, Marjorie Suchocki, Ted Peters, Phil Hefner, and a host of others. We will investigate the problem of destructiveness in three overlapping areas of life: the natural realm, the psychological realm, and the social or systemic realm. We will attempt to see the issue of evil from all three dimensions while refusing to collapse one dimension into another. I am deeply suspicious of reductionistic views of evil. For instance, in a previous generation, we witnessed a psychological reduction of what was also social and systemic evil. And today, as I shall argue, we are often seeing psychological or personal destructiveness reduced to sociopolitical sources. If an earlier generation became excessively preoccupied with an individual "self" disconnected from its social context, we are currently in danger of losing the self in the system. While social ills are very real, they do not provide a full account of the intrapsychic struggles we have to face.

Also, the destructiveness in nature must be taken with deep theological seriousness. While some may hesitate to use the word *evil* to describe natural processes, there is little doubt that nature is often bloody, relentless, and destructive. For religious believers, of course, such destructiveness built into nature raises immediate questions about the ultimate design of things, and therefore calls into question a God who is both loving and powerful. Put simply, who would create a world in which the raw ability to survive seems to be the final trump card? Why must the world be set up to "eat or be eaten"? Nature often seems quite void of compassion.

As one might guess, I make an intimate connection between evil and destructiveness. Scott Peck has described evil as "that force, residing inside or outside human beings, that seeks to kill life or liveliness."[1] For the purposes of this book I accept Peck's general definition and understand evil as *that which destroys the flourishing of life*. I am quite aware that definitions of "evil," as well as whether or not the word *evil* should even be employed in the social sciences, could be debated forever. The point, however, is that evil *is* being discussed by both natural and social scientists. Theology and philosophy no longer have a monopoly on the "problem of evil." For example, social psychologist Arthur G. Miller[2] has compiled a group of seventeen essays by some of the world's leading social psychologists who cannot resist commenting on what they call "evil." Some of these individuals have built most of their academic careers on the social scientific study of evil.

The word *evil*, then, has been frequently secularized for everyday use among nonreligious perspectives. While religious and theological beliefs must wrestle with the issue of how God and evil can coexist (theodicy), nontheistic perspectives must also account for how human beings can do such dastardly things to each other (anthropodicy). Put another way, both theists and nontheists share the burden of explaining why there is so much destructiveness in the world. And the question quickly becomes whether or not a strictly secular understanding can do justice to the full complexity and mystery of this destructiveness. Stated a different way, can we adequately grasp the character of evil on the basis of a naturalistic ontology that denies, from the very beginning, any notion of a transcendent realm, a metanormal dimension to life?

I have chosen to bracket the question concerning the ontological reality of an evil force, presence, or entity that stands outside of individual and social decisions and has been referred to as "Satan." While this is a fascinating issue, and one often debated in contemporary Christian theological circles, other books offer a careful and rich exploration of this issue. While Judaism has understood Satan as an external projection of inward temptation, Christianity has, since its inception, been persuaded that a transhuman source of evil is involved in the world's destructiveness. While this concept does not let humanity off the hook or make us less responsible, it has been a central belief until the Enlightenment. And for the majority of Christians, the idea of Satan as an external, personal presence in the world is very real. Lutheran theologian Carl Braaten put it this way:

> Who would possess the authority to grant us license to remove the Devil from Christian teaching? To rid theology of something so thoroughly anchored in Scripture and the Christian tradition assumes that one can derive Christian truth from some other sources. . . . Any theology that does not take the devil seriously should not itself be taken seriously. . . . The first thing we learn is that the decision for or against the existence of the devil is a decision for or against the integrity of Christianity as such. We simply cannot subtract the Devil, along with demons, angels, principalities, powers, and elemental spirits, without doing violence to the shape of the Christian tradition, our primary sources. . . . Christians ought to be careful—"sober" and "watchful"— about flirting with the assumptions of modern skepticism that call into question belief in the existence and relevance of the Devil, for the same assumptions can go to the jugular of belief in God.[3]

For Braaten, it is not enough that we believe in a generalized notion of evil; instead, we must acknowledge the devil as a personal agent and intelligent force working in the world. If we reduce the notion of Satan to a projection of our own destructive inclinations, then what will keep us from reducing God to a projection of our own goodness?

For Walter Wink, even though evil can never make full sense as a concept, it must be symbolized. "Without a means of symbolization . . . evil cannot come to conscious awareness and thus be consciously resisted. Like an undiagnosed disease it rages through society, and we are helpless to produce a cure. *Evil must be symbolized precisely because it cannot be thought.*"[4] Thus the symbol of "Satan" points toward a very real experience of life that cannot be adequately conceptualized.

Other theologians also believe that the concept of Satan should be understood in a symbolic manner, but should not be confused with an actual ontological entity. For instance, Peter Hodgson believes that the serpent in the Garden story actually represents the self-deceit of the first mythological couple.[5] In other words, the serpent's temptation is really occurring inside the minds of Adam and Eve. Because they could not own full responsibility for their actions, they blamed their decisions on the external snake. This is projection pure and simple. For Hodgson, Satan is a symbol that evil exists before we make our first choice. When we come into this world, there is already a "serpent in the Garden" in that evil is an established reality ready to corrupt us as well. Satan, therefore, is a word that points to this collective evil, but not to a transhuman, ontological reality.

Rosemary Radford Ruether represents another contemporary theologian who understands the concept of Satan as a symbol of collective social evil. She states her thesis well:

> The ancient religious writers of late Judaism and early Christianity were not wrong in suggesting that there is a pervasive "atmosphere" of malevolent influences that dispose the self to choose evil more often than good. But they were wrong in scapegoating women for the advent of these forces or in abstracting evil into demonic powers beyond humanity. Powers and principalities exist as the precondition of evil choices. But these powers and principalities are precisely the heritage of systemic social evil, which conditions our personal choices before we choose and prevents us from fully understanding our own choices and actions. . . . Long before we can even begin to make our own decisions, we are already thoroughly its product.[6]

For Ruether, then, a literal concern with "Satan" represents a detour from the real sources of evil—namely, the social structures that surround us. While it is true that this systemic injustice seems like an "external" power, it is nevertheless a humanly constructed evil and not an ontological being standing apart from us.

Yet another angle on this question is offered by the sociologist of knowledge, Peter Berger, whose occasional theological writing is always interesting. Berger admits that he stammers as he tries to point to the source of evil, yet he refers to it as a flaw in nature. He suggests that it is

. . . a countervailing power that causes both evil and suffering—a
flaw that can only be repaired by God's own suffering, by His
participation in the agonies of his creation. It goes without saying
that all speculation about the origin and nature of this flaw can only
be extremely hesitant (a "stammering" indeed). But two further
implications can be stated: The notion of a power opposing God will
probably have to be personalized, as it was from early on in the figure
of Satan—and one may say that *this* notion has gained credibility in
the context of the more-than-human evil manifested in the Holocaust.
And further, the flaw in history cannot be limited to human history—
for there is the immense pain driving evolutionary process long before
human history began, with entire species of animals suffering and
being swept into oblivion by the inexorable selection of biological
evolution. In other words, the flaw in creation must have a meta-
historical, perhaps even a cosmic dimension—and so, if follows, must
the process of its redemptive repair . . .[7]

It is important to notice Berger's point that the twentieth century, and
particularly the Holocaust, seems to bear witness to an evil that is "more
than human." Indeed, for those individuals who are unable to any longer
make sense out of the old idea of Satan, it may be worthwhile, throughout
this study, to ask the question as to whether the evil we encounter demands
this "more-than-human" explanation. As Berger humorously puts it, we are
all "metaphysically underprivileged"[8] when it comes to a precise account of
these ultimate questions, but it is nevertheless important to ask.

Perhaps the best description of the historic Christian understanding of
Satan is offered by Jeffrey Burton Russell.

The heart of the concept is that a cosmic power exists other than the
good Lord, a power that wills and urges evil for its own sake and hates
good for its own sake, a power that is active throughout the cosmos,
including human affairs. The power is not a principle independent of
God but rather a creature of God. The evil in him proceeds not from
his nature, which was created good, but rather from his free choice of
hatred. God permits him to choose evil and to remain evil because true

moral freedom is necessary to the divine plan: God creates the cosmos for the purpose of increasing moral goodness, but moral goodness entails freedom to do evil. The Devil, whose will is wholly given over to hatred, wishes to distort the cosmos as much as he can; to this end he tries to corrupt and pervert the human race. This is the center of the concept and the crucial judgment must be made upon it.[9]

I agree with Russell that one should make one's judgment about the existence or nonexistence of Satan based on this description because it captures the concept's historic meaning.

No doubt some readers will have a strong belief in the actual *being* of Satan, while others will understand Satan as a symbol of humanly derived destructiveness. My hope is that bracketing the philosophical question of Satan does not detract from my attempt to investigate evil. While Satan has been a prominent part of historical Christianity, I do not believe that a belief in this cosmic force is *necessary* for one to be considered Christian.

THIS BOOK'S DIRECTION

The first two chapters of this book deal with the colossal issue of what so often seems like brutality, destructiveness, and ultimate purposelessness in the natural world. Granted, this state of affairs is not perhaps as unnerving to an atheist as to a theist, but for anyone who wants to believe there is purpose and meaning in the larger scheme of things, it is deeply problematic. So we will explore Darwin's great challenge to traditional views of providence and illustrate how his observations of a cold and cruel universe brought into radical question the notion of a benevolent Creator. We will further examine post-Darwinian theologies of providence, most notably the thought of John Haught and Langdon Gilkey. We will contrast these perspectives with those of atheistic evolutionists such as Richard Dawkins and Daniel Dennett. This chapter will call into question the entire plausibility of a loving Creator in the face of evolutionary destructiveness. Then, in chapter 2, we will investigate the controversial issues surrounding evolutionary psychology and its explanation of human destructiveness. The underlying question is, "How far can we extend Darwin to describe psychological, as well as biological, life?" The question of ethics will be a primary concern of this chapter.

Our next section (chapters 3 and 4) will examine the issue of human destructiveness from a psychological perspective. Chapter 3 will deal exclusively with a psychoanalytic portrait of evil, starting with Freud and then moving to Erich Fromm and Ernest Becker. This psychoanalytic exploration will be followed by a theological critique, particularly as it is found in the works of Paul Tillich and Reinhold Niebuhr. Chapter 4 will then explore a cognitive perspective on evil, and more particularly, the work of Aaron Beck. For Beck, evil can largely be explained as cognitive distortion in the face of threat and anxiety. As our anxiety escalates, we overreact with primal thinking, and hence, engage in destructive behavior. We will then look at the interesting work of Carl Jung, particularly through the perspective of Jungian analyst and expert on evil, John Sanford. And finally, we will survey the work of the important pastoral counselor and theologian, David Augsburger, particularly concerning the issue of hate.

The next section (chapters 5 and 6) turns to social and systemic explanations of evil. In chapter 5, we will look at the important work of social psychologists on the issue of evil. The work of such persons as Stanley Milgram, Philip Zimbardo, and Roy Baumeister will be outlined and analyzed. The fundamental question throughout this chapter will be whether evil can be best explained by a "dispositional" or "situationist" viewpoint. While the vast majority of social psychologists argue for a situationist view, we will explore potential shortcomings in this perspective. Then in the final chapter, we will examine the question of whether individual or social sin should be privileged in a discussion of evil. The theologies of sin in Langdon Gilkey and Reinhold Niebuhr will be brought into contact with feminist and liberation perspectives.

A few years ago, a colleague of mine, Cindy Epperson, and I decided to offer an interdisciplinary course on evil. That course has mushroomed into multiple sessions largely because the issue of evil is perennially fascinating, even though it is disturbing. Destructiveness in the world seems to invite, or sometimes demand, commentary. My hope is that this book, even in a small way, contributes to a deeper understanding of the dynamics of evil and the courage to believe that evil never has the final word.

CHAPTER ONE

EVIL AND EVOLUTION

DARWIN AND THE BRUTALITIES OF NATURE

The universe we observe has precisely the properties we should expect if there is, at bottom, no design, no purpose, no evil and no good, nothing but blind, pitiless indifference.
—*Richard Dawkins*

It is not by exhibiting flawless "design" but by carrying a promise that the cosmos also finds its fundamental "purpose."
—*John F. Haught*

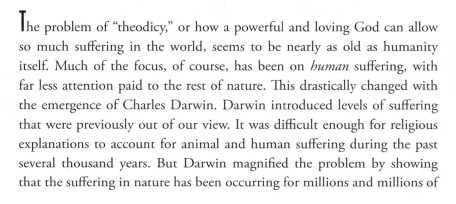

The problem of "theodicy," or how a powerful and loving God can allow so much suffering in the world, seems to be nearly as old as humanity itself. Much of the focus, of course, has been on *human* suffering, with far less attention paid to the rest of nature. This drastically changed with the emergence of Charles Darwin. Darwin introduced levels of suffering that were previously out of our view. It was difficult enough for religious explanations to account for animal and human suffering during the past several thousand years. But Darwin magnified the problem by showing that the suffering in nature has been occurring for millions and millions of years. In fact, suffering seems to be "built into" the very process of nature. If evolution is a story about anything, it is a narrative about how the vast majority of creatures do not survive. Darwin's vision of the world was a bloody one. In fact, it is perhaps well expressed in Darwin expert Stephen Jay Gould's frequent comment that those who find great comfort in nature have no idea what goes on there. Darwin pulled back the curtain and exposed levels of suffering that humanity had not previously understood. If the Holocaust raised the central question about *moral* evil in the twentieth century, natural selection raised the central question about *natural* evil in the nineteenth century.

Countless volumes have been written on Darwin's central ideas, the controversy they raised, and the implications for a science and religion dialogue. Darwin's name still arouses an enormous scientific reverence in some and a disdain in others. Buried in Westminster Abbey beneath Sir Isaac Newton, Darwin is considered one of the most important figures in the history of Western thought. It is obviously far beyond my scope, and exceedingly far beyond my abilities, to provide a comprehensive picture of Darwin's theory and its implications. Besides, biographies of Darwin, overviews of his thought, and theological reflections on his implications for religion (theistic, agnostic, and atheistic) are plentiful. My aim is much more modest in exploring Darwin—namely, to understand some of the ramifications of his theory for our topic of evil, and particularly natural evil.

In this chapter, I hope to (*a*) offer a brief, skeletal overview of how Darwin's findings created such a problem for the traditional concept of divine providence, (*b*) indicate ways in which Darwinism has sent theologians "back to the drawing board" and necessitated a rethinking of the relationship of God and natural evil, (*c*) explore Darwin's own perspective on whether natural evil can be "transcended," (*d*) look briefly at the heated argument as to whether Darwinism demands a purely materialist, and hence atheistic, view of the universe, (*e*) examine Alister McGrath's recent critique of atheistic Darwinist Richard Dawkins, and (*f*) investigate a post-Darwinian view of providence and evil, especially as it is developed in the work of John Haught.

NATURAL HISTORY WITHOUT RELIGION

Biomedical ethicist Harold Vanderpool suggests that the overall impact of Darwin's thought has been connected to its disengagement from any need for religion to account for human and natural history: ". . . the over-arching issue involved the way Darwin divorced knowledge about the nature of man and the biological world from cardinal Western religious convictions. Man and nature were understood apart from the existence of God and his creation and providence. This is the essence of naturalization—the removal of things from a religious or spiritual realm to the realm of the natural and ordinary."[1]

Is religion superfluous to an adequate account of the world? Has it outlived its explanatory usefulness concerning how the world came to be "governed"? Is the world, in fact, not governed at all? Darwin's perspective did not offer a complimentary, scientific layer to the overarching explanation of natural theology. In fact, his view of an evolving universe seemed irreconcilable with the rational, orthodox, natural theology of early nineteenth-century Anglicanism. For Darwin, nature seemed to be without a moral direction or a metaphysical foundation. Was the previous courtship between science and religion, which certainly dominated the first half of the century, now abruptly divorced? Had secular science now replaced, rather than complimented, the revealed truth of religion? Yet surely many scientists were also clergy. Even Darwin himself had studied for the ministry and looked forward to the days of furthering his scientific interests as a country clergyman. Had not William Paley shown that the universe is intricately designed like a watch? Wasn't there, in fact, a divine watchmaker? Wasn't science the handmaiden of theology? Surely if there were inconsistencies between science and Scripture, then a more detailed understanding of science or a clearer reading of Scripture would eliminate all such contradictions. The Bible could, after all, be considered a trustworthy historical and scientific guide as well as a spiritual resource.

Perhaps as much as anything else, the Darwinian world seemed to deliver a deathblow to a human sense of specialness. For Darwin, the long evolutionary history of the natural world—a time that spread over millions of years and not several thousand—was hardly laying out a red carpet for the arrival of humanity. In fact, we are "latecomers." While our arrival may seem like the quintessential moment *to us,* the universe seems rather indifferent as to whether or not we even showed up. Thus Stephen Jay Gould is fond of saying that Darwinism is the great antidote to cosmic arrogance. Or, as Vanderpool puts it, "At once the inherited concepts of creation and design were undermined, and with that man was to experience a fall second only to Lucifer's exclusion from heaven. Only instead of into hell, man was to fall into the gap of a naturalized world."[2]

Enlightened, orthodox Christianity had largely defined the human condition. Darwin himself had at one time believed all thirty-nine articles of the Anglican creed. He had rather masterfully learned Paley and was most familiar with the use of scientific evidences in a Christian apologetic. But all of this was changing at a very fast pace.

THE VOYAGE AND THE EMERGING CONVICTION OF NATURAL SELECTION

When Darwin left England in 1831 to be a part of the voyage of the HMS *Beagle*, his official degree from Cambridge was in theology and the classics. His real interest, however, was in being a naturalist. This was his passionate hobby and primary motivation. The idea of being a minister was largely his father's idea. As a country clergy, however, Darwin would be free to pursue his scientific interests. He was simply not cut out to study medicine; he was too sensitive even to observe, much less perform, surgery. This tender side of Darwin can be found throughout his life. And this is perhaps one of the reasons that the brutalities he found in nature affected him so much.

Aboard the small *Beagle*, Darwin experienced seasickness right away, yet seemed enormously excited when he arrived on land. The mission of the boat was to explore the shoreline of South America. The trip had originally been planned for two years, but it turned into a five-year adventure. The captain of the boat was Robert FitzRoy, with whom Darwin was a social companion and dinner guest throughout the voyage. Stephen Jay Gould makes the interesting, and probably accurate, speculation that if we could have been a "fly on the wall" listening to the dinner conversations between Darwin and FitzRoy, we would have probably heard Fitzroy drone on and on about the glorious design in nature and the fact that nature is clearly a mirror of God. FitzRoy, as an enthusiastic advocate of the argument for design, was likely proclaiming such things precisely when Darwin was beginning to discover the horrendous struggles and cruelties of nature. But more than that, Darwin was becoming increasingly, even if privately, convinced that nature did *not* display the handiwork of a benevolent, loving God. Quite the opposite: the brutal struggles and immense suffering seemed to point more toward a cold and indifferent context of life. Again, given Darwin's sensitive, nonaggressive demeanor, these progressively cruel findings must have been especially difficult. There was nothing even friendly or civil, much less benevolent, about what he observed. It was bad enough discovering what he was finding during the day, but it was perhaps compounded by having to listen to FitzRoy pontificate each evening about the divine order and regularities of nature. According to Gould, FitzRoy's natural design fanaticism may have at least partially irked Darwin into the challenge of proving him wrong.[3]

Darwin returned from the voyage convinced that species change over time and that the traditional understanding that all species were "set" at creation cannot be accurate. Darwin had become convinced of Charles Lyell's notion of "uniformitarianism," which emphasized that the earth is much older than we had ever imagined, and that it has changed very slowly over time. These changes, contrary to catastrophism, another opposing theory, had not occurred as a result of sudden, dramatic shifts or catastrophes. Previous theologians had worked to "square" the book of Genesis with catastrophism by suggesting that each "day" of creation actually matched a major geological shift in the earth. Each day, then, referred not to a twenty-four-hour period but to a geological epoch that preceded the next major change. If one believed that these cataclysms explained geological changes, one could hold onto the notion of a much younger earth, a position that could thus be reconciled with the Genesis account. But Darwin was utterly convinced that nature gradually evolved. He simply needed to understand the mechanism by which this slow process of evolution had taken place.

As is widely known, a key turning point in Darwin's thought occurred when he read Thomas Malthus's "Essay on the Principle of Population," written in 1838. This essay communicated the simple idea that the world contains an overpopulation, and hence, those individuals most equipped to survive will indeed persist while the weaker individuals will not. Both plants and animals overproduce; this initiates a struggle for limited resources. Nature "selects" the most competent competitors, and thus produces more of them. The reason is simple: they have the best chance for survival. The implications of this simple idea were staggering. The older concept of a designed and benevolent order was radically threatened by a new law—that of chance, variation, and brute strength. The repercussions of this idea for the traditional notion of providence, including the devout faith of his dear wife, pushed Darwin to withhold the idea for over twenty years as he collected more and more data. One can only imagine the burden of this "secret" he carried within him throughout this time. Aware of the enormous turmoil and condemnation he would trigger—particularly as a conflict-avoidant person—Darwin kept silent. Darwin knew "what he was in for" if his idea became known.

Nevertheless, a single letter changed his mind about publishing his ideas. This was a letter sent to Darwin from Alfred Wallace, surely one of the most important correspondences in the history of Western thought. Darwin was amazed to find out that Wallace, quite independently from Darwin, had discovered much the same idea! This prompted Darwin to write fast and furiously. The result was the enormously influential *The Origin of Species,* written in 1859. Darwin had been working on a very long, methodical treatment of natural selection. His writing speed was very slow, much like the evolutionary process he was describing. But Wallace "lit a fire" under Darwin.

Again, Darwin believed that natural selection replaced, rather than complimented, the theological understanding of creation. In fact, reality could be explained naturalistically without any appeal to supernatural forces. The world is self-contained. One need not resort to theology to explain the natural order; science could handle the job quite well. Organisms have their origins in preexisting types and are not individually and specially created. The notion that God created all the species "according to its own kind," which Genesis affirmed, was no longer feasible. *All* species, in fact, emerged from the same primordial pool of life.

NATURE'S CRUELTY: PHILOSOPHICAL AND RELIGIOUS IMPLICATIONS

The idea of human life gradually emerging over a long period of time was very troubling to biblical literalists, who represented the vast majority of Genesis readers. But it was equally damaging to hear about the long, cruel, and bloody struggle at the heart of nature. Natural selection didn't pull any punches: nature was indifferent, unjust, capricious, and void of benevolence. What sort of "God" did it represent? Where was divine goodness in this viciously competitive war for survival? Paley had argued that design not only demonstrates the *power* of God, but also God's *kindness*. But again, what sort of God would create such a world, a world that ruthlessly favors the powerful over the weak? How could God honor brute force as the final criteria for survival? Who would write such a bloody play? Who would "design" such a scheme?

Previously many theologians had blamed the cruelties and injustices of nature on the fall of human beings. Nature had been peaceful, gentle, and harmonious before the disastrous choice of Adam and Eve. As a fallout of this dreadful rebellion against God, the entire natural world suffered the consequences. If the world looks bloody, it's the fault of the first human pair. All suffering, human and animal, is attributable to sin.

This notion, of course, presupposed that humanity arrived first on the scene and that a long history of creaturely suffering did *not* precede human involvement. But that view could no longer be used. Nature struggled for survival long before humanity offered its own sinful contribution. Again, much of Western thought had presupposed the notion of a paradise in our collective past, a literal, historical period in which "unfallen" creatures were perfectly created. Human beings had deteriorated from this wonderful beginning. Darwin, however, radically questioned any such notion of a golden era in our past. Instead, life had emerged from "lower" forms, not fallen from a perfect state. Evolution provided absolutely no evidence that everything had at one time been ideal or even close to perfect. Instead, life was emerging toward greater and greater complexity. Even though Darwin never endorsed the notion that human evolution is morally progressive, he did claim that life has become more sophisticated and complex than it was millions of years ago. We have not fallen from a *high* state; we are emerging from a *low* one.

Darwin's blow to religion was especially felt by a period in English history that had nearly canonized Paley and made divine design a little too obvious. In fact, some theologians, including John Henry Newman, believed that Paley's apologetics of nature was excessive and that it monopolized other sources of religious truth.[4] Put simply, Paley put too much stock in the design argument, an argument that only led to Deism anyway. Oxford theologian Aubrey Moore did not approve of leaning so heavily on the argument from design.[5] Even if the argument is useful, it is a big step from the notion of a distant designer to a Christian understanding of a God who reveals Godself in the Bible. Moore liked the idea that God set in motion the world's potential for self-organization. He believed that the notion of a "special creation" of human beings was not necessary to see a divine purpose in the evolutionary process that led to human beings. He even stated that an evolutionary view is "more Christian" than a special-intervention theory. As he put it, "Those who opposed the doctrine of evolution in defense of 'a continued intervention' of God seem to have failed to notice that *a theory of occasional intervention implies as a corrective a theory of ordinary absence.*[6] For Moore, there needed to be a far-greater emphasis on the immanence of God working in nature.

Yet this is precisely what Darwin did *not* find. Saying that God is immanently involved in the cruelties of nature is asserting that this God is either powerless or sadistic. How is the Divine "immanent" in a system of nature that seems devoid of benevolence? How does such language have any meaningful referent whatsoever?

Darwin's blow to Christianity involved far more than merely pointing out a couple of flaws in the design argument. His thought brought to the shores of providence a tidal wave of dissonance. Theologians such as Charles Hodge in America *knew* what was at stake for a traditional conception of God's relationship to the world. This is why he was quite anti-Darwinian. He grasped the implications. Many clergy believed that they were fighting for their lives, or at least the life of pre-Darwinian belief. A major paradigm shift was underway.

> Hodge was aware, from statements of Darwin and Huxley and others, that the Darwinian denial of design implied atheism, though it did

not demand it. The focus of Hodge's critique of Darwin was directed toward exposing this implication. For Hodge the peculiar character and danger of Darwinism was neither in its advocacy of evolution, or even natural selection, but in its rejection of teleology.[7]

Quite understandably, Hodge believed that the notion of a directionless, purposeless universe in which humanity appeared by accident was completely incompatible with a picture of a providential God.

Perhaps some clergy and theologians, in an excessive eagerness to eliminate any conflicts between science and religion, uncritically and unthinkingly embraced Darwinism without "thinking through" its theological conclusions. Hodge is to be affirmed for clearly seeing those conclusions. For he was right: while a strict Darwinism did not necessitate atheism, it certainly hinted in that direction.

Nevertheless, Christian evolutionists affirmed Darwinian evolution, but understood it as the mechanism by which God achieved God's purposes. Evolution was the way God chose and continues to choose to do things. While evolution's design is ultimately not without purpose, some theologians did conclude that the traditional understanding of fall and redemption needed to be greatly revised. For Lyman Abbott, the notion of a fall from a "higher state" simply had to be eliminated.[8] This idea completely contradicted new scientific evidence and had outlived its usefulness. Sin, then, was seen as a relapse back to a more primitive way of being. When each of us moves from a higher form of consciousness to less developed ways of thinking and behaving, we "fall." Abbott's view actually has much in common with the views of contemporary psychiatrist Aaron Beck, who argues that destructive behavior comes from our anxiety-induced, primitive thinking (see chapter 4). Yet rather than agreeing with Darwin's nonprogressive view of evolution, Abbott "theologized" the evolutionary story into a "slow but certain victory of Christian love, freedom, and fraternal democracy over selfish individualism and paternalism."[9] Liberals applauded Abbott's perspective, and conservatives accused him of being unbiblical, as well as downplaying the divinity of Christ. Yet Abbott and other theistic evolutionists offered a much rosier picture of the world than Darwin had depicted. Darwin had no assurance, for instance, that our moral values are indeed progressing. Again, nature's law was not the "survival of the most moral," but instead the survival of the strongest. In spite of this, many liberal theologians used Darwinian evolution to emphasize their own concept of progress. The twentieth century would rip asunder many of these optimistic hopes and point us again to the brutalities of nature—especially *human* nature.

DARWIN'S STRUGGLE WITH THEODICY

I have already mentioned that Darwin had a reputation for being a kind and gentle person, one who greatly disliked and avoided conflict. For a person with such a disdain for conflict, a front-row seat for the savage battles in nature must have been most distressing. Evolution seemed to produce so much waste, such pointless destruction of entire species. The cold cruelty of nature seemed paramount. Perhaps Darwin's own questions were quite similar to those of a Darwin reader who wrote a letter to theologian John Haught:

> How could a loving God have planned a cruel system in which
> sensitive living creatures must either eat other sensitive living creatures
> or be eaten themselves, thereby causing untold suffering among those
> creatures? Would a benevolent God have created animals to devour
> others when he could have designed them all as vegetarians? What
> kind of deity would have designed the beaks which rip sensitive flesh?
> What God would intend every leaf, blade of grass, and drop of water
> to be a battle ground in which living organisms pursue, capture, kill,
> and eat one another? What God would design creatures to prey upon
> one another and, at the same time, instill into such creatures a capacity
> for intense pain and suffering?[10]

The transition in Darwin's religious pilgrimage moved from being a fairly orthodox Anglican, to Deism, and then finally to agnosticism. In his autobiography, Darwin described how unbelief crept over him gradually.[11]

An additional indication of Darwin's empathy and sensitive nature can be seen in his early struggle with the concept of hell or eternal damnation: "I can hardly see how anyone ought to wish Christianity to be true; for, if so, the plain language of the text seems to show that the men who do not believe—and this would include my father, brother, and almost all my best friends—will be everlastingly punished. And this is a damnable doctrine."[12] Darwin carried the extra burden that if his devout wife, Emma, knew all of his views, she would then be tormented by the thought that her husband and she may well be separated for eternity. She would worry relentlessly about his soul, a worry he did not want her to experience.

Darwin, unlike some of his current representatives, took no delight nor felt any Promethean liberation in the gradual erosion of his faith. His was not a rebellious apostasy, not a bitter rejection of divine things. And he certainly felt no need to attack or undercut anyone else's faith.

Along with the theoretical problem of theodicy, Darwin faced some heavy personal injustices in his life. In addition to losing his invalid mother at an early age, Darwin helplessly watched his ten-year-old daughter, Annie, die over Easter weekend. She had been very special to Darwin, and her loss must have seemed dreadfully unfair. Perhaps in part because of Darwin's unusual sensitivity to the suffering of his children, Annie's death marked one more example of the unfair cruelties of life.[13] He also endured health problems most of his adult life, a condition that often allowed him to work only a few hours per day. Theodicy was not just a theoretical problem. The absence of God was not only seen in nature, but experienced in his own life. One cannot help wondering if his personal suffering and sense of the tragic did not enormously add to his conviction that nature is quite cruel.

Perhaps Darwin ended up agnostic rather than atheistic because of his great reservation to make pronouncements without adequate evidence. Atheism perhaps seemed to claim too much. Also, atheism often had a tone of aggression or belligerence toward religion, and this was not consistent with Darwin's nature. As he eventually put it, "I cannot pretend to throw the least light on such abstruse problems. The mystery of the beginning of all things is insoluble to us, and I for one must be content to remain an Agnostic."[14] Thus Darwin moved from an early, pre-Beagle, theistic belief in the thirty-nine articles of the Church of England, to Deism, which seemed to underlie *The Origin of Species,* to his eventual agnosticism. Darwin saw religion as essentially prescientific speculation. He firmly believed that both historical and scientific evidence undermined the accuracy of both the Old and New Testaments. Earlier, prescientific religion reflected a world of ignorance and credulity. The rational argument from design, in which he had originally put so much stock, now fell asunder. Darwin rejected biblical literalism and was also not very impressed with the nonliteral, symbolic, or mythic use of religious language. Darwin allowed Paley to be the all-important representative of Christianity. And when Paley's argument went down, so also did the entire edifice of Christian faith. While some biblical scholars prior to Darwin had pushed a metaphorical reading of Genesis, this seemed to have little impact on Darwin.

Indeed, if religion is nothing more than the eighteenth- and nineteenth-century rational orthodoxy that Darwin knew, then Darwin's discoveries effectively rebuked religion. Post-Darwinian arguments for the existence of God based on design are utterly riddled with problems. While one might rationally hold that the "original conditions" for the emergence of the universe were most unlikely without a designing Creator, the wasted species, the long trail of blood, and the savage patterns of nature point in the opposite direction.

> Darwin's interpretation of nature was infinitely more damaging to a Christian vision of the world than the revolutions of Copernicus or Newton. If theories of these earlier scientists forced certain readjustments in the Christian's conception of man's and God's place in nature, they did not essentially threaten the Christian drama of Creation, Fall, and Redemption. Darwinism challenged the entire Biblical account of man's unique creation, fall, and need for redemption. The doctrine that man was the product of a long evolutionary process from lower to higher species was simply incompatible with the traditional interpretation of the Fall in Genesis. In Darwin's opinion man had risen from a species of dumb animal, not fallen from a state of angelic perfection. How could one impute a sinful fall to a creature so superior to his brutish ancestors in intellect and morals? And if man is the *chance* product of natural

variation, what sense does it make to say that man is the crown of God's plan, created in the very image of his Creator?[15]

Process, change, and diversity were replacing the traditional role of underlying, immutable laws. Static views of the world would not be able to accommodate the new science.

DOES EVOLUTION NECESSITATE ATHEISM?

It's perfectly appropriate and quite necessary for biological evolution to work within a naturalistic framework. Evolutionists need not become theologians as they investigate natural phenomenon. Perhaps, however, they *should* look at the pretheoretical, precritical assumptions they bring to their investigations. The question then should be, Have I ruled out, a priori, any possibility that a metanatural realm may be a part of reality? A *methodological* naturalism can easily assume an *ontological* naturalism. When this happens, science has become philosophy. Physicist and theologian John Polkinghorne puts this issue beautifully.

> Science, by its self-denying modesty of ambition, which is also the
> enabler of its great and limited success, has foresworn the attempt
> to wider questions of meaning and purpose and confines itself to
> prosaic issues of process, the causal sequences by which things happen.
> Scientists themselves have been less austere in practice than their
> ostensible principles would require them to be. Although officially
> they foreswear metaphysics, covertly they love it and lace their popular
> writings with *obiter dicta* of that kind. Hence the claims either to
> discern the mind of God or to dispose of God altogether. I am not
> against such metaphysical indulgences, for it seems to me quite
> impossible to live without them in one form or another. It belongs to
> our humanity to wrestle with questions of significance and purpose
> that, contrary to the claims of some that are meaningless issues, are in
> fact so meaningful for us that they insistently clamor to be addressed.
> I am simply eager that we should be clear in our minds about what is

the character of discourse in which we are engaged and what authority and success in one kind of inquiry should not be invoked to settle illegitimately issues in a different domain of discussion.[16]

Theologian of evolution John Haught readily admits that one's presuppositions or disposition toward the data makes a huge difference in how one interprets the evolutionary process: "[A] theology of evolution is suspicious of scientific literalism as well as biblical literalism. It will try, therefore, to make the case that the raw ingredients of evolution flow from the depths of divine love, a depth that will show up only to those whose personal lives have already been grasped by a sense of God. By definition this deeper reading of evolution will be rejected by the literalist, whether scientific or biblical."[17]

Presuppositions or dispositions of the heart seem to guide one's search. None of us approaches this complex topic without what philosopher Hans-Georg Gadamer frequently called an "effective history," or a tradition of beliefs and faith assumptions in which we have been saturated. No one comes to the question of evolution "in the raw." We each bring orienting assumptions, or what Peter Berger often calls a "plausibility structure," to every theoretical issue. Yet while every perspective *begins* in these faith assumptions, it can distance itself from these assumptions and engage in critical dialogue. Unfortunately, as we shall see, much of the religion and science debate over evolution involves two forms of fundamentalism—one scientific and the other biblical—locked into a refusal to look beyond their own controlling assumptions. In such a situation, no alternative views are taken into perspective.

Some members of the so-called Religious Right are not completely wrong when they point out the hidden philosophical agenda of some materialist scientists. Operating with the assumption of Auguste Comte that the human "stage" of theology is over, science can now deliver the final answers. Philosophical materialism, which is actually unnecessary to conduct good science, gets smuggled in with science itself. Atheists as well as theists can have their own proselytizing agendas. Thus much of the so-called warfare between science and religion is in fact a warfare between two fundamentalisms—biblical literalism and scientism. Granted, scientific creationism is not science; it is a religious perspective. But science should not become an all-encompassing metaphysical faith. This is beyond its method. As theologian Langdon Gilkey puts it:

> To the creationists, therefore, evolution science—and all the
> astronomical, geological, paleontological, botanical, and biological
> theorems associated with it—is not merely science, not merely a
> set of tentative hypotheses dealing with a circumscribed, carefully
> delimited area or level of experience. It represents, on the contrary,
> a *total* explanation of the origins of all things, a view of the universe
> as a whole, a complete account of how all things came to be. Since
> evolution science is a total explanation of origins in terms of matter in
> motion, of blind chance, or purposeless flux, it is for them essentially
> atheistic, godless, and anti-religious in form.[18]

Gilkey goes on to say that scientists often confuse *proximate* origins with *ultimate* origins. The question of proximate origins involves the exploration of how certain things within the universe have come to be. This has to do with the emergence of special entities and their relationship with other entities. These questions can and should be investigated through science. If science is to remain coherent, it must take on a naturalistic viewpoint. This means that it purposely limits its inquiry to the goings-on of nature. This does *not* have to mean that nature tells the *only* story, or the *whole* story, of reality. Again, it holds a *methodological* naturalism, but not necessarily an *ontological* naturalism. Ultimate origins, on the other hand, concern why there is anything at all. Where did the universe itself come from? What, if anything, is its ultimate purpose? What is the source of this grand reality in which we find ourselves? These have always been religious questions.

Now there is certainly nothing wrong with scientists speculating on these ultimate questions as long as they recognize that they are no longer simply speaking as scientists. They should clearly declare that they are now speaking as philosophers or quasi-theologians rather than scientists. The problem, once again, is that they often attempt to smuggle their metaphysical convictions into their "empirical" science. Pronouncements about ultimate reality go beyond the strict methods of science. Many philosophers and theologians would welcome these speculations to their discussion if they would dismiss the pretension that they are still doing science.

Historically, one of the distinctions between religion and science has been expressed through the terms *primary* and *secondary* causation. Primary causes have to do with the ultimate cause or question of why there is anything at all. For instance, what is the meaning of the cosmos? Secondary causes, on the other hand, have to do with specific cause-and-effect relationships we can observe in the natural world. For example, when we see a newborn child, we look at its parents as the secondary cause. Yet this does not rule out the possibility that the primary cause of the child is the ground or source of life we call "God." It is even possible that primary causality can work through secondary causality. Again, secondary causes are natural, historical, and finite. They are open to public scrutiny, and are not "revealed." Put differently, they are secular. Without them, the regular, dependable, natural patterns that science investigates would not be possible.

For many scientists, of course, there is no need to even bring a "primary cause" into the discussion. They are quite content with a completely natural explanation. But the conclusion that there cannot possibly be another "level" or "dimension" to this experience is itself a philosophical, and not a scientific, conviction. Science cannot prove that matter is all there is. All they can say is that, given the limits of scientific method, they don't *see* anything else. But once again, they make this claim as a philosopher and not as a scientist. Yet they often deny that they are making a metaphysical leap, and instead want to claim that they say these things with both feet on empirical ground. They do not. Some scientists even believe that science will eventually eliminate any need for philosophy, much less religion. Eventually we will understand everything about the universe. Yet, as I have suggested, this still leaves open the question of why there is a universe *at all,* and whether or not it serves a larger purpose.

By failing to see that religion addresses issues of ultimate or primary causes, scientists often believe that religion is nothing more than pseudo-science in its meager attempt to explain secondary causality. If Genesis is read strictly as an attempt to explain history and science, it fails miserably. But what serious biblical scholar understands it as an attempt to explain natural causes? It is a poetic story about ultimate origins, about God's relationship to the world, and not a technical manual about how the world came to be.

To exclude God from the scientific method is not to exclude God from the universe. The same could be said for the study of history, psychology, or any social science. If God "pops up" in a random, nature-denying way, then how could we possibly speak of a consistent science? The supernatural would constantly interrupt the natural. Science would be impossible.

Also, how could science possibly investigate a concept such as creation *ex nihilo*? Science must have "materials" or "stuff" with which to work. Creation *ex nihilo* says that God worked with nothing. God brought all the elements that would form the universe into being. This is utterly incomprehensible to science, yet the question of ultimate beginnings won't go away. Science does very well with post-big-bang investigation. But what about pre-big bang? Once again, what is the primary cause? As Gilkey says, "The fact that science omits God is a result of the *limitation* of science, not of its atheism. Science is limited to finite causes and cannot speak of God without making God into a finite cause."[19] Again, arguing that evolution science excludes God forgets that all sorts of other disciplines—including law and medicine—also leave God out of their investigations. Excluding God from a particular discourse does not mean *denying* God. If it denies God, it has ceased to be scientific.

As Gilkey suggests, creation science is a *reactionary* perspective, but the blame for this reactivity is not the sole fault of the creation scientists. Science itself has often taken a smug, condescending, *scientistic*, rather than scientific, view of reality. Unconsciously carrying a religious bias and being negatively fused to their own religious background, many of the scientists *have* had an axe to grind. They've developed their own form of fundamentalism—a fanatical allegiance to positivism. Science is not without its own faults in its battles with religious conservatives. As Gilkey suggests, "science and technology can be creative and not destructive in social existence *only* if these other complementary aspects of culture—its literature and art, its law, morals, and social theory, its philosophical and religious assumptions—are also strong and creative, and if the relation of scientific and technological developments to them is rationally assessed and humanely enacted."[20]

Clearly science provides a very important "reading" of the universe.

But, as John Haught suggests, there are multiple "levels" or "readings" of the "text" of the universe. Scientific materialism often reads the text of nature like religious fundamentalists read the Bible. This involves a cosmic literalism that does not enter into the depths of what may very well be happening. As Haught puts it, "if textual literalism is a way to avoid the deeper dynamics of sacred texts, cosmic literalism for its part now keeps out of view the vast domain of nature's own depth."[21] As we have seen, a certain methodological materialism is necessary for science. Yet, again, science often jumps from methodological to ontological materialism. Put another way, science tells us a very important story about the evolution of the universe, but it does not tell us the *only* story. We can fully agree with the scientific description of the unfolding of nature without believing the metascientific hypothesis that materialism tells the whole tale. Theology needs to listen to science describe the world, but it also needs to have a "metaphysics alarm" that goes off every time science attempts to inject ultimate explanations about *why* things are the way they are. It's almost as if some scientists are saying, "Leave us alone and let us explore the *physical* world," while theologians and philosophers are saying in return, "But you've entered a *meta*physical world." Thus many scientists are wonderful empirical investigators but very limited philosophers. More specifically, they don't seem to realize when they are changing roles. As they speak metaphysically and philosophically, they think they are still operating as scientists.

Thus theology balks at the claim that evolution is not merely an important explanation of the cosmic past, but that is the *ultimate* explanation, or the *only* explanation. Darwinism, in the hands of materialistic philosophers who see it as the ultimate explanation of everything, even believe they can account for religion and morality. In the next chapter, we will explore this evolutionary account of religion and morality. While some atheistic Darwinists are more sympathetic to religion and say that is has been an adaptive illusion, many encourage us to face the way things really are—meaningless and purposeless. In fact, those who believe that they are encountering the presence of God simply need to understand the many illusions of which the mind is capable. Our complex brains can see "patterns" when none is really present. Whereas Freud believed we project an image of the protective Father onto God, some evolutionists believe we project our need for a warm and receptive providence to escape the cold, unfriendly realities of a brutal world.

> To satisfy our longing for meaning in an age of science, some of us may turn to piety or poetry. But enlightened evolutionists caution us that religion and art are merely heartwarming fiction. Our genes, they claim, have created adaptive but essentially deceptive brains and emotions that spin seductive spiritual visions in order to make us think we are loved and cared for. But in fact it is all illusion. Darwin has allowed us at last to naturalize religion completely.[22]

Thus, according to some evolutionary views, our deepest spiritual aspirations are in reality the pawns of our own manipulative genes, genes that want one thing: survival! Religion supposedly provides consolation, moral conviction, and meaning for persons in a cosmic setting that is ultimately meaningless. Religion is simply the "band-aid" for our woes. But how long do these evolutionary views of religion think people will continue to trust in religion upon realizing it points to nothing ontologically real? If religion is nothing more than psychotherapy for the cosmically wounded, then let's drop the metaphysical claims and allow psychology, not religion, to do its job. If we believe that there is any truth in the Freudian notion that we human beings need to become adjusted to the reality principle and live consistently with "what is," then according to atheistic evolution, religion needs to go. Again, I will deal much more fully with this evolutionary interpretation of religion in chapter 2.

EVOLUTION AS RELIGION: RICHARD DAWKINS AND ALISTER MCGRATH

One would be hard pressed to find a more interesting celebrity intellectual than Richard Dawkins. Extremely bright, wonderfully articulate, handsome, and enormously capable of translating difficult scientific concepts into everyday language, Dawkins has sometimes been tagged "Darwin's Rottweiler" because of his spirited and direct attacks on his conceptual enemies. He is universally recognized for his brilliance in science, but he is not always applauded for what many consider to be his outrageous claims about religion.

In all fairness to Dawkins, he really seems to believe that he is engaged in a public service when he attacks the foolishness of *all* religion. Frequently referring to it as a "virus" of the mind, Dawkins believes it is prescientific nonsense, even dangerous nonsense, in that it tends to promote irrational behavior. Blind faith, as he often calls it, should be considered one of our foremost enemies. And indeed, the notion of reasonable religion is an oxymoron. The so-called adaptive significance of religion is not honored. Instead, we must make a choice between God and Darwin. While Dawkins can forgive, and even admire, William Paley, post-Darwinian theology is self-deluded. One simply cannot have both Darwin and theology.

Alister McGrath, one of the world's most productive and leading theologians, happens to be dually trained as a scientist and a theologian. For years, McGrath has admired Dawkins's scientific genius, and back in McGrath's atheist days he would perhaps have agreed with some of Dawkins's attack on religion. But along the way, he found himself converting to Christianity and becoming a very accomplished philosopher and theologian as well as a scientist. Quite frankly, he can no longer "take" Dawkins's rants on religion without blowing a whistle on him.[23]

> Dawkins writes with erudition and sophistication on issues of evolutionary biology, clearly having mastered the intricacies of his field and its vast research literature. Yet when he comes to deal with anything with God, we seem to enter into a different world. It is the world of a schoolboy debating society, relying on heated, enthusiastic overstatements, spiced up with some striking oversimplifications and more than an occasional misrepresentation (accidental, I can only assume) to make some superficially plausible points—the sort of arguments that once persuaded me that atheism was the only option for a thinking person when I was a schoolboy. But that was then. What about now?[24]

While Dawkins is emphatic about how his involvement in the natural sciences led him to atheism, McGrath says that atheism is "tacked onto his evolutionary biology like intellectual velcro."[25] McGrath is convinced that this so-called necessary movement from science to atheism is a conclusion Dawkins has reached on grounds other than purely scientific ones. In fact, McGrath believes that Dawkins moves from biology to theology (or antitheology) while pretending to be a "pure scientist" the entire time.

Rather than trying to usher in a theological apologetic to combat Dawkins, McGrath prefers to challenge him on the turf of the philosophy of science. Stated bluntly, McGrath believes that Dawkins's atheism is not the logical conclusion of science that Dawkins claims. Yet Dawkins elevates Darwinism into an entire worldview, a metanarrative of human experience, an ultimate explanation of all of reality. For Dawkins there is no higher or deeper explanation than that of evolutionary science. In the passage with which I began this chapter, Dawkins says the following: "In a universe of blind physical forces and genetic replication, some people are going to get hurt, other people are gong to get lucky, and you won't find any rhyme or reason in it, nor any justice. The universe we observe had precisely the properties we should expect if there is, at bottom, no design, no purpose, no evil and no good, nothing but blind pitiless indifference."[26]

Again, Dawkins believes that his atheism is a logical conclusion drawn from the conditions of the world. Surely any notion of God worthy of our belief would have done a much better job with the world. Thus Dawkins makes the reverse argument of Paley and offers an apologetic for atheism. While we may think we see "patterns of design" that necessitate a Creator, these patterns have emerged through changing variations over billions of years. Given enough time, complex organisms can indeed involve from something much simpler.

But, as McGrath points out, Dawkins doesn't stop with agnosticism. Darwinism, in Dawkins's hands, doesn't merely create doubt for religious views; instead, it wipes them out! Darwinism, for Dawkins, does more than cause religious people to rethink their conception of providence. It pulls the rug out from under *any* type of faith in God. Thus Dawkins would say to the vast array of religious individuals who "naïvely" believe they can have their faith and Darwin too: "You are utterly deceived." The issue is black and white. In this much he agrees with the creation scientists: one cannot have Darwinism and a belief in Creation within the same worldview. Yet many scientists remain agnostics or even believers, in spite of Dawkins's proclamation that it is impossible. Again, this is a crucial point about Dawkins: he doesn't merely say that evolutionary science creates dissonance for theism or that it leaves us with agnosticism; instead, he claims that this evidence demands atheism. While many foes of Dawkins would not object if Dawkins merely claimed that the evidence has led him *personally* toward an atheistic conclusion, they *do* object when he claims that atheism is the *only* conclusion that can be legitimately drawn from the evidence. Indeed, Dawkins is hard pressed to demonstrate his own atheistic conclusions. Many of his coscientists make no such leap. Darwin himself, Thomas Henry Huxley, and Darwinist Stephen Jay Gould, for instance, argue that agnosticism, not atheism, is as far as one can go. As Huxley put it, "Agnosticism puts aside not only the greater part of popular theology, but also the greater part of anti-theology."[27] And Gould is even more forceful in his conviction that Darwinism must not be equated with atheism: "To say it for all my colleagues and for the umpteenth millionth time (from college bull sessions to learned treatises): science simply cannot (by its legitimate methods) adjudicate the issue of God's possible superintendence of nature. We neither affirm nor deny it; we simply can't comment on it as scientists."[28]

Science is "stuck" working with natural explanations. It has no comment on God. McGrath says, "The bottom line for Gould is that Darwinism actually has no bearing on the existence or nature of God."[29] In my view, however, this is an overstatement, one that I suspect Gould would contest. Saying that Darwinism does not disprove the existence of God is far from saying that it does not offer evidence that makes belief in God highly problematic. While Gould did not believe that science could prove the God question one way or another, he *did* understand the world to be blind, materialistic, and purposeless. He simply believed that science had no business trying to answer ultimate, metaphysical questions. Those questions were, for Gould, "too direct an assault on eternity."[30] Thus Gould may very well have thought that the evidence from evolutionary science makes theism most unlikely, yet he refused to speculate on such things "in the name of science." Dawkins is not so modest.

As McGrath suggests, if the scientific method cannot prove or disprove the existence of God, then we should (a) abandon the question or (b) recognize that we must answer the question on other grounds. These "other grounds" should not violate what we know from science, but they will, of necessity, go beyond science.[31] But Dawkins is clearly not going to "let go" of the larger religious question. In fact, he has become as widely known as an advocate for atheism as an advocate for Darwinism. (He would of course, argue that the two go hand in hand). Dawkins continues to make philosophical arguments as if they are "laws" of science. He simply digs in deeper and insists that the whole discussion be conducted on the turf of science. Yet, according to McGrath, it is Dawkins himself who unwittingly changes the turf to philosophy while he pretends to play on strictly scientific ground. Dawkins will admit the need for a "turf switch" when it comes to ethics. In fact, he argues that science is simply not equipped to provide us with our ethical ideals. Yet he does not extend this courtesy to matters of religion. But this is because Dawkins insists upon viewing religion as nothing more than pseudo-science, an illusory precursor to science, an infantile virus of the mind. Atheism is self-evident. Yet Dawkins's atheism does not seem "self-evident" to others.

In short, McGrath believes quite strongly that one can use the evidence from evolutionary science to defend an atheistic, agnostic, or theistic perspective. Natural processes do not demand an atheistic interpretation. God may have very well created the world so that it is self-regulatory, as many contemporary theologians believe.

In all fairness to Dawkins, however, I believe that McGrath sometimes exaggerates the extent to which Dawkins's criticisms of religion are in fact targeted at only a specific, historical view of divine design that emerged in Victorian England. McGrath is quite right that this view was especially vulnerable to Darwinism because it had placed far too much emphasis on the authority of nature to demonstrate God. It was indeed dangerous to put all of one's "apologetic eggs in one basket."

> Dawkins' assessment of the theological implications of Darwinism is excessively dependent on the assumption that Paley (or Paleyesque) approaches to the biosphere are typical or normative for Christianity. He also seems to assume that the intellectual case for Christianity

rests largely, if not totally, upon an "argument for design," such as that proposed by Paley. Yet Christian theology does not hold that Christian belief is irrational or lacking positive epistemic status without the kind of arguments that Paley develops. Dawkins makes a superb case for abandoning Paley. Sadly, he seems to think this also entails abandoning God.[32]

I believe that McGrath, as an outstanding historical theologian, is quite right in saying that Dawkins's argument, like Darwin's, is especially aimed at the inflated natural theology of Paley. Yet Dawkins knows quite well that Darwinism started a tidal wave for *all* of Christian thought, not just Paley's version. Prior to the eighteenth century, the vast majority of people read Genesis historically and scientifically. Darwin's ideas must have at first seemed utterly incompatible with the world they had taken for granted. Of course, some theologians made rather quick theological accommodations to Darwin, but it certainly took some cognitive maneuvering in order to do so. Thus, Darwinism did not simply challenge Paley's perfectly ordered world; instead, its focus on the brutal sufferings in nature questioned whether there was *any providential care in the world at all.* Darwinism, for the past century and a half, has not pushed religious people to simply back off from their enthusiasm over the design argument; it has instead pushed them toward wondering if the notion of divine providence makes any sense at all, particularly given the suffering and evil so basic to nature. This is not just a problem for Paley; it is a problem for all monotheistic traditions.

EVOLUTION AND THE GOD OF CLASSICAL METAPHYSICS

The type of God most incompatible with evolutionary science, and the God that some process theologians have worked so hard to transcend, is the powerful, sovereign, unchanging, unfeeling, and coercive God of classical theistic metaphysics. This is a God who could never "let the universe be," because that would mean withholding omnipotence and ceasing to control all that happens. This God does not encourage human beings toward autonomy and freedom; instead, this God constantly reminds creation that it is controlled by its omniscient designer. This is a God who governs by force. As Haught puts it:

> Such a stingy and despotic forcefulness, by refusing to favor the independence of creation, would clearly be less influential in the final analysis than a God who wills the independence of the world. A world given lease to become more and more autonomous, even to help create itself and eventually attain the status of human consciousness and freedom, has much more integrity and value than "divine designer." If by persuasion rather than coercion something greater than a puppetlike universe is permitted to come into being, then we can say that persuasive power is more influential than brute force.[33]

Haught goes on to say that this coercive power is not only incompatible with human freedom, but that it is also incompatible with the pre-human evolutionary spontaneity of the world.

The immutable, impassible, all-powerful, and all-controlling God perhaps found its most classical expression in the airtight providence of John Calvin. For Calvin, whatever God wills is right, because God wills it. This is absolute freedom. God owes no one an explanation, even if God acts inconsistently. God always has "secret reasons" for what God does even if we cannot see them. This is because we are finite creatures who simply don't understand the big picture. God never changes, and any notion of God "changing his mind" (Gen. 6:6) must be read figuratively. Also, God does not "feel" our sorrow because this would interfere with God's Self-sufficient happiness and serenity. Further, sovereignty essentially means domination. There is no mutual relationship between God and God's creatures. In fact, Calvin's universe is a kind of cosmic stimulus-response theory. God chooses us and we are therefore determined to respond. Human choice is completely unable to resist the will of God.[34] It's not just that God has foreknowledge of what happens; God *decrees* it. Also, this God is completely isolated, self-sufficient, and invulnerable. Again, it's the God of classical Greek metaphysics. As theologian Clark Pinnock puts it, this is "an aloof monarch, removed from the contingencies of the world, unchangeable in every aspect of being, as an all-determining and irresistible power, aware of everything that will happen and never taking risks."[35] Pinnock goes on to make the interesting observation that while this classical Greek metaphysical picture of God has often dominated historical theology, it has not been the God acknowledged in religious experience. That God tends to be more relational, more affected by human suffering, and more responsive to human needs.

Again, this classical, omnicausal image of God is very difficult to defend in the light of the long history of evolution's brutalities. It is difficult enough for *any* theodicy to wrestle with the question of why God *allows* suffering. But Calvinism, if one follows its logical implications, argues that God not only allows it, God decrees it! Evil is all somehow a part of a greater wisdom that we limited, finite types simply cannot grasp. But when we object to God's endorsement of cruelty, we are simply told that we dare not question divine wisdom. But the notion that the Holocaust, the 2005 Southeast Asian tsunami, or the 9/11 attacks on the World Trade Center and Pentagon were all a part of God's will is a violation of everything sacred about God. Who could love such a monster? Yet hardcore Calvinists keep repeating themselves: God does not have to answer to us and God operates on a completely different level than we do. But let's be clear about what Calvinists are really asking us to believe: our deepest experiences of love, compassion, justice, fairness, and kindness are utterly useless when it comes to understanding God. God transcends all our feeble human experiences, and sometimes acts in direct opposition to our understanding of what is good, just, and right. God need not explain Godself to anyone. If God's character violates our own moral standards, then so be it. While there may be a danger of overextending human analogies when considering divine matters, it is also a very frightening world when an idea about God doesn't even meet the standards of moral personhood. Indeed, when we as human beings are more compassionate, loving, and concerned about human suffering than our God, perhaps it's time to find another God. To say that the world's history of bloodshed, violence, cruelty, cancer, exploitation, oppression, and dying children are all part of the will of God is enough to make even the most submissive person rise up in protest. When we make God the all-controlling cause of everything, then this God is profoundly blameworthy. Philosopher William Hasker asks a penetrating question for strict Calvinists: "Is God as you conceive him unable to create a world in which there are free creatures who voluntarily enter into a relationship of love and friendship with him? Or does he prefer a world in which he alone monopolizes control, leaving nothing to be decided by his creatures? And why should we think that he would prefer a world like that?"[36] Indeed, why *would* God would want a world in which people are puppets? Clearly a God who prized relationships *would not*.

As theologian Sallie McFague suggests, the model of God with which we operate often greatly influences our own behavior.[37] More specifically, we often imitate the God we believe in, and if we happen to believe in a highly controlling, dominating, nonmutual portrait of God, our own dominance and oppression may not be far behind: "Our doctrines of creation and providence do not stand alone: they are offshoots of our deepest beliefs about the nature of God's relation to the world. If this belief is that God and the world are wholly other, creation and providence will be seen in that light. If this belief is that God and the world are intrinsically intimate, creation and providence will be understood from that perspective."[38]

The traditional story of providence has emphasized God's power over God's love, God's distance over God's relatedness. And in turn, this control model has been imitated on our planet, with the environment ending up in very bad shape because of it. A dominating God has also indirectly justified unfortunate hierarchies of power and dominance, particularly men over women. And as theologian Daniel Migliore reminds us, "Torn out of its context, the divine command to humanity to 'have dominion' over the earth (Gen. 1:26) has been twisted into an ideology of mastery."[39] Clearly we need to be shaken from our narcissism and realize that we *share* this earth with other creatures. But a self-sufficient, dominating God reinforces our narcissism, because such a God is the ultimate narcissist. Perhaps we need to be reminded that those billions of years before we happened to arrive were not just a "pregame show."

So the classical image of a stagnant, yet dominating God runs into major problems with evolutionary theory. As Pinnock puts it: "We do not limit God by saying he can be surprised by what his creatures do. It would be a serious limitation if God could not experience surprise and delight. The world would be a boring place without anything unexpected ever happening."[40] For Pinnock, omnipotence does not refer to God's power to determine everything, but instead to God's omnicompetence to deal with anything that comes up. Divine determinism and human freedom mixed together are not a "mysterious paradox," but instead a logical impossibility. Further, while omniscience may mean that God knows everything there is to be known, this does not include the outcome of decisions that have not yet been made. The future is open to multiple possibilities.

Again, the God of classical metaphysics is a God very difficult to "square" with the science of evolution. Clearly this was the God rejected by Charles Darwin, and the God dismissed by many contemporary evolutionists such as Dawkins and Daniel Dennett. And this is also the God who has been rejected by many contemporary theologians.

Yet the question remains as to whether a theology of evolution is possible, and whether or not it can possibly do justice to the enormous amount of pain and suffering in the natural world. Put simply, is a post-Darwinian view of providence possible? Can the brutalities of nature be fully acknowledged within a theology of evolution? It is to this challenging question that we turn.

PROVIDENCE AND PURPOSE AFTER DARWIN

John Haught, a major theological interpreter of Darwin, has said, "I believe that even now, at the beginning of a new millennium, we are still reeling from the shock Darwin apparently delivered to many traditional beliefs."[41] While the battle between "creation science" and Darwinism still rages in some sections of America, many religious thinkers have attempted to "theologize Darwin" in a way that acknowledges the legitimacy of his evolutionary findings, while refusing to embrace the materialist philosophy in which Darwinism is often presented. These theologians refuse to divide the world between biblical literalists and materialistic atheists or between religious fundamentalists and scientific fundamentalists. Instead, they believe that "it does not diminish God's providential role at all if the natural world is so extravagantly gifted that, at relevant points of its unfolding, random events open the door abruptly to a creativity that gushes forth in astonishingly new and unpredictable ways."[42] While this post-Darwinian theology has called for a fairly dramatic rethinking of traditional notions of providence, it nevertheless insists that a cosmic purpose still guides what at times can seem like a brutal and arbitrary process. Thus part of the emphasis of this theodicy is to "think bigger" in terms of cosmic design rather than examining the intricate details of nature. We are part of a larger story than the earth's evolutionary history. Redemption involves the entire universe, not just human beings. The challenge, of course, is to point toward a universe that is loved and nurtured by God in spite of what appears to be nature's brutal indifference toward the earth's creatures. Haught displays a great deal of courage to take on the following awesome task: "I shall argue . . . that Darwin has gifted us with an account of life whose depth, beauty, and pathos—when seen in the context of the larger cosmic epic of evolution—exposes us afresh to the raw reality of the sacred and to a resoundingly meaningful universe."[43] Haught readily admits that the classic conception of an all-powerful God engaged in coercive control of the world has indeed been wrecked by evolution. Yet this is part of Darwin's "gift" to theology. Older notions of Sovereign design, for Haught, have outlived their usefulness, and in fact were never descriptive of God's actual relationship with the world. Notions of a traditionally framed, micromanaged "divine plan" for the universe have dissolved in the light of the slow, often random, and wasteful journey of evolution. As theologian John Macquarrie puts it, "The process of evolution on the earth's surface looks much more like a groping procedure of trial and error, with fantastic waste, than like the carrying through of a preconceived plan."[44] Thus it was easy to believe—when the earth was understood to be around six thousand years old and an all-seeing God resided in the heavenly realm above the earth—that nature had a direct plan and purpose. But when we recognize that the universe stretches out over approximately fifteen billion years, that billions of those years were occupied by nonorganic life, that dinosaurs dominated the planet for some 150 million years, and that humanity represents only a fraction of a minute in the universe's time scheme, the notion of providence has its work cut out for it. As we have seen, rather than being a clear manifestation of intelligent design and protective guidance, the world is riddled with violence, a very brutal drama in which the weak, disadvantaged, and ill-prepared are simply destroyed. Religious skeptics want to know, If providence is such an obvious reality, why have the vast majority of all species been extinguished? What sort of "plan" is behind the predatory nature of the world? Where is the fine-tuned design in a world so full of excessive suffering, waste, and cruelty? As we shall see, Haught argues the case for *purpose* rather than *design*; for God's *vision*, rather than God's controlling *plan*.

For Haught, theology will not be taken seriously until it comes face-to-face with the Darwinian challenge. Haught doesn't merely attempt to answer the theological problems raised by evolution; instead, he embraces evolution as offering a deeper context for doing theology. Far from assuming that evolution is the enemy of faith, Haught believes it is a necessary element within that faith. Science is the enemy of an outdated, classical metaphysical framework that upholds a static, coercive God. That image of God needs to be exorcised from a serious conversation between theology and science.

Any attempt to provide a theology of evolution will clearly be attacked from two sides. On the one hand, creation scientists are utterly convinced that Darwinism is so deeply enmeshed in a materialistic, atheistic philosophy that it represents a hopeless dialogue partner for theology. The notion of "evolutionary theology" is therefore an oxymoron. On the other hand, materialistic evolutionists such as Dennett and Dawkins would also agree that one can't have Darwinian evolution without materialism and a purposeless universe. Haught readily agrees that if the universe has no sort of purpose or meaning, then Dennett and Dawkins are right: there is no place for religion. While theological adjustments can be made to accommodate scientific advancement, *all* religious traditions are in trouble if the universe is pointless and without any overarching meaning. A purposeless universe is certainly a Godless universe. But beyond this, even nontheistic traditions such as Buddhism believe that "ultimate reality" or "the sacred" is full of meaning. If there is no point to this "ultimate reality" then all religious traditions are examples of Sisyphus futilely rolling a rock up a hill only to have it tumble back down for all eternity. While one may withdraw from this cosmic meaninglessness and temporarily rebel against it by carving out a fleeting meaning for oneself, this is *not* a religious outlook. Again, *the backbone of religion is the conviction that the deepest layers of reality have purpose and meaning.* Whether or not one is a Christian, Jew, Muslim, Hindu, or Buddhist, stripping the world of ultimate purpose is also stripping it of religion. Most religious traditions would argue, of course, that what Dennett understands as meaninglessness actually has a deeper, hidden meaning, or a purpose that his materialist assumptions will not allow. For if one reads Darwinism as a treatise on the inescapable meaninglessness of the universe then atheism is obviously the next step. In that case, religion in general, and particularly theology, cannot survive Darwin. If that were true, theology would only still be around because it has not fully grasped the implications of Darwin's theory. Theology would be a mere walking corpse.

Navigating between both creation science and atheistic evolution, Haught sets forth his understanding of evolutionary theology:

> Evolutionary theology, unlike natural theology, does not search for definitive footprints of the Divine in nature. It is not terribly concerned about "intelligent design," since such a notion seems entirely too lifeless to capture the dynamic and even disturbing way in which the God of biblical religion interacts with the world. Instead of trying to prove God's existence from nature, evolutionary theology seeks to show how our new awareness of cosmic biological evolution can enhance and enrich traditional teachings about God and God's way of acting in the world. In other words, rather than viewing evolution simply as a dangerous challenge that deserves an apologetic response, evolutionary theology discerns in evolution a most illuminating context for our thinking about God today.[45]

Haught often suggests the following analogy: just as God so desired freedom for humanity that God allowed evil to come into human existence, so God so valued the world's independence and capacity for self-regulation that God took a noninterventionist stance. In other words, God wanted to respect the cosmic "boundaries" of life and allow the universe to differentiate itself from its Creator. This is a nonimposing God, a God who purposely restrains divine power out of love.

Simply stated, the God of Christian faith is not one who overpowers

the world and forces it to confirm to a rigid plan. Instead God wills
that the world "become itself" as fully as possible. This means that
the world must be allowed the space and time to wander about,
experimenting with various possibilities. While the mind of God is the
source of all the alternative possible paths the universe may travel on
its evolutionary adventure, we can safely suppose that a God of love
would not compel it to follow a prefabricated itinerary unyieldingly.
If God loves the world hen we can assume that God concedes to the
world a certain degree of freedom to experiment with an array of
possibilities in becoming.[46]

Evolution is thus experimental, loose ended, wandering, and open. The
universe, like a youngster leaving home, is discovering itself, expanding,
and growing. In the same way a loving parent allows a child to differentiate
and find his or her own way, so a noncontrolling God allows the universe
to be self-regulatory. The narrative of the universe is primarily a tale of
experimentation, slip-ups, and new possibilities. In the same manner that
human destructiveness and suffering, perhaps most profoundly expressed in
the Holocaust, is the price paid for human freedom, so suffering paid in the
long history of the natural world is the price paid for nature's independence
and freedom. As John Polkinghorne puts it, "God wills neither the act of a
murderer nor the incidence of cancer, but allows both to happen in a world
to which he has granted the freedom to be itself."[47] Or as Haught puts it,
"Theology should not have been surprised, but should have expected that
the created world be open to the kind of contingency and randomness we
find in life's evolution."[48]

Theologian Ted Peters, on the other hand, is somewhat suspicious of
this justification of nature's suffering in order for the natural world to be
free and independent from God:

> As for me, I am not sure I would want this price to be paid. I find
> the argument for God's self-limitation to permit suffering in order
> to attain human freedom less than fully satisfactory. I recognize that
> Christian theologians for two millennia have espoused variants of this
> position; and I am aware that esteemed contemporary theologians

find it compatible with evolutionary theory. Yet, somehow I find it less than satisfying. Suffering, whether due to natural evil such as defective genes or moral evil such as concentration camps, I find too high a price to pay for what we have been describing as freedom. If the cosmic marketplace could make the offer, I would gladly exchange my freedom to put an immediate end to it. Conceptually, I would find it easier to consign past evil to mere indeterminism, to contingency and chance, rather than to a divine plan.[49]

Perhaps Polkinghorne or Haught might say in return that the "divine plan" *is* contingency and chance. Nature must be allowed to go in its own direction. God's self-restraint and respect for the universe's independence necessitates the kind of suffering we can witness in the natural world. Again, God is like a loving parent who allows the world "to be."

But perhaps Peters has a point. Does the Divine-human parallel not break down? For instance, a loving father will allow his children to work out their own arguments and frustrations, thus helping his children effectively deal with conflict. But what loving father would allow these children to poke out each other's eyes or hit each other with baseball bats? The policy of noninterference would not be worth it; the "lesson" would be too severe. Does God see nature's indeterminacy as so important that a tsunami can wipe out thousands of lives? Does God "allow" human beings to be free enough to kill over one million children during the Holocaust, some of whom had their small heads bashed into concrete walls right in front of their mothers? Is "tinkering with nature" or intervening in human suffering too much to ask? If a young boy is drowning in a lake, should his father take a "loving," noninterference approach? Does love require this sort of "hands-off" policy in order to guarantee freedom? We would hold such a detached father in contempt. Thus there are limitations in using a divine-human parallel of nonintrusive freedom. Again, is Peters right? Are the stakes too high? If the universe is set up to run autonomously without any interference from God, we might eventually ask whether this type of "tough love" doesn't really sound more like "bystander apathy."

For Haught, however, evolution is an expression of God's humility. Theology points toward a self-humbling, self-emptying of divine power in order to express the love of "letting the universe be." Yet one wonders: If Darwin were alive today, would he ask how a story of nature's brutality can be transformed into a story about divine love? Divine love is precisely what he did *not* find in nature. Yet Haught and other contemporary theologians would no doubt encourage Darwin to look at the larger, cosmic picture rather than the crude behavioral patterns of insects or even humans. While it is often said that previous religious thinkers would have changed their minds if they would have understood today's science, would previous scientists, such as Darwin, have changed their minds if they understood today's theology? Darwin clearly rejected an early nineteenth-century view of providence. It is unknown whether he would have rejected the notion of providence offered by theologians today. I strongly suspect that he would have remained agnostic and simply said that it goes beyond the boundaries of what we could possibly know.

Haught goes so far as to argue that the hiddenness of God in nature can be seen as evidence of God's love. "The very possibility of giving an aesthetic interpretation of evolution," argues Haught, "is that God's creative love humbly refuses to make itself available at the level of scientific comprehension."[50] To some, this will seem like an enormous stretch. The absence of evidence of God indicates God's love for us? Granted, we should not expect God, as a metaphysical reality, to be fully revealed in nature, but should we call God's apparent absence an argument in favor of God's being there? Any naturalist would be astounded that a "lack of evidence" is used as a form of evidence. Perhaps the issue can thus be stated sharply: a theological evolutionist argues that the long course of nature, so seemingly directionless, is in reality a part of a cosmic process that is still ultimately in God's hands. God participates in the world by means of the secondary cause of evolution. God, in order to allow nature to have autonomy and integrity, generally maintains a "hands-off" policy at the level of micromanagement. An evolutionary materialist, however, will "read" the clumsy, wandering, bumbling, and directionless trail of nature as evidence that there is no cosmic purpose, at least none evident to human beings. There is simply too much chaos, waste, and suffering to believe in an ultimate sense of purpose and direction. There are too many brutalities within nature. While evolutionary theists often claim that the God of evolution is a God of novelty, randomness, and new possibilities, naturalists will no doubt argue that this is still another example of theology's frantic attempt to try and find a place for God in a universe that clearly appears godless. Theological evolutionists, on the other hand, will argue that divine providence can be seen in the "original conditions" that allowed life to spring forth after the big bang. Surely God provided the right conditions for this most unlikely scenario of life to emerge. Yet naturalists such as Dawkins will argue that there was nothing even remotely like intelligence at this time. Intelligence had to evolve; it was not a part of the beginning.

Theistic evolutionists argue that if God had completely designed the world, then the world would have no future. It would be "dead set," frozen, and fixed. God, argue these theologians, is still creating the world. Also, when we fault God for not intervening in the world, perhaps we should ask this question: If God *did* intervene, where would it end? If God ends one child's leukemia, is God not obligated to take away another woman's breast cancer? This could go on and on. When does one's own expectation for a miracle become an entitlement claim? According to Haught: "Our demand for a perfectly ordered universe is implicitly a demand that providence take the form of dictatorship. But God apparently has other ideas about what providence means."[51]

Yet one wonders if this comment doesn't suggest an unnecessary all-or-nothing view of providence. Is there not a strong difference between God being a "dictator" and God demonstrating a genuine nurture and protectiveness for God's creation? The options are not simply between "God as a busybody controller" and "God as uninvolved." Since when does *guidance* have to mean *dictatorship*? Haught goes on to argue that while natural selection works indiscriminately, so do the other laws of nature. In other words, natural selection is no different than the law of gravity. "In principle, therefore, the remorselessly consistent character of natural selection should raise no more serious theological problem than do the laws of physics."[52] He also asks us to think about what sort of universe we would have created ourselves. Would it be one without "challenge?" Yet again, does the extinction of the vast majority of species represent a "challenge?" If so, it is a case of "overkill." Nature's "challenges" are often enormously destructive rather than informative or educational. If the sufferings of nature are an "obstacle course for growth and development," then perhaps some will wonder if the God who watches it all evolve is not himself a sadist.

METAPHYSICAL IMPATIENCE AND EMERGING PURPOSE

For Haught, the definitive view that the universe is without purpose, a claim central to atheistic forms of evolution, reveals a metaphysical impatience. Put simply, the game is "too early to call." This might sound strange, given that the universe has existed for some fifteen billion years. Nevertheless, we cannot adequately say whether or not there is a deeper promise or purpose within the overall scheme of things. While nontheistic evolutionists insist that the universe bears no obvious signs of design, Haught looks not so much for design, but for promise. Purpose means that the universe is *in the process* of realizing something *good*.[53] So this is a central message in much of theistic evolution: *Cosmic purpose must be understood in terms of promise, not design.*

> Within the massive bombardment of our perceptivity by the universe, religious awareness claims to discern, at least vaguely, a dimension of reality that science must deliberately ignore in order to establish its own distinctive identity as science. That the theological reading will always be "dim" or "vague" is not a defect; rather, it is the consequence of religion's referring to a reality that lies *too deep* for human thought and language. Since the effort to arrive at scientific clarity impels us to ignore so much of reality's complexity, only a cloudier but richer kind of medium—that of myth, symbol or metaphor—can put us in touch with ultimate depths of things. By permitting ourselves to be grasped by religious symbols, we are pulled down into a domain that often unsettles us at first, but one that eventually leaves us more satisfied than before. This dimension, at least to those who have allowed themselves to be grasped by it, will impress them as being much closer to *what is* than any of the abstractions of science can claim to be.[54]

For Haught, as for Paul Tillich, we must allow ourselves to be pulled into this depth of life. We don't so much comprehend this depth; instead, this depth comprehends us. We do not discover this depth on the basis of our own scientific investigation. Again, it grasps us and necessitates that we speak in symbolic language and metaphor to describe its ultimacy. This is not an "ambush" but a powerful lure. It moves us beyond scientific literalism and the demand for an empirically verifiable purpose to the entire drama.

Also, we must come to understand that *we cannot get an adequate "reading" on an unfinished universe*. The story is not over. We are in the midst of a narrative that is still going on. We can only get a partial glance at this cosmic meaning. It is very much in process and it points us toward the future. Thus the point can be made directly: if we insist upon finding a definite design in the unfolding of nature so far, then the randomness, brutality, and even cruelty of the natural world may well convince us that atheistic materialism has the last word on evolution. But if we examine the goings-on of nature with an image of a noncontrolling God who perpetually invites nature and humanity into greater complexity and benevolence, then evolutionary theism cannot be ruled out. Stated another way, atheistic materialism usually rejects the God of omnicausality, the God who governs everything in a micromanagerial style. Yet a theology of evolution can say, "Good, so do we!" But when one looks for a self-giving God who *persuades, invites, and encourages* rather than *controls, dictates, and demands*, there may very well be room for a loving God within the parameters of evolutionary theory.

To put it another way, cosmic pessimism is premature. The universe is still very much in process. And this process is still loaded with promise:

> . . . I propose that we cease looking for design as evidence of purpose and instead look deeper—into what I have been calling the promise of nature. The notion of promise is much more flexible and more realistic than that of design. Unlike design, promise is logically consistent with the ambiguity that evolutionary science finds in the natural world and that we encounter in natural history. The notion of cosmic purpose need not be forced to coincide simplistically with the stiff and lifeless idea of divine "intelligent design." There is wonderfully intricate patterning in nature, of course, but there is much disorder and

suffering as well. By anyone's reckoning, the universe is not a perfectly ordered one, and all instances of order eventually dissolve into the torrent of entropy. Thus, if today we are to speak once again of cosmic purpose with our eyes wide open, it must be in such a way as to take nature's present disorder and eventual demise fully into account.[55]

The question then becomes whether or not the beauty, personal meaning, enjoyment, and sense of fulfillment that many individuals *have* discovered in their lives is utterly inconsistent with a cosmically indifferent, unjust, uncaring, meaningless, and purposeless universe. Some atheistic evolutionists believe that we are denying the very fiber of life when we insist that the whole scheme of things makes sense and has an ultimate purpose. Yet theistic evolutionists may argue that these very experiences of hope and meaning reflect the ultimate depths of life and the direction the universe is headed. Atheistic evolutionists say, "Wake up and smell the coffee: There is no meaning or purpose to any of this." And theistic evolutionists in turn respond: "You have given up too early. You have already concluded a pessimistic ending before the play is even close to being over." Atheistic evolutions might say: "Look, we've had fifteen billion years without any clear evidence of a designer." And theistic evolutionists might retort, "Yes, but there are hints of the direction the story is headed. It is moving very slowly because a noncontrolling God invites the universe toward self-actualization, and out of love refuses to dominate and control the process."

If we "read" the universe as a long narrative of the unfolding of life, a story that contained the possibility of life in the very conditions of the big bang some fifteen billion years ago, we may not prematurely conclude that the whole thing is meaningless. Granted, a post-Darwinian world looks very different than the world assumed by a pre-Darwinian worldview. But perhaps the universe is unfolding as it is precisely because God loves it enough to let it be autonomous and move in its own direction. Perhaps God works with nudges, invitations, and persuasions rather than divine design and control. From our own personal relationships, we know that genuine love does not force or compel. Refusing to see the universe as a simple extension of God's own being, God may indeed want relationships rather than puppets. Perhaps nature emerges experimentally precisely because it is not under God's rigid hand. If God is self-restraining, and wants to extend to prehuman nature the very autonomy that God wants human beings to experience, then what sort of universe should we have expected? Could the slow rate of evolutionary forces indicate a benevolent providence behind it? If we understand the Divine as "infinitely patient," then why must God move things along according to our own timetable? Further, instead of "pushing things along," perhaps God is "pulling them forward," or at least inviting, loving, and persuading the world to emerge in more complex and beautiful ways. Like a patient psychotherapist who invites and waits on a client's growth but does not force it, so perhaps God invites the world to actualize its potential, a potential that was embedded in the big bang itself. The world is allowed to become distinct from its creative ground.

Again, if someone such as Dawkins insists that the only God for theology is the God of deliberate design and careful planning, then he is right: this God doesn't exist. But what if that is *not* our conception of God at all? What if God is far less of a "planner" and more of an "inviter" or "persuader"? Then we do not make the same demands on this God for a tidy, providential world. But Dawkins's God is so tied to the notion of cosmic design that he won't seem to look at other theological perspectives. For Dawkins, the only God is the God who controls. Obviously, then, the universe appears to be godless. Dawkins has every right to blast away at this God of airtight design. Just as Darwin dismantled Paley, so Dawkins dismantles intelligent design. But the problem, again, is that Dawkins continues to attack an image of God that many contemporary theologians have also abandoned. Haught insightfully describes a different view of God, a God compatible with evolution.

> Nature's contingencies and evolution's randomness are not indicative
> of a divine impotence, but of a God caring and self-effacing enough
> to wait for the genuine emergence of what is truly other than God,
> with all the risk, tragedy and adventure this patience entails. A God
> who loves extravagance and diversity is able to rejoice in the evolving
> autonomy of a self-organizing universe. Such a God is also vulnerable
> enough to suffer along with life in its occasions of failure, struggle and
> loss. . . . [W]e should not be surprised that a divine power rooted in

the depths of an infinite love would not crudely stamp a prefabricated blueprint onto the creation. A divine providence that takes the form of self-humbling love would risk allowing the cosmos to exist and unfold in relative liberty. And so the universe would take on an evolutionary character not in spite of but because of God's care for it.[56]

For many contemporary theologians, God is primarily infinite love, and infinite love constantly restrains itself in order to let us be. If God conveyed an unrestrained omnipotence, then there would be no room for anything other than God. God's control would prescribe any self-determination we might have. But God chose the path of a humble retreat in order to allow creation to develop and evolve toward greater autonomy. "So if ultimate reality is essentially self-giving love, and if love in turn entails letting the other be, then theologically speaking, both the world's original coming into being and its indeterminate Darwinian transformation through time would be completely consonant with the Christian experience of God."[57]

Intimacy always preserves "otherness." God's love allows (even insists!) that the universe be ontologically separate from God. A theory of emanation does not secure such intimacy. The world is not simply a "chip off the old block," or "God, Jr." The indeterminacy at even the most minute levels of physical reality point toward an autonomy that is divinely supported. Using an analogy from family-systems theory, God wants a differentiated, rather than a fused, world. Intimacy demands separateness, but not isolation. God neither smothers the world with sovereign control, nor distances Godself in deistic abandonment. The laws of nature, including natural selection, are part of the world's autonomy. Yet God is always inviting the world to transcend itself and act in more loving and just ways. The ultimate story of the universe, then, is one of promise rather than tragedy. Jerry Korsmeyer, in his helpful book *Evolution and Eden: Balancing Original Sin and Evolutionary Science*, describes how the God of classical theism could not do this.

> A God with classical omnipotent power who could create anything at a word, would not produce the universe as we know it today. The messy aspects of evolution, the diversity of life bursting into all niches

available after extinctions, the dead ends of evolution, dinosaurs in vast array living for hundreds of millions of years, the parasites, the disease bacteria, nature "red in tooth and claw"—all these things become more understandable in the light of a persuasive God and co-creating creatures. The evolving universe makes no sense whatsoever if divinity has the characteristics of classical theism. No wonder the idea of evolution is so repugnant to biblical literalists.[58]

For Korsmeyer, God has been calling forth nature from the beginning, inviting nature to develop greater complexity, greater consciousness, and greater beauty.

SUMMARY

In this chapter, we have explored the implications of Darwin's discovery of the brutalities of nature. We have seen how this discovery largely dismantled the naturalistic apologetic of William Paley, and how it posed a severe problem for the classical metaphysical understanding of God and the world. We examined the philosophical question as to whether Darwinism demands atheism, and particularly examined Alister McGrath's recent evaluation of Richard Dawkins. We then investigated the creative work of theologian John Haught, who has offered a highly interesting and informative theology of evolution. Taking Darwin very seriously, Haught sets forth a view of providence that, in my view, is consistent with Darwin's findings. Is Haught's theology of evolution void of problems? No. All theological perspectives, as thought adventures, are limited and finite. The evils of the world still sting. A "completely fulfilling" theodicy will fade away every time. Nevertheless, Haught has thought long and hard about a "Darwinian theology," and offers a perspective that, in my view, leads in the right direction.

Perhaps a final emphasis is in order concerning a major point Haught and others frequently make: human beings usually do not decide about the "God question" on the basis of a detached, calculated "reading" of the universe. As Blaise Pascal was so fond of saying, we often do not even seek God unless we have already been found by God. Or to echo Tillich's understanding of faith, we do not conjure up our ultimate concerns; instead, *they grasp us*. This is not being irrational. Rather, it is recognizing that the issue of faith goes beyond what reason itself can provide. But perhaps it is helpful to keep in mind that *everyone* goes beyond reason, atheist and theist alike. Our lives are built upon metaphysical assumptions we take for granted, but which we cannot demonstrate. In fact, we normally reject one faith in the name of another faith. We go beyond the evidence to make claims about the nature of ultimate reality. We may *claim* to be making these claims as scientists, but in reality, we are as philosophical as the most devout believers. No one escapes the "faith" enterprise. Even the notion that science is the final arbiter of all reality *is itself* a philosophical faith in science, not the result of scientific discovery.

Evolution has radically exposed the destructiveness in nature. Theologians simply *must* deal with this destructiveness or natural evil if their promises of hope are to be meaningful. Evolutionary theory also has a lot to say about human beings, ethics, and religion itself. What, for instance, is the relationship between evolutionary theory and what we have traditionally called "sin"? It is to this further investigation that we now tun.

CHAPTER TWO

EVIL, ETHICS, AND EVOLUTIONARY PSYCHOLOGY

Morality, or more strictly our belief in morality, is merely an adaptation put in place to further our reproductive ends. . . . In an important sense, ethics as we understand it is an illusion fobbed off on us by our genes to get us to cooperate. It is without external grounding. —*Michael Ruse and Edward O. Wilson*

If we have been puppets all along, how can we suddenly become the puppeteer? —*Ted Peters*

Perhaps it would be helpful to begin this chapter with a central question: How far do we push Darwin? In other words, how much do we draw on Darwin's evolutionary theory to account for *all* of human behavior, including evil? For instance, can Darwinism explain human ethics, social behavior, and even religion? As John Haught suggests, "The leap from 'Darwin got it right' to 'Darwin tells the whole story' has proven increasingly irresistible."[1] Some believe that Darwinism can provide us with far more than an evolutionary theory; instead, deep Darwinism can offer an entire worldview, including a scientific understanding of human behavior.

In fact, Darwinism may well serve up exactly the kind of metanarrative for which the scientifically inclined have been searching. Nothing would be off-limits. Given the assumption that all things can be examined from a naturalistic ontology, science would then be free to investigate matters that have been previously seen as taboo. Cultural explanations of behavior, for instance, might well take a backseat to biological explanations. This approach would obviously eliminate any appeal to the metanatural. Science can handle the job—the *entire* job. Even the existential questions previously addressed by mythic, religious, and metaphysical interpretations could then be placed under the microscope of science. As philosopher of religion Mikael Stenmark puts it:

> Science is, therefore, taken to be the candle in the dark in a demon-haunted world. It is our only hope to avoid superstition and safeguard our cultural achievements and our planet. Consequently, if there is no truth to be found outside science, scientists must become missionaries and bring the gospel to the pagans and unenlightened people. The broad agenda must be to strive to incorporate many other areas of human life within the sciences, so that rational consideration and acquisition of knowledge can be made possible in these areas as well.[2]

In this chapter, I will first explore some of the broad themes of sociobiology, or what is now often referred to as evolutionary psychology. Second, I will investigate the efforts of some Darwinian theorists to account for the origins of morality, "evil," and religion. Third, I will provide a theological critique of these efforts to explain both religion and morality from a purely naturalistic basis. And finally, I will examine whether the traditional Christian understanding of sin, and particularly "original sin," still makes sense in a post-Darwinian world. The overall purpose of this exploration is to gain insights from evolutionary psychology while questioning its metascientific philosophical foundation. Stated a different way, I will attempt to extract some of the empirical findings of evolutionary psychology as a valuable resource while simultaneously questioning the exhaustive naturalism that frequently accompanies those insights. As in the first chapter, I will argue that one can benefit from evolutionary psychology's contributions without buying into the total narrative of a naturalistic ontology. The goal will be to provide a deeper understanding of the nature and dynamics of evil, and particularly human destructiveness.

EVOLUTIONARY PSYCHOLOGY, SOCIOBIOLOGY, AND DARWINIAN ANTHROPOLOGY

A brief comment on terminology is necessary to begin an investigation of evolutionary psychology. I use the terms *evolutionary psychology*, *sociobiology*, and *Darwinian anthropology* interchangeably. While not everyone in this broad field would agree with this equation of terms, I believe the differences between the terms are minimal, and in fact have more to do with political connotations than with significant theoretical departures. For many, sociobiology, from the beginning, became associated with a form of social Darwinism, or at least a highly suspicious bias against some groups of people. Evolutionary psychology, they believe, does not have this baggage and is more acceptable in the academy. Others, and I am one of them, find the same essential arguments offered regardless of the banner under which it is flown. Richard Dawkins makes an interesting comment on this issue of terminology:

> I think it's awfully easy to exaggerate the difference between
> evolutionary psychology and sociobiology. I've always assumed the
> reason for the new name was public relations. A whole lot of people
> have been brought up to think that sociobiology is a dirty word, so
> we'd better have a new word. The phrase "behavioral ecology," was
> invented for exactly the same reason: to distance the subject from
> sociobiology, which in ignorant circles has been taken up as a sort of
> red-rag word.[3]

Regardless of the terminology employed, evolutionary psychology or sociobiology largely believes that evolution can explain *both* cultural and natural phenomena. Edward O. Wilson, whose controversial book, *Sociobiology: The New Synthesis,* established him for many as the founder of sociobiology, argues that sociobiology is "the systematic study of the biological basis of all social behavior."[4] Evolutionary psychology assumes that our thinking process and many of our behavioral patterns are largely inherited rather than learned. These thinking processes are built around nature's master narrative—*the perpetuation of our own genes*. Reproductive success is the primary goal of all life. It drives human behavior in the same way that Freud thought the unconscious drives it. "Fitness" is the all-encompassing preoccupation of life, the ultimate principle that explains everything. This basic understanding of evolutionary psychology and sociobiology will be used throughout this chapter. But before examining some specific themes of this new perspective, let's look briefly at Darwin's view of ethics.

DARWIN AND ETHICS

We saw in the last chapter that Darwinism is based on some rather simple observations. First, all species overproduce. They produce more than the environment can manage. Second, this overproduction creates a struggle for survival. Limited resources demand competition. Third, because differences exist within each species, the members with the greatest capacity for local adaptation survive. The notion of an organism's "fitness" refers to its capacity to survive and reproduce. It has nothing to do with progress or superiority. Natural selection is simply nature's selection of those most adapted. This competition can be brutal and poses a problem of evil for those who yearn for a fair universe.

Darwin's famous "bulldog," Thomas H. Huxley, made a special point of insisting that evolution did *not* provide a foundation for ethics. Herbert Spencer had argued that ethics could be grounded in an evolutionary framework and essentially endorsed the notion that the more "fit" human beings have appropriately survived while the weak have not. This "social Darwinism," as it was later called, was a very unfortunate misunderstanding of Darwin. Again, Darwin never postulated that organisms who survive are "better" or "superior" to other organisms. They are just more equipped to adapt to their immediate environment.

In contrast to Spencer, Huxley argued that there will always be a conflict between the higher aspirations of human beings and the crude laws of nature. We should *not* simply imitate the law of survival as we see it in nature. Evolution has equipped us with the intelligence and capacity to rise above this. Only a fool looks for the rules of ethics in nature. After all, nature's hostility is in conflict with our capacities for empathy, compassion, and aesthetic judgment. To endorse nature as a good guideline for ethical behavior is to dismiss the higher functioning of human beings. Human life has evolved to the point in which we can critically reflect upon the laws of nature, restrain our instincts, and sometimes move against nature's tug. Darwin was in complete agreement with Huxley's views. What is somewhat ironic about Huxley's argument is that while many were accusing Darwin of bringing humanity down to the level of the beasts, Huxley, in a sense, was arguing that the process of evolution had led humanity to its higher functioning and more sophisticated status.

Charles Lyell, who had greatly influenced Darwin, did not believe that natural selection, by itself, was capable of accounting for the ethical, aesthetic, and unique features of humanity. For Lyell, there must be another factor involved, a factor that transcends nature. Without rejecting the notion of natural selection, he simply wanted to add something to it. Natural selection could not be stretched far enough to account for all of human uniqueness without an additional creative factor. Surely some divinely inspired leap forward was necessary to explain the differences between human beings and the rest of the animal world. The shift from inorganic matter to highly developed, civilized people goes beyond natural selection.

Like Lyell, Alfred Wallace also believed that natural selection could not explain the "higher reaches of human nature," to borrow a phrase from Abraham Maslow. It seemed unthinkable to him that symphonies, great works of art, philosophy, and poetry resulted merely from natural selection. Humanity has a special faculty, a fundamental quality that is different from the rest of the animal world. While this human factor may be hidden to the direct observations of science, it is surely there. Thus Lyell and Wallace argued the case for natural selection *plus* an additional, metanatural factor that "created" human beings.

Darwin, on the other hand, did not see a need for such a transnatural ingredient. Natural selection has provided the human species with a much larger brain. This, and this alone, is the explanation for humanity's higher aspirations. There has not been a qualitative break or discontinuity with lower forms of life. Human uniqueness simply emerged from evolution's gift of a larger brain. Both Darwin and Huxley saw a continuity in all organisms and felt no need to move beyond natural selection. The word *creation* had outlived its usefulness. Thus, "by demonstrating man's proximity to the animal kingdom, Darwin and Huxley did wound man's pride; but this wound was healed by their intense appreciation of man's functional superiority and their expectations of his further development in the future."[5]

Harold Vanderpool provides a brief but informative overview of Darwin's view of ethics.[6] First, human beings are social animals with identifiable familial affections. Second, because human beings have developed brains, they can remember and evaluate their previous actions. This helps us develop a sense of conscience, ethical guidelines, or sense of what is "right." Third, the development of language allows us to communicate this sense of "ought" and moral conduct to each other. And fourth, standards of right and wrong are greatly strengthened by habit. As Darwin puts it: ". . . as man gradually advanced in intellectual power, and was enabled to trace the more remote consequences of his actions . . . and as his sympathies became more tender and widely diffused, extending to men of all races, to the imbecile, maimed, and other useless members of society . . . so would the standard of his morality rise higher and higher."[7]

Darwin held onto a kind of eschatological hope that humanity's lower impulses would have less and less influence on human behavior. Perhaps this internal warfare between "higher" and "lower" natures will eventually decrease and it will be possible to rise above our previous patterns. But this does *not* mean that we are on a royal road to progress.

> Man's functional superiority in comparison to the animals hardly
> places man at the center of the cosmos. A better image would be
> to place man on the top of the heap, on the top of the billions of
> organisms whose desperate struggles for survival gave birth to man.
> Clearly Darwin had abandoned his orthodox Christian view of man.
> Man has no "soul." He is neither created nor designed by God. The

idea of Adam, who had been created by God, was dead.[8]

But evolution has also produced human culture and the possibilities of rising above our brute survival impulses. Natural selection, in a sense, has competition—namely, our emerging sense of morality, compassion, and empathy. This allows evolution's creature to step outside of natural selection, refuse to be determined by raw survival, and use our intelligence to act justly and fairly. We have an opportunity to care for the weak, to lift up those with disabilities, and to be concerned with the less fortunate. Clearly this tendency can combat the cruel indifference of nature. Culture thus reduces the pressure of natural selection. And it is our duty to combat this dimension of nature. As Richard Dawkins says, we alone are capable of *resisting* our "selfish genes."[9] We do not have to be slaves to our genes and natural selection does not have to have the final word on our ethical decisions. For Dawkins, our ethics can rise above our selfish genes and create a world vastly different from what we observe in the past.

A great deal of controversy surrounds the issue of whether it's possible to transcend our evolutionary background while simultaneously believing we are determined by it. As we shall see, some believe a contradiction emerges in evolutionary ethics. On the one hand, all human behavior is naturalistically determined, and even our more noble behavior is reduced to selfish genes. On the other hand, some evolutionary psychologists encourage us to rise above this determinism and assert socially liberal ethics. Some critics wonder how we can be both determined and admonished to defy this determinism. Which is it? And if we are to rise above the selfish genes of our nature, on what basis are we to do this? But before we investigate this problem more thoroughly, it is important to get a better understanding of some of the central tenets of evolutionary psychology.

FROM DARWIN TO EVOLUTIONARY PSYCHOLOGY

As we saw in chapter 1, Darwin developed his theory without a knowledge of genetics and therefore assessed fitness in terms of number of offspring rather than gene replicas. While the direct replication of our genes through producing children is the most obvious form of survival, it is also possible to protect our genes by assisting and aiding our relatives, who also carry our genes. As psychology professors B. R. Hergenhahn and Matthew Olson put it: "The fact that persons can perpetuate copies of their genes into subsequent generations either by having offspring or by helping relatives survive and reproduce significantly expands traditional Darwinian theory. It is this expanded theory of evolution which is accepted by sociobiology."[10]

Thus we can invest energy in making sure that our genes are perpetuated, but this process involves more than simply our own particular reproduction. Instead, it refers to our kin as well. This expanded understanding is called "inclusive fitness" because it refers to more than our own particular reproduction. For sociobiology, a great deal of social behavior can be understood and explained through this concept of inclusive fitness. Again, this concept exposes the fact that our primary goal in life is to perpetuate our own genes. This motive of gene perpetuation is largely unconscious. As evolutionary psychologist David Barash puts it: "Genes need not know what they are doing in order to function effectively, and—here is the painful part—neither need we. We can spend a whole lifetime serving their purposes without ever knowing it."[11]

So the major motive of our lives is to replicate ourselves. Much like the Freudians, evolutionary psychologists ask us to look beneath our everyday behavior and find unconscious motives. In the case of sociobiology, however, the motive is clear-cut—survival and the extension of our genes into the future. Social behavior has hidden purposes. Issues such as dating and courtship, group attitudes, child rearing, and family life can be much better understood in the light of natural selection. Stated differently, evolutionary theory helps us understand more than biology; it helps us understand psychology as well. Sociobiologists argue that much of our current behavior exists precisely because it was adaptively advantageous for our ancestors. We *currently* behave, often unconsciously, in ways that have *worked in the past.*

Sociobiology is opposed to any perspective that argues the Lockian position that we are born with a blank slate. This strictly empirical position argues that we are shaped completely by our experience and that we do not come into this world with innate dispositions or inherent tendencies. As evolutionary psychologist David Buss puts it:

> This old paradigm holds that we have no essential nature when we
> are born, aside from a general capacity to learn. The content of our
> character gets written onto this blank slate as we develop. Our "nature"
> is shaped by outside influences: parents, teachers, peers, society,
> the media, and culture. . . . Evolutionary psychology, by contrast,
> contends that we come into the world factory-made—equipped
> with a mind that is designed to solve a range of adaptive problems
> our ancestors grappled with throughout human history. This
> psychological equipment helps us to handle challenges of survival and
> reproduction—the adaptive problems that have confronted generations
> of predecessors going back into deep time. People do not spring from
> the womb, of course, with these adaptations fully formed. Men are not
> born with fully developed beards and women are not born with fully
> developed breasts. They develop later on to help solve problems during
> the reproductive phase of our lifespan. Similarly, our psychological
> adaptations appear at the appropriate time over the course of our
> development.[12]

Perhaps the most pronounced form of this empiricism is represented
by B. F. Skinner, who has argued that our behavior is dominantly shaped
by environmental factors. Sociobiology, on the other hand, leans more
toward "essentialism," or the view that our essential traits are a part of our
biological package. This viewpoint is in opposition to social constructivism,
which often argues that even human "nature" is a socially derived notion.
Predictably, sociobiology is concerned with *universal* elements within
the human condition. These cross-cultural universals that evolutionary
psychology highlights are hotly debated by the more social-constructivist
wing of the social sciences. Also, the postmodern emphasis on diversity and
pluralism runs counter to evolutionary psychology's search for universals.
Stated differently, evolutionary psychologists and postmodern sociologists
don't get along very well. While evolutionary psychologists attempt to
make psychology more scientific by pointing toward universal human
tendencies, postmodern thinkers, and especially sociologists, argue that

evolutionary psychologists minimize the particular gender, socioeconomic, and race issues connected with the individual's context. While evolutionary psychologists claim to recognize these cultural differences, they want to look beneath those differences and find universal elements of the human condition.

> Human beings are, after all, still human beings, and as such, there is a certain range within which their behavior will fall. They may develop distinctive customs and of dress and adornment, perhaps parrot feathers in one place, strange patterns of head shaving in another, the ritual carving of deep scars on cheeks and foreheads in yet another, but some pattern of dress and adornment is always found. Similarly marriage in one place might be sanctified by a ceremonial sharing of food, or maybe by the union of menstrual blood with semen, or by the payment tokens from one partner to the other or by signing a document and utterly officially approved words, but some ritualized sanctioning of male-female association seems almost always to take place. . . . While it is true that culture makes people, people also make cultures, and there is much to gain by looking at what remains the same about people underneath their customs and habits.[13]

Evolutionary psychologists often use the term *biogrammar* to describe these universal structures behind human behavior. While grammar structures refer to the rules of language that make verbal communication possible, biogrammar refers to the structure or rules of social behavior that make social actions possible. Just as there are many languages, so there are many social behaviors, but an underlying structure is always concerned with genetic reproduction.

According to evolutionary psychologists, the blank-slate theorists in psychology, those whose extreme empiricism has led away from any unifying themes about the human condition, have blocked the development of a *scientific* psychology. A scientific psychology dares to make claims about human nature, about the human condition in its universal essence. This minimization of inherent qualities and innate dispositions has led psychology to the dubious conclusion that we simply are what we experience. Psychology has thus provided very little information about why people behave in certain ways. Again, evolutionary psychologists want to ground human nature in a much larger evolutionary theory. They insist that human beings do indeed have a nature. And, "according to the sociobiological theory of human nature each human being is well endowed at birth with the genetically determined behavior tendencies that allowed his or her ancestors to perpetuate their genes."[14]

Evolutionary psychologists frequently acknowledge both *proximate* and *ultimate* causes as they describe human behavior. Proximate causes refer to the immediate factors that influence behavior (environmental factors, level of motivation, and previous experience). Ultimate causes, on the other hand, reflect the larger evolutionary picture of survival. A love of a child, for instance, involves both causes. The proximate causes are that children are helpless and need us, they make us feel good, and they are cute. Yet the ultimate cause is that they guarantee our gene survival, so attachment to them makes sense. This is evolution's way of assuring that our species continues. Children have what ethologists call "internal releasing mechanisms" that "hook us" into caring for them. "All of the usual reasons given by parents for loving their children, such as because they are so cute, or helpless, or because it feels good to love them, constitute proximate causes of parental love. The ultimate cause, however, is the fact that surviving offspring perpetuate the genes of the parents."[15]

We are programmed to "like" what is in our survival interest. This is unapologetically selfish. These inherited behavioral tendencies make us adaptive. Yet this biogrammar is more of a tendency than a determination. It provides a "general game plan for our behavior."[16] We inherit the *structure* of our biogrammar, but culture is also another major factor. As David Barash puts it: "Culture is, in fact, one of the most important biological adaptations, and it therefore need not be opposed to biology. In behaving culturally, we are also behaving biologically. Our culture is natural to us, just as quills are natural to a porcupine."[17]

Culture, however, has limits. While human nature is socially influenced, it is not socially constructed. In fact, our biogrammar pushes culture to be compatible with our biological nature. Thus we become genetically inclined to create institutions that further our fitness and survival. Wilson frequently calls this the "leash principle." Our genes hold culture on a leash. It may be a long leash, but it is still a leash.

THE CONTROVERSIAL ISSUE OF ALTRUISM

For sociobiology, "pure" altruism does not really exist. There is always a hidden motive. We may help each other if we are genetically related (*kin altruism*) but the underlying motive is really our own gene perpetuation. This, as we have seen, is part of inclusive fitness, which recognizes that one of the best ways to perpetuate our own genes is to help our relatives. Sometimes this is also called "kin selection" or nepotism. Because this tendency appears to be universal, sociobiologists believe it is biological.

Another dimension of altruism is *reciprocal altruism,* which argues that we cooperate because this helps our own chance for survival, a kind of "I'll scratch your back, you scratch mine" mentality. The admonition, "Do unto others as you would have them do unto you," actually imagines the need for our own help in the future. Understanding that we, too, may need help some day, we are motivated to help someone else now. The focus is on our future need, not just the other person's current need. Therefore, hidden motives underlie our "pure" self-giving gestures. Evolutionary psychologists, then, have similarities with the seventeenth-century philosopher Thomas Hobbes, who argued that all ethics can be boiled down to psychological egoism and that altruism is really just a disguised form of self-interest. For Hobbes, our own survival is the driving force behind all ethical considerations. Any interest in society is merely for the sake of how it enhances our own survival. Charity is cynically reduced to self-concern. Put in more contemporary language, the ultimate purpose of life is dictated by the desire for gene replication.

Ted Peters and Martinez Hewlett, however, believe that this view of altruism falls short of a Judeo-Christian understanding of altruism.

> The difficulty, of course, is that genetically driven altruism is reciprocal, limited to one's close genetic kin group, and finally reducible to governance by the selfish gene. Altruism as a principle of evolutionary

adaptation is not what Christians would call love because love in its most ethical sense aims at improving the welfare of someone who is other. Limiting love to genetic kin removes the element of seeking benefit for the other. So, if altruism is reducible to disguised selfishness, it does not pass the test the ethicist would exact.[18]

Loving only one's kin is a far cry from the ethical vision of Jesus, who exhorted us to love even our enemies.

Don Browning, however, makes the interesting claim that many of the key themes about kin altruism were anticipated in the theological work of Aquinas, and even in the earlier philosophical writings of Aristotle.[19] Aquinas clearly recognized the natural tendency to show greater preference for those children to whom one is biologically related. While exceptions may exist, they do not negate the general human tendency to show partiality and preferential treatment to our own offspring. Human infants need far lengthier and greater care than other species. This creates a long and intense tie to the mother. A major factor in the male joining the female/child dyad is the male having a fair degree of assurance that the baby is really his and does not represent the genes of another man. As Aquinas put it, "Man naturally desires to be assured of his offspring and this assurance would be altogether nullified in the case of promiscuous copulation. Therefore the union of the man with the woman comes from a natural instinct."[20] The male may also feel inclined to join the mother-child dyad in order to achieve mutual assistance and regular sexual exchange.

While Aquinas sounds, in some ways, like an evolutionary psychologist, some caution is necessary as we bring him into the discussion. First, as Browning suggests, Aquinas probably overstates the case when he talks about a natural instinct for the human male to join the female, something that is often not done among other mammals. Browning, with warrant, suggests a revision of this natural inclination thesis: "among conflicting male tendencies, there are some which, when faced with the dependency of an infant that a human male recognizes as his, can be channeled into enduring male-female family arrangements for the purpose of caring for the infant."[21] Thus this "natural inclination" offers no guarantee that the male will join the female. Also, it does not cancel out conflicting natural tendencies. Browning, following William James, believes that we each have a plurality of instincts, not just one or two that compete with each other. Also, Aquinas himself believed that ethical arguments must be made to establish further the goodness of marriage. While these arguments were built upon natural inclinations, the natural inclinations alone could not sustain the reasons for marriage.

Browning's argument certainly does not endorse the subordination of women as does Aristotle's and Aquinas's position. Clearly, throughout his work, Browning makes a strong case for mutuality and equal regard in the marital arrangement. In fact, he believes that feminists are quite right in their criticism of self-sacrifice as the highest form of care for which we should strive. While self-sacrifice is important, it is a transitional ethic, a temporary position, in service of the larger good of *mutuality* and *equality*. Both males and females may well be called upon to make sacrifices for the good of the other. Stated simply, this is part of "going the extra mile," which all couples need to do at times. However, this should not exist as a permanent pattern. Mutual respect, care, and equality are the goals, not ongoing agape. Thus self-sacrifice is not an end in itself, but a transitional moment to ultimately reinforce love as mutuality, friendship, and equal regard. Constant agape in our relationships leads to resentment, as we inevitably see the nonreciprocal unfairness.

So these natural inclinations, well described by both Aquinas and evolutionary psychology, need reinforcement from cultural values, narratives, and symbols. The realities of evolutionary psychology provide us with important information about the human condition. To deny this biological dimension is to distort our human inclinations. Yet a theological perspective is willing to go beyond this form of altruism and invoke images of the other as a child of God. We are called to act lovingly toward others regardless of whether we are related to them.

Philip Hefner, a Lutheran theologian with a very sophisticated grasp of science, makes the interesting point that altruism is not antievolutionary.[22] In fact, it is part of a much larger evolutionary process that can be theologically understood as the purpose of God. Trans-kin altruism is the possibility toward which God is inviting us. Because God's ultimate purpose is the renewal and perfection of all creation, human beings have an opportunity to actualize a new stage of evolution. For Hefner, the billions and billions of prehuman years do not subtract from the significance of human beings because we are "created co-creators." Hefner's work has nearly become synonymous with this phrase because it captures the heart of his theory. We are utterly dependent upon the prehuman evolutionary processes from which we emerged. Our existence is a "derived" or "created" one. We are not self-generating. Yet through the gradual development of self-consciousness and greater freedom, we have an opportunity to cocreate with God, to help bring about the ultimate purposes of God through our own choices. A strict genetic evolution has moved into a cultural evolution. We are biological animals who have also become cultural beings. Metaphorically speaking, we have "two natures." Our biological instincts push us in the direction of self-centered survival. This is the legacy of our prehuman history. As Hefner puts it, "we bring stone-age biological drives into a contemporary technological milieu to which our biological equipment is but poorly adapted."[23] Our cultural evolution offers us an opportunity to transcend natural selection. We do not have to allow our immediate selfish genes to prevent the possibility of care for nonrelatives. There is tension and struggle between these two competing inclinations, but even the evolutionary past has always, argues Hefner, envisioned the possibility of this type of freedom. It has not been blind and without purpose. In fact, the story of evolution, even from the big bang forward, is a story about the gradual emergence of creative freedom. On the one hand, the ongoing legacy of our survival thinking has left on us a mark of selfish opportunism. On the other hand, our emerging cultural evolution with its sense of cooperation, higher values, and concern for all people (not just our kin), invites us toward a higher plane of existence, an evolutionary shift. As a theologian, Hefner believes that Christ is the symbol of this hope.

> In his life, death, and teachings, Jesus offers us the possibilities
> for raising human living to a higher plane, one which will reveal
> new ways of adapting to the reality system of nature and of God.
> Jesus' proposal for the love-principle—a universal love that crosses
> boundaries of kinship—is a new way of life that stretches and bends
> the requirements of adaptation in novel ways. This proposal for trans-

kin altruism is scandalous to many, because it appears to be a formula for maladaptation if not extinction. Yet theologically, we want to say that the cross and resurrection represent the divinely willed direction for future cultural evolution.[24]

For Hefner, it is important to recognize that while this "battle" between genes and culture may seem like a dualistic framework, our higher aspirations have in fact emerged out of lower ones. The tension between genes and culture is a developmental struggle and not a fixed and permanent dichotomy. In a sense, then, Hefner is saying that values are "built into" the evolutionary process, lying dormant all along until their time to emerge. Thus Hefner can assert:

> The human being is created by God to be a co-creator in the creation that God has brought into being and for which God has purposes. . . . The conditioning matrix that has produced the human being—the evolutionary process—is God's process of bringing into being a creature who represents creation's zone for a new stage of freedom and who therefore is crucial for the emergence of a free action. . . . The freedom that marks the created co-creator and its culture is an instrumentality of God for enabling the creation (consisting of the evolutionary past of genetic and cultural inheritance as well as the contemporary ecosystem) to participate in the intentional fulfillment of God's purposes.[25]

Hefner also mentions John Hick's point that if it is God's intention to create a world of genuine freedom, then even that freedom itself must be chosen. Put another way, if God had given humanity its freedom "all at once" it would have been less meaningful. We would have played no role in our own developing freedom.[26] Thus, for Hefner, out of the conditioning matrix of our prehuman evolutionary history, the goal has always been greater freedom and the possibility of cultural evolution.

Does Hefner go too far in pitting genes against culture and identifying sin with our biogenetic context of selfishness? Does he therefore imply that sin is intrinsic to our vary nature and thus necessary? We will turn to these questions later in the chapter when we examine views on how the notion of original sin may still make sense in a post-Darwinian world. For now, we must turn to evolutionary psychology's link between violence and reproductive competition.

AGGRESSION AND REPRODUCTIVE COMPETITION

We saw in the first chapter that nature is quite bloody. While this is certainly true, it is perhaps a mistake to jump to the conclusion that nature is therefore extremely aggressive. Predation, the pursuit of other animals for food, seems to result primarily from a desire to survive and not from a primitive form of aggression for aggression's sake. Stated differently, aggression serves the purposes of survival. As we will see in the next chapter, the seasoned Freud believed that aggression is a drive separate from libido, a drive that must find some form of discharge. For evolutionary psychologists, we engage in aggressive behavior because it is advantageous for us. Aggression is purposeful, a strategy to aid survival and fitness. "The sociobiological position is that humans inherit the capacity to act aggressively but will do so only when it maximizes fitness. For example, humans are likely to fight among themselves in environments where valuable resources are scarce. Should circumstances change and resources become more plentiful, aggression among humans decreases."[27]

Aggression, then, emerges when there is a limitation of resources, and hence a threat to survival. Thus competition provokes aggression. This competition may be for food, territory, or mates. And it is particularly over mates that most aggression occurs in mammals. Males are especially aggressive with each other in the pursuit of females. As we have seen, females who invest heavily in the process of reproduction can afford to be quite "picky" about their partners. With a limited amount of reproductive possibilities, they can wait on a male who can provide resources and aid their child-rearing efforts. Males, on the other hand, expend very little energy in the process of reproduction. Historically, it has been reproductively advantageous for males to have many partners; the more partners, the more children, and therefore the greater the replication of one's genes. For women, on the other hand, it has been reproductively advantageous to choose a single partner with resources. They need a partner who will put greater investment into the limited number of children they can have.

David Buss is very interested in connecting the relationship between reproduction competition and aggression. In a very extensive and impressive research project that investigated various factors in murder, Buss discovered that most violent crime is committed by men. On average, around 87 percent of all murders in the United States every year are committed by men, most of whom are between twenty to twenty-nine years of age. Further, most of the victims are also men in that same age range. "What these numbers reveal is that murder increases dramatically as males enter the years of reproductive competition."[28]

It is also important to note that these numbers are cross-cultural. They don't seem to differ much in developed or undeveloped countries. This is important for Buss because it questions the widespread idea, championed especially by Albert Bandura's social-learning theory, that male violence in developed countries results primarily from the imitation of aggressive, macho images of maleness conveyed in the media. Bandura's well-known argument is that human beings acquire social behavior by imitating others, and a huge influencing factor is violence on television. Men are consistently portrayed as fighting and violent, and for social-learning theorists, young males simply imitate what they see. Thus men *learn* to be violent.

Buss disagrees. He does not think this is an adequate account of male violence for a couple of reasons. First, as I mentioned above, Buss believes that these aggressive male tendencies occur in societies that are not saturated with media images of violent males. In fact, he argues that the propensities toward male violence are about the same regardless of whether or not men are exposed to violent images in the media. And second, Buss argues that the media conveys many different types of male images. "The models range from nice men who perform heroic deeds, to evil, sneering bad guys who get punished for having been violent. And we are taught from an early age that murder is wrong and that crime doesn't pay. Nothing in the theory can explain whom we will choose to imitate from the vast array of models to which we are exposed."[29]

Buss also comments on "pathology" theories of murder. These

theories argue that killing is frequently related to brain damage or severe psychological dysfunction. In a major study of Michigan murders, however, Buss found that neither brain disease nor psychopathology was the cause. Brain-damage-related or psychopathological murders would most likely be random and senseless, often with bizarre elements. Such was not the case. Also, most human beings with brain damage do *not* become violent.

Another perspective on murder comes largely from sociology. This explanation sees violence as connected to unfortunate aspects of the larger society such as poverty, economic inequality, or even capitalism itself. Buss recognizes economic inequality as a factor in crime. In areas full of economic disparity, robberies and muggings clearly increase. Yet in areas in which poverty dominates across the board, there is not necessarily an increase in crime. Also, according to Buss, there is no evidence that murder or any other sort of crime is more common in capitalistic societies than in socialist cultures.[30] Further, Buss argues that sociological theories do not tell us *why* people would react to economic disparity with murder rather than some other response.

Buss locates a great deal of murder and male violence in reproductive competition. The competition to reproduce, he argues, is a major force in our lives. Every generation has a fixed number of reproductively viable men and women with whom to mate.[31] "Each man and woman is ultimately in competition with other men and women for 'shares' of the ancestry of the next generation."[32] Though it is disturbing to say, in the process of reproductive competition, murder is a successful way of promoting our own gene replication. Though we are now more civilized, and have developed rules against murder, throughout most of our evolutionary history, murdering a rival was a sure way to guarantee our own gene reproduction. This seems cold-hearted, but it has worked as a survival mechanism.

As Buss suggests, from an evolutionary perspective, being murdered is doubly bad. Not only is one dead, one's ability to pass on one's genes is destroyed. Every opportunity for reproduction is now eliminated. And further, if one has a mate, that mate is now available and eligible for other men to perpetuate *their* genes. Again, it is reproductively advantageous to get rivals out of the way.

In the murder cases that Buss examined, a common theme had to do with sexual rivalry. "Sexual reproduction added a whole new element of competition, that of members of the same sex vying to hook up with the most appealing potential mates. That intense competition opened the door for murder."[33] In developed countries, this competition plays out in financial resources, expensive cars, the ownership of property, and status. It's usually wallet competition or a battle over who has the greatest resources. For women, it is physical beauty and a healthy, youthful appearance. As Buss suggests, "members of each sex, in essence, become willing victims to the whims and desires of the opposite sex. Those who don't compete go to bed alone."[34]

Buss is also very interested in the manner in which men and women "put down" members of their own sex when they are in the presence of the opposite sex. These denigrations usually revolve around what they perceive as important to the opposite sex. For instance, women often comment on infidelity and physical ugliness in regard to other women. Knowing that men value fidelity in a partner, a woman can suggest that another woman is quite "loose" sexually or "sleeps around." Similarly, men put down other men in the presence of women by pointing toward another man's lack of achievement and resources, "loser" quality, or junky car. If another man is presented as an ambitionless nobody meandering about, there will be a significant loss of female interest in him.

Evolutionary psychologists thus suggest that there are deeper evolutionary reasons for our so-called "shallow" concerns in mate selection. The criticism that men are preoccupied with physical attractiveness and youth, according to an evolutionary perspective, misses the point that they have an underlying concern to perpetuate their genes. Similarly, the criticism that a woman is a "gold digger," or only interested in a man's resources, misses the underlying concern for the survival of her own children. Thus the evolutionary perspective suggests that we don't simply shop for *partners*; we also look for *parents* of our children. Once again, the master motive of gene replication is the determining factor. The person with the most genes wins.

So for Buss, it is this sexual competition that often promotes a propensity for violence. In fact, it is this male competition, more than any other factor, that explains aggressive behavior. In this, humans are not dissimilar to other mammals. "When we witness two male hamadryas baboons going at it tooth and claw, two male elk crashing antlers, or two male sea lions attempting to gore each other to death, invoking 'pathology' or 'media exposure' or 'parenting practices' obviously doesn't get to the core of the matter."[35]

Again, for evolutionary psychology, this motivation to reproduce is not usually a conscious intention. It functions beneath the surface. Similarly, motivation for murdering other males may well exist below human awareness as it is connected with the reproductive task. Men mainly kill other men and they do so during the primary years of reproductive fitness.

Buss has accumulated a very impressive body of research and has distinguished himself as an outstanding theorist. The evolutionary perspective on male violence and murder, particularly as it is related to reproductive competition, makes sense. The question, however, is whether this explanation tells the *whole* story of human destructiveness. I suggest that it does not. While sexual competition may be a significant factor in male aggression, we will see in the next two chapters that there are effective psychological explanations that need to be added to the evolutionary perspective. Human destructiveness is more nuanced and complicated than a strict evolutionary theory allows.

In addition to providing the reasons for human aggression, many sociobiologists also believe they can provide an evolutionary account of religion. These claims may be the most controversial dimension of the sociobiology perspective.

EVOLUTIONARY PSYCHOLOGY AND RELIGION

For many evolutionary psychologists, religion is a carryover of our primitive brain's attempt to create illusions and bizarre beliefs.

> Most representatives of the present generation of Darwinian
> anthropologists now agree that religion is an irritatingly obsolete
> but stubbornly ineradicable human tendency. Our religious
> orientation seems to be so deeply rooted and so pervasive that it

cannot be understood simply as a cultural invention. Religion must
be connected more closely to the specific kind of brain we have, to
cerebral systems that served the cause of survival during the course of
human evolution. Thus, the ultimate explanation has to do with gene
survival. Genes need vehicles that will allow them to replicate faithfully
and prodigiously. And it now appears that vehicles equipped with a
tendency to be religious were among the most suitable to human gene
survival.[36]

Our genetic capacity to create illusions is the primary reason for
religion. Religion is not connected to actual encounters with the Divine
or revelation, but instead, can be explained as the brain's evolutionary
tendency to create a protective God to help us feel safe in a dangerous
world. Religion has helped us adapt by providing a sacred sense of ultimate
protection and a metaphysical grounding for our moral behavior. Religion
promotes "fitness" in that it aids our conviction that we are not alone in a
cold universe. Religion keeps us from seeing the universe as the impersonal
place it actually is. It provides an ultimate sense of order, meaning, and
purpose that distracts us from the reality that the universe is really pointless.
We "function better" when we believe in ultimate meaning. Thus, to
use metaphorical language, our own genes have spun out this elaborate
network of symbols, myths, and rituals to help promote their survival. Our
genes have a greater chance of surviving when we believe in the illusions of
religion. Religion is the shield and protection against the anxieties of cosmic
aloneness. It is epistemologically soothing and cognitively reassuring. In
short, religion has historically helped us continue to survive because it has
assured us that it is all worthwhile.

This new "biology of religion" gives us the *scientific* answers we need
to understand the religious impulse throughout our evolutionary history.
While we may have previously thought our religious inclinations were real,
we are now free to admit that they are long-lasting, adaptive fictions.

Note here that many evolutionary psychologists are not as critical of
religious beliefs as someone such as Freud, whom we will consider in the
next chapter. For Freud, religious beliefs stunt psychological growth as
one refuses to grow up and let go of the projected father figure named

"God." Evolutionary psychologists clearly see the adaptive significance and functional importance of religion. Yet, like Freud, they believe it is a trick the human brain plays on itself. While it has functional value, it is not based on anything in reality. And scientists, of course, are what Peter Berger frequently calls the "reality experts." So religion has been both ignorant and useful. "As a result of natural selection, our ancestors' genetic constitution made their brains and anxiety-prone nervous systems fertile soil for the implantation of a kind of religious conjecturing that in turn has abetted the cause of gene survival. And because our gene sequencing is essentially the same today as it was 100,000 or more years ago, can there be any wonder that religions are still around?"[37]

Cultural changes will not eliminate religion because the roots of religious belief are deeper than culture. Instead, religion is rooted in an evolutionary mental process, a cognitive inclination deeper than cultural learning. The naturalistic explanation provides the important biological basis for why religion persists. Walter Burkett and Pascal Boyer are examples of two contemporary voices who believe that cultural explanations will never get at the basic persistence of religion.[38] They "biologize" religion to demonstrate its adaptive function. Religion is a splendid invention of our self-serving genes. While culture supplies the *content* of many religious ideas, it is our genes that are behind the religious impulse. The particularity of our religion is, of course, deeply influenced by our culture. But the *fact* that we are religious comes from our genes.

As John Haught suggests, it is revealing to look at how Darwinian anthropologists deal with the question of truth. As we have seen, they refuse to attack religion on the grounds that it is illusory, and hence not true. Most critics of religion have argued that an "untruth" needs to be pointed out even if it has *functional* value. Not to point out a falsehood would be immoral. Evolutionary psychologists, however, argue that we may not even have survived as a species if it were not for religion. Again, metaphorically speaking, our genes saw the value of religion. This was a necessary deception, a life-promoting illusion. Thus we are in a most precarious position: we must expose the very illusory world that has carried our species along. In fact, for some evolutionary thinkers, we may want to "leave well enough alone" when it comes to challenging people's religious views. Scientists, of course, "know better," but many human beings may need religion in order to survive. As philosopher Loyal Rue has put it, "the role of deception in human adaptive strategies has been so important that we may suspect it to be essential for survival."[39] This deception is a defense against the *real* world, which is nihilistic. Our deception protects us against the survival-threatening despair of meaninglessness. This deception is similar to the necessary deception Freud described in the early life of a child. Defense mechanisms come to our rescue and protect us from facing truth we cannot handle. We "lie" to ourselves out of necessity. The problem, for Freud, is that these early strategies become permanent fixtures in our psyches, and even as adults, we hide the truth from ourselves. Similarly, these evolutionary lies have been necessary for our biological survival as a species. Otto Rank and Ernest Becker, whom we will encounter in the next chapter, argue that human beings must create "vital lies" in order to cope with the world. "Apparently, it is just those who are courageous enough to look at reality nakedly and without illusions who will be most prone to psychosis. The healthy-minded among us should give thanks for our species' capacity to evade truths that would surely sicken us if we looked straight at them."[40] Thus the enlightened now know the truth and must swallow the pill. The unenlightened still need religion and we should recognize that it may be essential to their survival.

Once again, evolutionary adaptation becomes the all-inclusive, "objective" explanation of life. These Darwinians somehow "know" that while religious people *claim* to encounter the presence of the Divine, they are actually only imagining this because it has evolutionary survival. In actuality, all religious ideas simply serve gene production.

An evolutionary account of religion can be helpful, but the problem is that this approach claims to offer the *ultimate* explanation, a perspective so comprehensive that its renders all other perspectives useless. By "naturalizing" that which the majority of humans claim to be metanatural, evolutionary thinkers move from method to metaphysics. Once again, scientism, rather than science, raises its head. Spirituality is reducible to a biological connection designed to further the species. But this approach moves beyond the appropriate naturalistic method. It ushers in a naturalistic metaphysic, which makes claims about ultimate, and not just empirical, reality. Science has once again become philosophy as it "believes" or "has faith that" there is absolutely nothing but the strictly empirical world. If this is self-consciously announced as a philosophical view about the nature of science, then it is perfectly legitimate. But announcing that a "purely scientific" investigation has led to this conclusion is not legitimate. It is an overextension of science. Scientists are quite free to speak philosophically and theologically, but they should not pretend to be scientists when they do so.

As this evolutionary approach inappropriately reduces religion to gene survival, it also dehumanizes religion. The quest for personal meaning and the long history of theological thought is but a by-product of what is really going on—the relentless demands of our genes. Personal agency seems quite irrelevant. We are mechanically pushed by our biology. The dignity of our quest for meaning is reduced to raw, biological survival. "Contemporary gene-enchanted Darwinism, however, has exiled living beings, including human subjects, from their natural home in the sphere governed by the logic of achievement. Simultaneously, it has projected the deracinated attribute of centered striving onto atomic genetic units that both physical science and common sense are normally obliged to consider incapable of any kind of commitments or personal agency whatsoever."[41]

This is a fairly common criticism of the "selfish gene" theory—namely, these evolutionists infuse inanimate and impersonal genes with qualities of personhood. The gene attempts to "get ahead," "achieve," "survive," and so on. Further, these genes seem "manipulative" and even "cunning" in their ability to get what they want. While these evolutionists have insisted that they are speaking metaphorically about an impersonal process, many critics believe that they are, in fact, injecting genes with personal motives and characteristics.

Ironically, "striving" is denied to personhood and attributed instead to an impersonal gene, a most strange anthropomorphism. Impersonal genes are thus given a level of subjectivity that the overall human organism is denied. While human subjectivity is never treated as the primary cause of motivation, the selfish gene is provided with a kind of subjective intentionality that goes unquestioned. Yet I would argue instead that we project onto the gene a subjective striving and ambition that comes from our own psychological experience. For many evolutionists, our own aspirations and choices do not have subjective credibility as "reasons" for our behavior. Yet the aspirations and choices of our genes are accepted at face value.

DETERMINISM AND TRANSCENDENCE: THE CENTRAL PROBLEM

I am hardly the first to point out a controversial issue surrounding sociobiology's understanding of determinism—namely, that it is self-contradictory to speak of complete genetic determinism on the one hand, and encourage the tendency to rise above such determinism on the other. Some evolutionists argue that they do not operate on the basis of such a determinism. The problem with any form of radical determinism is this: the declarations of the determinist claim an immunity from the very process that he or she is describing. Theories of determinism seem to have a paradoxical (contradictory?) moment in which someone steps outside the conditioning factors to admonish a particular way of life. Skinner steps outside of his own environmental conditioning to tell us how to engineer a healthy society; Dawkins steps outside of his selfish genes long enough to tell us how to be unselfish. No matter how much a metanarrative denies genuine freedom, that freedom finds a way of sneaking back in. Otherwise, Skinner's vision of a good society is nothing but the limitations of his own conditionedness and Dawkins's discussion of a just world is simply another manifestation of his selfish genes talking. Some evolutionary psychologists work with a genetic metanarrative that eliminates from the outset the possibility of human freedom, then employs human freedom to help us step outside the deterministic flow.

Ted Peters has suggested that there are three factors which must be considered when examining the human predicament: genetics, the environment, and human freedom.[42] An exclusive focus on any one of the three at the expense of the others will not allow for a comprehensive portrait of humanity. Evolutionary psychology, for Peters, involves "puppet determinism," a view which states that our genes define who we are, that DNA is the ultimate determiner of our lives. Freedom, as we have seen, is an illusion. In this genetic essentialism, there is no "self" other than DNA.

This view is also fatalistic.

> To speak of "genetic fatalism" or to say "It's all in the genes," is
> to assume that genetic influences are unchangeable, that we are
> immutably destined to act as our DNA programs us to act. The
> psychological corollary to genetic determinism is clear: what we assume
> to be personal freedom is only an illusion. The ethical corollary to
> genetic determinism is also clear: we are not responsible for what we
> do; our genes are. We have natural innocence in a new form: blame my
> genes, not me.[43]

Peters then describes what he calls "promethean determinism," named after Prometheus, who stole fire from the sun so that the earth could have a source of heat and light. Promethean determinism is paradoxical, if not flatly contradictory. It suggests that by figuring out how our genes control us, we can then "outsmart" our own genes in such a way that we can control them. Because genes are always working behind the scenes, scientists need to identify and reveal this genetic determinism so that we can gain some degree of control over our genes. Ultimately, this is an attempt to control nature.

It is not always clear how these two "sides" of genetic determinism work. We're controlled by our genes, but genetic knowledge and technology can liberate us from this control. Like the unconscious, selfish genes prefer to work unexposed and in the dark. Selfish genes exploit our ignorance and are most content when we have the illusion that we are in control. This makes us more cooperative toward the real aim of life—genetic reproduction.

Some evolutionary psychologists, once again, denounce genetic determinism and argue that *both* genes and culture determine behavior. They would be what Peters calls "two-factor" determinists.[44] Single-factor determinists focus on the genes or the environment *alone* as the all-inclusive story of human life. Those who argue that genes offer a complete account of human existence would be obvious examples of single factor determinism. Thus the "gene story" is a single-factor metaphysical story, framed in scientific language, about the totality of existence. Two-factor determinism, on the other hand, would combine both genetics and environment. Peters believes that Harvard scientist Richard Lewontin offers a good example of two-factor determinism. In his criticism of single-factor determinism, Lewontin writes, "We must insist that a full understanding of the human condition demands an integration of the biological and the social in which neither is given primacy or ontological priority over the other."[45] While Lewontin and his colleagues argue against a one-factor puppet determinism, they nevertheless argue in favor of a two-factor determinism—genes *plus* environment. Both our genes *and* our environment pull our strings, but our strings are still being pulled. But Peters raises an important concern: "The logical question is this: If the genes have been our puppeteer, did they themselves give us what we need now to cut the strings and to take control? Is human freedom itself a gift of the genes? If not, what is the condition that makes possible transcendence of our genetic inheritance? If we have been puppets all along, how can we suddenly become the puppeteer?"[46]

Edward O. Wilson is quite direct in answering this question: "The agent itself is created by the interaction of the genes and the environment. It would appear that our freedom is only a self-delusion."[47] While we may consciously *feel and think* we are free, this is born out of an ignorance concerning the real factors that are pushing and pulling us. "Even more to the point: our lack of conscious awareness regarding what determines us is not an accident. It is part of nature's design. We have been programmed to by our genes to be ignorant of their power over us. The delusion of freedom with which we operate is a delusion perpetuated on our consciousness because it serves the designs of genetic interest, namely, adaptation."[48]

Free will is thus a useful fiction. For one thing, it helps limit crime. If we tell people that they are free and then threaten punishment, this may deter crime. If the legal system is going to be possible, we must perpetuate the notion of freely chosen behavior. Otherwise, no one could be held responsible for crimes. We are determined by DNA and yet we must rise above DNA. In fact, our sense of morality necessitates rising above it. "And what moral means here is clear: engaging in acts of love which no personal gain—or reproductive gain for one's own genes—is the goal.[49] Selfish genes are unconsciously influencing our reason, desires, and instincts. But again, how does this theory explain the manner in which our "higher morality" arose in the first place? Further, how is this higher level of ethical thinking related to our selfish genes? When did the trans-selfish overshadow the selfish? On the one hand, we are driven by a near-cynical view of the selfish gene; on the other hand, we hope for a just, fair, nonsexist, liberal social agenda.[50] Perhaps we must once again ask: Isn't the evolutionary psychology theory *itself* the very product of determinism? How did these scientists manage to step outside of evolutionary determinism long enough to figure out the big picture? "It appears that evolutionary psychologists, once they have made the deterministic argument, suddenly wake up and realize that they live in a liberal society; and they want to speak of liberty. Freedom gets reaffirmed, and liberation becomes our task. It's like inviting prisoners in a concentration camp to a freedom pep rally, and when it's over, asking them to return to their cells."[51]

Holmes Rolston III does not like the idea of applying a moral category such as "selfishness" to premoral genes. He believes that by doing this, we are anthropomorphizing biology as we turn genes into conscious agents. In order for something to be *selfish*, it must have a *self*. Only an entire self, not its genetic parts, can be described as moral. Further, Rolston adds: "Just where is Wilson getting these *oughts* that cannot be derived from biology, unless from the insights of ethicists (or theologians) that transcend biology? This no longer sounds like a biologist biologizing ethics and philosophy. It sounds like a biologist philosophizing without acknowledging his sources."[52]

Wilson's norms are clearly extrabiological. And yet he remains convinced that Darwinism will eventually describe all dimensions of life. As Peters puts it, "Wilson's belief in the final explanatory power of the neo-Darwinian model in every feature of human nature seems to justify Gould's characterization of him as a Darwinian fundamentalist."[53]

The theologian Langdon Gilkey also sees much of the same problem.[54] He faults evolutionary psychology for borrowing language from the region where human freedom is found, applying it by analogy to natural processes, then concluding that so-called freedom is determined by biological processes. For Gilkey, the problem is that evolutionary psychologists are using the language of purpose from human experience to describe an evolutionary process that they believe has no purpose. Teleological language is used to describe a nonteleological process. Or stated differently, this is a nonpurposeful application of purposeful language. Conscious purposes are used to describe unconscious processes. Language that describes the *whole* organism is employed to describe only one unit of the organism—namely, the genes. Thus Gilkey believes there is enormous linguistic confusion in this discourse.

As we have seen, evolutionary psychologists claim that our minds are quite deceptive. They convince us that we are altruistic, when in fact we are working in the service of self-preservation. Yet they claim they are able to climb out from under this natural deception and name it for what it is. Gilkey raises an interesting point:

> The reader cannot help but wonder why, if this theory is valid,
> the moral sentiments expressed by the scientific authors, however
> persuasively argued, and their scientific conclusions, however
> empirically verified, should not themselves be products of this
> intricate, infinitely devious, and quite ruthless process of deception,
> designed or programmed to deceive the reader into altruistic
> political acts (pacifistic ones) helpful to the interests of the biological
> community and their genes. One can only assume that somehow to
> these authors these moral sentiments and rational arguments represent
> a sort of morality and rationality different from those described in the
> theory, and so again we encounter a sharp dualism.[55]

Gilkey suggests that people such as Dawkins clearly transcend mere selfishness, the very selfishness that, according to their own theory, dominates and manipulates consciousness and morality. But Dawkins provides no explanation for why we should trust his perspective as genuinely rational, "objective," or altruistic. How do we know his own theory is not utterly driven by powers of manipulation and deception? In short, how do we know that his talk about a selfish gene is not itself the result of a selfish gene? How does he escape this conclusion? Dawkins is an advocate of a nondiscriminatory social system that serves altruistic purposes. How does he pull this off? What is the mechanism by which he transcends his selfish genes?

> Morality is thus ultimately self-interested, at least on the part of
> its prime or ultimate instigator, the gene; and, therefore, altruism,
> while perhaps descriptive of the individual, is seen biologically as a

function of genetic self-interest—and of moral realism as a mode of propaganda or corporate deception—does not explain at all the clear and "high" moral sense of the authors themselves, which systematically if not explicitly defies this genetic and group self-love and seeks, as an authentic obligation, a just, fair, universal society based on science and so not on deception.[56]

Dawkins commits hubris insofar as he claims to rise above his own selfish genes and speak from an altruistic, objective place of science. Even this "higher morality" of Dawkins has its ambiguity and self-interest. Again, Dawkins does not account for his own gene transcendence.

The evolutionary psychology claim to have the objective truth about life, to be the metanarrative for our self-understanding, may very well expose its own dark side of self-interest and misguided grandiosity. As Gilkey suggests, evolutionary psychology sees itself as *the* central discipline to which all others need to listen. It claims a scientific basis for its *prescriptive*, not just its *descriptive*, agenda. It teaches us to be suspicious while being unsuspicious of its own teachings. "Again, what is needed is not only brilliant and articulate defense of what one knows in one's discipline but also humility about the limited character of what one knows and about its cooperative place in the entire panorama of human understandings. Then what is called for is a synthesis of all these perspectives, each of which sheds its own light on the larger mystery."[57]

Also, evolutionary psychology, according to Peters, should not be equated with natural science. It offers no experiments that confirm or falsify its claims. It is an interesting speculative philosophy. It is imaginative and provocative, but it is a *philosophical* perspective, and not a scientifically governed viewpoint. Like all forms of scientism, it moves from methodological reductionism to ontological reductionism. And this is a philosophical, not a scientific, move.

[W]hen we confront Darwinian theory we confront far more than merely the science of biology. Trying to get to the science is like trying to get on one's e-mail for the day. Pop-ups and advertising and junk messages clutter the computer screen, just as social Darwinism and genetic reductionism and materialist philosophy clutter the basic Darwinian theory. For the theologian trying to assess the potential value of Darwinian theory for understanding human nature or divine creativity, the clutter makes reading the message more difficult. Yet, it is no less interesting, and no less worth the effort.[58]

Once again, it becomes important to separate Darwinian science from Darwinian metaphysics.

In summary, Peters and Hewlett identify three major problems with evolutionary psychologists providing a comprehensive ethic in the name of science. Evolutionary psychologists typically insist on eliminating the vocabulary of "purpose" from their theory and research. Yet, while eradicating the notion of purpose in their research methodology, it is smuggled back into their assumptive world as they explain the "point" of human behavior. Second, despite claims to the contrary, their attempt to ground ethics in nature alone commits the naturalistic fallacy. Philosophically, we cannot base an *ought* on an *is*. On what basis does evolutionary psychology draw its image or vision of the good toward which we should strive? Third, how does it help us to appeal to nature for our moral options, when nature itself is quite ambivalent about the issue. One can find a justification for brutal selfishness or for some forms of altruism. If nature provides more than one pattern, on what basis do we decide between them? Herbert Spencer and Adolf Hitler appeal to evolution to enact their social agenda. Richard Dawkins's evolutionary ethic encourages us to not simply imitate nature but to defy our selfish genes. Whom do we trust and why?

ORIGINAL SIN AND EVOLUTIONARY PSYCHOLOGY

Many believe that evolutionary psychology has rendered any notion of "original sin" obsolete. After all, the traditional idea of original sin was part of an overall package that included a very young earth, a historical Adam and Eve, and a world void of suffering before humanity's "fall." Astronomy, cosmology, geology, and biology have revealed an earth that is much older than what we had previously thought. Besides, there is no evidence whatsoever of a golden period in humanity's past, a prefallen paradise exemplifying peace, harmony, and nonviolence. Disease and death occurred long before human beings arrived on the scene. In fact, every serious evolutionary scientist would see all these premodern elements of the "original sin package" as part of an untenable faith that belonged to a previous generation. I agree. The sooner Christian theology fully admits this state of affairs, the better off we will be. While we cannot blame theologians prior to the nineteenth century for not knowing this, today we know better. And theological insights into the human condition will be ignored if they persist in a scientifically untenable insistence on a literal, historical fall from "paradise." One can appreciate the deep insights of premodern theologians while equally recognizing that they simply didn't have access to our understanding of the natural world. Thus it is simply no longer plausible to argue the case for original sin based on this premodern "package." Yet does that mean the concept of original sin has lost all semblance of meaning for our world today?

Beyond historical and scientific problems with the fall from paradise, many believe there are also theological problems. For Augustine, no one else in the history of humanity has ever experienced the "created goodness" that Adam knew for a brief time. According to Augustine, when Adam rebelled, all of us, even babies born in our world today, were somehow involved in that decision. This mysterious solidarity with our first ancestor sets us up not only for original sin, but for *original guilt,* because we, too, somehow made that choice in Adam's loins. Consequently, the next logical, but deplorable, Augustinian step is to say that even infants, if unbaptized, are damned because of the taint of not only original sin, but original guilt as well. Thus, in this causal explanation, everyone since Adam is indeed born in sin, a kind of genetic predisposition toward evil. Again, Adam may have at one time had "essential goodness" but that element has been completely lost to the rest of humanity.

So in a sense, the practical, existential implication for each of us is that we *are* created evil. We are guilty for simply existing. Yet *our* existence, not some mythical existence of our first parent, is all we know. We thus come into this world inherently flawed and corrupt. For many, this is a theologically unfortunate and psychologically abusive doctrine. Paul Ricoeur powerfully addresses this issue in the following statement:

> The harm that has been done to souls, during the centuries of
> Christianity, first by literal interpretation of the story of Adam, and
> then by the confusion of this myth, treated as history, with later
> speculations, principally Augustinian, about original sin, will never be
> adequately told. In asking the faithful to confess belief in this mythico-
> speculative mass and to accept it as a self-sufficient explanation, the
> theologians have unduly required a *sacrificium intellectus* where what
> was needed was to awaken believers to a symbolic superintelligence of
> their actual condition.[59]

We might want to put the issue this way: Augustine's brilliant, but
exaggerated, explanation of original sin, an explanation that attempted to
salvage human goodness from the Gnostic idea that created existence is
evil, was sabotaged by his development of original guilt. For now, the world
into which each of Adam's descendents is born is indeed a world whose very
structure is evil.

The other questionable theological point in the Augustinian tradition
is the catastrophic manner in which God reacted to the first sin. If we
think in literal terms, getting banished from the Garden, being sentenced
to death, being condemned to the vicious pains of childbirth, and for most
of humanity, being eternally damned, seems like a harsh overreaction. If we
even begin to employ any sort of parental analogy to this scene, we would
be aghast at such a harsh, even cruel, parental reaction.

In an effort to escape some of the problems with the traditional model
of the fall, theologians from Schleiermacher to John Hick and Matthew
Fox have turned to Irenaeus.[60] Irenaeus was clearly the most significant
theologian of the second century. He offers a theological anthropology
notably different from that of Augustine. Irenaeus employs the two words
associated with the *imago Dei*, image and likeness, in a manner differently
from most Western interpretations of Genesis 1:26. For Irenaeus, *image*
refers to the bodily powers, reason and choice, with which each of us is born.
Image is automatically given in creation and does not have to be developed.
Likeness, on the other hand, refers to a cultivated sense of taking on God's

character. This requires a process of growth. It is not a readymade gift of creation. As Irenaeus puts it: "A mother, for example, can provide perfect food for a chid, but at that point he cannot digest food which is suitable for someone older. Similarly, God himself certainly could have provided humanity with perfection from the beginning. Humanity, however, was immature and unable to lay hold of it."[61]

While Adam carried the image of God, he was not yet created with God's likeness. Adam was not perfect because he was a *created* being, and for Irenaeus, only *uncreated reality* can be perfect. Adam could not have handled perfection. Consequently, God set up a strategy whereby Adam could grow into a stronger and stronger commitment toward goodness. But Adam did not have what later Western theology would call "original righteousness." Theologian Stephen Duffy provides a helpful description of Irenaeus's view of the first human.

> Morally and intellectually he was a child-man not yet endowed with
> the Spirit of adoption. Adam, through a torturous process of growth
> in obedience, was meant to grow up into closer *likeness* to God. The
> whole sweep of history through the two testaments is to be for infanat
> humanity an educational process. However, due to his immaturity,
> Adam fell prey to a jealous Satan, disobeyed, and the process was
> hindered. Growth in the likeness of God, the divine strategy was
> retarded. This understandable, even inevitable, sin of Adam was
> freighted with consequences, for in him all lost what Adam lost.[62]

Irenaeus thus understands the fall not as radical evil, but as an understandable sin. Adam, being immature, was tempted and fell. His discriminatory abilities were not developed and he was easily misled.

It is interesting to contrast Irenaeus's view with the position Augustine later took in *The City of God*.

> The injunction forbidding the eating of one kind of food, where
> such an abundant supply of other foods was available, was so easy to
> observe, so brief to remember; above all, it was given at a time when
> desire was not yet in oppostion to the will. That opposition came

later as a result of the punishment of the transgression. Therefore the unrighteousness of violating the prohibition was so much the greater, in proportion to the ease with which it could have been observed and fulfilled.[63]

Thus, for Augustine, the first sin was completely inexcusable. In Adam's prefallen state, his desires were not yet unruly, so he was not impulsively overwhelmed. Instead, for Augustine, this first act of rebellion grew out of Adam's pride. Adam wanted to usurp God and make himself the center of the universe.

It may well seem at this point that Irenaeus is much more compassionate concerning humanity's ills. In fact, Irenaeus believes that the fall into sin is an inevitable part of growing up and learning about life. Whereas Augustine would later portray sin as prideful rebellion, Irenaeus sees it as an understandable mistake due to immaturity. Whereas Augustine would later argue that even all natural evil is a result of sin, Irenaeus said that disasters are trials necessary for us to develop. The punishment for the first sin, according to Irenaeus, is more a sign of God's compassion than of his wrath. The experience of sin makes us appreciate God's kindness. In a sense, then, getting kicked out of the Garden was a good thing. It was the path toward growing up. Sin and its consequences are our teachers. They allow us to encounter and appreciate God's compassion and love. Suffering, therefore, is not the horrible consequence of Adam's sin, but the vehicle of spiritual development. By concretely experiencing the differences between virtue and sin, we can come to a point of gradually preferring goodness rather than having it from the beginning, not adequately appreciating it, and hence losing it.

A major problem for our spiritual development, according to Irenaeus, is that we do not have patience. We want too much maturity too fast. He says:

People who do not wait for the period of growth, who attribute the weakness of their nature to God, are completely unreasonable. They understand neither God nor themselves; they are ungrateful and never satisfied. At the outset they refuse to be what they were made: human beings who are subject to passions. They override the law of human nature; they already want to be like God the Creator before they even become human beings. They want to do away with all the differences between the uncreated God and created humans.[64]

Thus we need to be patient with ourselves as we realize that we are a work in progress. Put another way, we need to work on being human before we work on being Divine.

Irenaeus's view has been reaffirmed by many in contemporary theology because it seems more evolution friendly. By that, I mean that some of the older problems with the Augustinian "fall model" fade into the background. There is no need to posit a paradise or a golden era in humanity's past because humanity was not created perfect. Spiritual development is an evolutionary process emerging from our immaturity. We are gradually moving toward the likeness of God rather than having dramatically fallen from it.

The creative theologian of science, Philip Hefner, whom we mentioned earlier, combines elements of both an Irenean and Augustinian framework. Like Irenaeus, Hefner does not see "the fall" as a catastrophic event in our ancient past, but instead as an evolving story of spiritual and ethical development. We are in a state of gradual development, and not in a condition of radical falleness from a perfect world. Natural processes are not the punishment for some primordial sin; instead, nature's habits are the context out of which we arose. Nature has always been equipped with promise. The discrepancy between our genetic tendencies toward selfishness and our cultural values of inclusiveness creates a certain guilt about our existence. But this condition is a natural inheritance, and not a result of a volitional fall in our past. This is the way life has evolved. Thus Hefner holds to a sort of Augustinian biological inheritance model. As he puts it, the inheritance of sin "is the evolutionary process itself that bequeaths to each individual and each generation the constituitive elements of life that bear the conditions of what we have called sin of origin."[65] While separating himself from Augustine's notion that Adam's sin has been passed on to each of us biologically, Hefner *does* believe we have inherited a prehuman genetic inclination toward survival thinking and selfish genes. He is quite direct about this point: "What we have called sin is inherent in human being because it is constituent of the processes that make life possible in the first place and that contribute to life's development."[66] Put another way, what we've called "sin" is in the very biological structures of life. It could not have been otherwise or life would not have developed.

Hefner's bold thesis makes some theologians uneasy. First, he seems to come dangerously close to a Manichaean world in which nature itself is fundamentally flawed, and hence, sin is not only inevitable, but necessary. Perhaps Hefner would say that these flaws are part of an evolving journey in which God is inviting human participation to renew the world. Perhaps he would also say that the Western tradition has overreacted to this "fall" and seen "sin" as a catastrophic condition rather than part of our collective, prehuman past. Yet some may indeed wonder how Hefner coordinates his view of "sin" with a notion of personal responsibility. Put simply, how are we accountable or in any sense "blameworthy" for that which is an inherent part of our nature?

The second concern for some is that Hefner seems to focus on the biogenetic context of sin so intensely that he overlooks the social and cultural transmission of sin. At times, he comes close to saying that the source of *all* sin is in the biological and genetic realm. Physicist and theologian Ian Barbour states this concern as follows:

> Philip Hefner proposes an *evolutionary interpretation* of the concept of sin. He identifies sin with the conflict between information in the genes and that in culture. Genetically based selfishness is in conflict with cultural sources of cooperation and altruism. Original sin consists in biologically based dispositions from the past that are not adaptive in the modern world. The problem with this analysis is that it tends to make genes the source of evil and culture the source of good. I would argue that social injustice, violence, racism, and militarism are products of culture and social institutions and of individual decisions as much as of inherited genes.[67]

In other words, Barbour believes that Hefner's view of sin is somewhat reductionistic. It does not adequately account for how sin emerges in our so-called "higher" nature as well. Sin is not something out of which we simply evolve. Greater capacities for freedom will bring new possibilities for sin.

Rather than renew the Augustinian concept of biologically inherited sin, other theologians believe that the Augustinian perspective offers a powerful disclosure of the human condition and the nature of human choice. In giving up the literal story, we do not have to lose all of Augustine's insight. In describing the universal inclination toward sin, Ted Peters says the following: "To make this point is the task of the doctrine of original sin. To make this point it is not necessary to posit the historicity of the Garden of Eden or to employ the disease metaphor wherein we inherit a predisposition of sinning. The paradise story and the concept of inherited sin are the dressing for the otherwise naked proposition that God and God alone is responsible for establishing a divine-human relationship that is salvific."[68] Thus, while we may no longer believe that we are mysteriously linked to the choice of a historical person named Adam, it may still be possible that Adam tells our story as well.

Langdon Gilkey also believes the symbol of original sin, which should never be literalized, discloses our situation as human beings. "The symbol of original sin does not explain our predicament by assigning to it a cause; it discloses that predicament by uncovering its hidden but destructive features and by revealing unsuspected new possibilities for renewal despite our apparent bondage."[69] Gilkey describes the ambiguity of our nature:

> We are destructive as well as creative. Even more, it is precisely through our creativity and human uniqueness, or spirit, mind, and intelligence, that we become anxious and through anxiety that we fall into aggression and self-destruction. Thus, paradoxically, we are destructive in our creativity; the two unite in a baffling mixture. . . . Our most lethal faults appear as distortions of our most creative powers: our religious capacities, moral striving (as ideology shows), and especially evident today, our scientific brilliance and technical gifts.[70]

Gilkey argues that sociobiology, or evolutionary psychology, sees our problems as arising from our biological inheritance and its solution appearing through a transcendent, almost supernatural, objective reason. Yet Gilkey believes our problems arise at *both* the level of genetic inheritance *and* mind or spirit. Manipulative, deceptive, and biased tendencies sneak into our scientific solutions. We cannot completely extract our scientific thinking from our own self-interest. The Augustinian understanding of original sin points toward this reality of egoistic bias in human thought. There are cognitive effects of our insecure self-centeredness. Finitude produces anxiety and the notion of original sin, in its most insightful form, describes how we often mishandle this anxiety and act in selfish and destructive ways.

Gilkey suggests that it is precisely because we are destined for infinity, or built for a relationship with God, that we desire an infinity of possessions. This infinite, inordinate drive to possess threatens others, the environment, and ourselves. Thus an infinite, restless desire for ultimacy propels our particular selfish fixations. We attempt to secure ourselves at the expense of everything. The problem is that our minds are capable of imagining an infinity of anxieties. We are driven to master a situation that is clearly beyond what any finite being can control. "When the self or its group loves itself inordinately, worships itself instead of God, the first result is injustice to the neighbor as the second result is the destruction both self and world."[71] It is important to remember that even the best science and technology can be tainted by this self-serving inclination.

> From each passing generation the new members of a culture have received and appropriated the institutions of their society, its social roles, rules, and customs, its expectancies and standards, its moral norms and ideals, and its camouflaged hostile attitudes, competitive habits, prejudices, anxieties, and hatreds, its modes of deception and manipulation of the other. What they have not emphasized, however, is how unjust institutions with their habits and demands (for example patriarchalism), how patterns of competiveness and self-love, group pride, and scorn for the other, how these, too, are passed on and inherited. These deeply ingrained forms of self-concern shape us as thoroughly as do the positive cooperative and creative sides of culture. This transmission of evil . . . is both objective, resident in the cultural and institutional patterns of bias that we inherit, and subjective, internal, latent in the inordinate self-love running through every social group and through every social institution. This inherited taint characterizes both religion and science; both are thus only part of the

answer to our ills but also part of the problem. Culture in all its facets is both creative and fallen.[72]

For Gilkey, then, faith in God, love of neighbor, and hope for the future are all basic structures of the human condition from which we have fallen. Because the connection between the self and our Source is the key to human life, distortion here affects everything. As Gilkey goes on to say, this has been described in the language of "inheritance." We are "born into" it. Yet we are *both* born into it and further it. "We know we, too, are involved in the world's evil, and yet continually we deceive ourselves that this is not so but that, on the contrary, we are righteous and the other is to blame."[73] This sense that we have participated in our estrangement problem suggests that our problem is not finitude itself, but what we have done with our finitude. We are not forced by the very structures of existence to sin. We may be tempted, but we are not coerced or forced. Our condition is one of anxiety. This anxiety becomes the precondition or forerunner of our sin or destructive behavior. As Gilkey puts it, "In this situation we 'fall' into a false security of self and a false fulfillment."[74] In spite of this, we also experience ourselves as grasped by a higher good, a good that goes beyond the ordinary morality of competition, self-centeredness, and a love for our own group.[75]

Also, in the allegorical story of the fall, according to Reinhold Niebuhr, another important existential truth is revealed about the nature of evil: none of us create evil in our lives *ex nihilo*. Evil exists prior to our first choices and is much larger than our individual decisions. The symbol of the serpent in the Garden points to the reality of evil before humanity made its first choice. As Robert R. Williams suggests, this notion of original sin moves beyond the secular conviction that evil can be reduced to institutional and social arrangements. It certainly moves beyond any myth of progress which insists that evil will eventually be scientifically and technologically eliminated. Thus, "the serpent symbolizes a mysterious depth dimension of evil that cannot be fully rationalized or absorbed into self-conscious, deliberate freedom."[76] When deliteralized, this story of the Garden is still pregnant with insight into the human condition.

SUMMARY

This chapter has taken us in several directions. I began with the question of how far we should push Darwinism in describing human behavior, including evil or destructive behavior. I then moved into a description of the central tenets of evolutionary psychology, tenets that point toward the master motive of gene replication. After looking at Darwin's perspective on ethics, I then described how evolutionary psychology differs quite radically from "blank-slate" empirical psychology. I examined the controversial topic of altruism and attempted to bring evolutionary psychology and theology into a fruitful dialogue. I then investigated the evolutionary psychology position on aggression and human violence, particularly David Buss's conviction that aggression is related to sexual and reproductive competition. While this is an interesting and informative perspective, I suggested that it does *not* tell the whole story of human aggression, violence, and destruction. Next, I explored in some detail the evolutionary explanation of religion, which essentially argues that religion has been a useful illusion in promoting human survival. And finally, I examined whether, in light of evolution, the traditional notion of original sin has any meaning for us today. When deliteralized, the Garden story describes our story as well. Further, it is not necessarily opposed to evolutionary theory.

Overall, we discovered in this second chapter some of the same issues we found in chapter 1. There we saw that evolutionary biology offers an extremely important and insightful understanding of the world. However, when it is inflated to a metaphysical theory that accounts for the totality of existence, it steps beyond its scientific method and becomes scientism. It forgets the difference between methodology and ontology. Similarly, in this chapter, we have seen how evolutionary psychology offers fascinating and important scientific discoveries about the human condition. However, it does not describe the totality of that condition. Evolutionary psychology moves too quickly from a limited investigation to grandiose claims about being the "master discipline," the final interpretation of human reality. When it does this, it becomes ineffective.

There are other rich and insightful perspectives on human destructiveness that move outside the parameters of evolutionary psychology. It is to these psychologies of evil that I now turn.

CHAPTER THREE

EVIL AND THE PSYCHOANALYTIC TRADITION

It would be difficult indeed for anyone who has a long clinical experience as a psychoanalyst to belittle the destructive forces within man. —*Erich Fromm*

The psychoanalytic tradition is one of the most comprehensive approaches to the human condition in Western intellectual history. Its daring attempts to look at hidden motives, concealed meanings, and unconscious dynamics beneath the surface of human behavior is far reaching. Since Freud developed his original ideas, psychoanalysis has evolved in ways that are somewhat similar to religious denominations. Traditional instinct theory, ego psychology, object relations theory, self psychology, and intersubjective theory represent the various wings of psychoanalysis. Rather than viewing these perspectives as competing dogmas, many psychoanalysts want ecumenical dialogue from within the ranks. Some, of course, want to demonstrate the certainty of their own conceptual tradition, but most seem to recognize the overlapping and complimentary character of these views. They feel a need to draw from multiple perspectives.

Some psychoanalysts are no doubt nervous with the word *evil*. They may very well see it as too connected to religion, myth, and even superstition. Yet they retain a deep interest in human destructiveness, malevolence, and sadistic behavior. Clearly not all psychoanalysts share Freud's atheistic, or even materialistic, assumptions. In fact, psychoanalysis probably remains the most dominant influence on the American Association of Pastoral Counselors. One can believe in both the reality of God and the existence of evil while working within a psychoanalytic paradigm.

In this chapter, I want to look at three psychoanalytic statements on the issue of human evil. The first, not surprisingly, is Freud himself. More particularly, I wish to review Freud's gradual turn to the death instinct as a biological rival of the life instinct. Freud's pessimism about the human condition grew as he aged. His mature reflections reveal a portrait of humanity most disturbing to anyone who wants to cling to an optimistic view of human nature. The second perspective is that of Erich Fromm, who is, in my view, one of the most interesting thinkers of the twentieth century. Fromm departed from Freud in some ways and extended Freud's analysis in others. The third view comes from Ernest Becker. Becker reinterpreted many key Freudian ideas to support his fundamental position that the fear of death is the most driving force of the human condition. Evil, then, results from this frantic attempt to deny our mortality, combat our finitude, and be our own "god."

While these three thinkers are not as "current" as some of the other authors explored throughout this book, I believe that they represent some of the richest discussions on the topic of evil in the history of the psychoanalytic tradition. They are provocative and they write with depth and insight. More contemporary psychoanalytic theory will be greatly benefited from a dialogue with this pivotal trio.

FREUD'S GRADUAL TURN TO THE DEATH INSTINCT

It is widely known that Sigmund Freud believed that human beings have two primary drives: sex and aggression. What is not so widely known is that Freud did not arrive at this conclusion until fairly late in his life. In *Civilization and Its Discontents,* Freud stated, "I can no longer understand how we can have overlooked the ubiquity of non-erotic aggressivity and destructiveness and can have failed to give it its due place in the interpretation of life."[1] He was slow to recognize aggression as an autonomous drive separate from sexuality. After 1920, Freud's view of the human condition became more explicitly pessimistic. In his earlier writing, Freud argued that sexual impulses and fantasies are blocked and forbidden by social norms, thus frequently creating a strict repression within the individual psyche. Analysis would, of course, help individuals uncover this repression and release the blocked energy that produced neurosis. Eventually, however, Freud's view of repression took on a less negative quality. Repression, he believed, was in fact necessary for civilization to go forward. Repression represents a form of social restraint that keeps individuals from their destructive, direct experience of the instincts. Psychoanalysts Stephen Mitchell and Margaret Black describe this move thusly: "Ideal mental life does not entail an absence of repression, but the maintenance of a modulated repression that allows gratification while at the same time preventing primitive sexual and aggressive impulses from taking over. [Freud's] turn toward a darker vision of instincts brought a more appreciative attitude toward social controls, which he now regarded as necessary to save people from themselves."[2] While there is no evidence that Freud read Thomas Hobbes, his final theory of the human condition looked quite Hobbesian. Hobbes had also emphasized the necessity of the social order to curb the highly egocentric, aggressive, and "brute" qualities of individual pursuits.[3]

Thus Freud moved toward the position that two competing drives dominate the human condition: *eros,* the life instinct, and *thanatos,* the death instinct. Freud described how difficult it was for him to finally embrace the notion of a destructive, life-denying impulse within humanity: "I remember my own defensive attitude when the idea of an instinct of destruction first emerged in psychoanalytic literature, and how long it took before I became receptive to it. That others should have shown, and still show, the same attitude of rejection surprises me less. For little children do not like it when there is talk of the inborn inclination toward 'badness,' to aggressiveness and destructiveness, and so to cruelty as well."[4]

Thanatos, the death instinct, rarely expresses itself directly. Instead, it emerges in the form of aggressiveness and hate. Eros, the life instinct, engages in a battle against the urge toward self-destruction. It blocks the death instinct from its internal expression and helps push it outward. This externalizing of the aggression is necessary for individual survival. By displacing the self-destructive tendency outward, the individual's safety is preserved. Others become the necessary targets to avoid the aggression toward, and hatred of, ourselves. Thus aggression becomes a necessary outlet for self-preservation. The experience of depression serves as an example. Depressed persons are often incapable of externalizing their aggression, so it attacks the self. Without an outside object, the self-contempt can push one toward suicidal thoughts.

While the death instinct has an autonomous source of energy, most of the time, thanatos and eros are mixed together. We don't see pure forms of either. As Freud put it, "the two kinds of instinct seldom—perhaps never—appear in isolation from each other, but are alloyed with each other in varying and different proportions and so become unrecognizable to our judgment."[5]

What, exactly, changed Freud's mind concerning the role of the death instinct within the human condition? The answer to this question is probably multifaceted. One factor, of course, was World War I. Prior to this violent outbreak, there had been a rather long period of comfortable, middle-class progression. Erich Fromm describes this context of Freud's thinking:

> There had been no war since 1871. The bourgeoisie was progressing
> steadily, both politically and socially, and the sharp antagonism
> between the classes was becoming smaller, due to the steady
> improvements in the situation of the working class. The world seemed
> peaceful and becoming even more civilized, especially when one did
> not pay much attention to the greater part of the human race living
> in Asia, Africa, and South America, under conditions of utter poverty

and degradation. Human destructiveness seemed to be a factor that had played a role in the Dark Ages and during many earlier centuries, but had now been replaced by reason and goodwill. The psychological problems that were being uncovered were those arising from the overstrict moral code of the middle class, and Freud was so impressed with the evidence of the damaging results of sexual repression that he simply failed to attach importance to the problem of aggressiveness.[6]

Freud biographer Peter Gay also adds that the slaughter of so many persons between 1914 and 1918 pushed Freud to recognize the full status of aggression. According to Gay, when Freud lectured in Vienna in 1915, he said that evil could not be excluded in the considerations of the human condition.[7]

In 1920, when Freud wrote *Beyond the Pleasure Principle*, he clearly began moving toward a revision of his instinct theory. Freud himself, however, was tenuous and not completely convinced. Yet a mere three years later, he *was* convinced. And by the time he wrote the *New Introductory Letters*, he stated the issue boldly: "It really seems as though it is necessary for us to destroy some other thing or person in order not to destroy ourselves, in order to guard against the impulsion to self-destruction. A sad disclosure indeed for the moralist!"[8]

Yet Gay also points out that Freud *had* considered the power of aggression before 1914, even though it had not made its way into his formal theorizing.[9] For instance, from his letters to his friend, Fleiss, as well as his *Interpretation of Dreams*, Freud confessed a death wish toward his younger brother, antagonistic feelings toward his father, and his own need for an enemy in his life if he were to be productive. Clearly Freud's achievement is related to the anti-Semitism he hated. Gay reminds us that Freud argued that the war had confirmed the psychoanalytic understanding of aggression; the war did not create it. So while the war clearly brought about a renewed focus on the dangers of aggression, psychoanalysis had already recognized aggression as a significant part of life.

Gay further suggests that Freud may have resisted the full embrace of aggression because both Alfred Adler and Carl Jung, with differing concepts, had also suggested its plausibility. Perhaps rivalry was a factor in this slow endorsement of a destructive impulse.

In spite of this rivalry and the social context of war, however, Gay believes, with good evidence, that psychoanalytic theory was internally moving toward a greater recognition of aggression and the death instinct. One such factor was Freud's observance of the human tendency to reenact painful experiences from the past. He saw this in the dreams of World War I veterans who had returned, what we would today call posttraumatic stress disorder. Repressing their memories would seem to be in the best interest of the patient. Freud had previously argued that the reduction of tension and the increase of pleasure are the primary human motivations. Repression, in this way, would serve the pleasure principle in that the analysand could avoid the pain. Yet this pain seemed to *want* to come forth. If the pleasure principle is the ultimate motivation of life, why would individuals keep returning to painful experience? There seemed to be a compulsion to repeat the painful experience. This repetition compulsion appeared to contradict Freud's previous understanding of the pleasure principle. Why would his patients ongoingly transfer onto Freud painful experiences and memories of a trauma? Why would the mind keep going back to such unpleasantness? It was here that Freud began to realize that his previous emphasis on the pleasure principle was quite unable to explain the experience of what seemed like masochism.

Sometimes children clearly want to repeat things that are pleasurable. Anyone who has read stories to a child knows that the entire story must be read or the child will object. There is satisfaction in hearing every detail of the story, even if the child is about to fall asleep. But why would adults retraumatize themselves through the repetition compulsion?

Freud also recognized this pattern with his eighteen-month-old grandson, Ernst. Ernst was attached to his mother and Freud noticed that his grandson played a little game when his mother, Sophie, would leave the room. As his mother left, Ernst would take a wooden spool tied with string and throw it over his curtained crib so that is was out of sight. Then he would say the word *gone*. He would then pull it back and greet the spool with the word *there*, as he acknowledged its return. This little game Ernst invented seemed to help him cope with his mother's disappearance. Freud interpreted it to mean that the little boy "was moving from the passive acceptance of his mother's absence to the reactive reenactment of her disappearance and return."[10] This anecdotal case seemed to offer more evidence that a disturbing experience was being directly sought out to reenact a trauma. The boy seemed to move from a passive acceptance of his mother's leaving to an active reenactment of it. As Gay puts it, "Indeed, Freud noted, patients who display this compulsion do their utmost to dwell on misery and injuries, and to force an interruption to the analysis before it is completed."[11]

This led Freud to the conviction that some drives are "conservative" in that they strive for an earlier, tensionless, inorganic state of affairs. Or as he famously put it, "the aim of all life is death."[12] Human organisms want to die in their own fashion. Thus the death wish was born.

But surely this seemed outrageously contradictory. The sexual drives are definitely life affirming, a part of eros. They hardly seek extinction. But for Freud, this drive now only represents one half of the picture. The other half, argued Freud, is the death instinct.

The death instinct thus has two dimensions to it. On the one hand, it has a passive tendency that seeks to reduce organic life to inorganic life. This is the tug of inertia, perhaps manifested in the contemporary slang of a "couch potato," one who prefers the lifeless existence of a television zombie to the struggles of real life. This perspective breathes new life into the traditional "deadly sin" of sloth.

The other form of the death instinct is active aggression. This can be turned inward against oneself or turned outward toward others. In order for civilization to persist, part of humanity's natural aggressiveness must be turned back on itself to where it originally began. This inward turn of aggressiveness is directed against one's own ego. More particularly, this aggressiveness takes the form of a harsh superego. This, of course, leads to chronic guilt and often manifests itself as a need for punishment.[13] As Freud put it, "civilization, therefore, obtains mastery over the individual's dangerous desire for aggression by weakening and disarming it and by setting up an agency within him to watch it, like a garrison in a conquered city."[14] The superego thus expresses an aggressiveness against the ego that keeps the aggressiveness from moving outward. It is a form of moral masochism that always results in undermining or sabotaging oneself because of an unconscious desire for punishment. The core of this aggressiveness is not usually suicidal. Instead of a physical death wish that would result in the destruction of one's own body, it is more often a destruction of one's own *self-agency*. In other words, it pushes us toward a passive form of self-disgust. Our guilt, then, is largely a fear of this aggressive superego.

Thus Freud ends up arguing that the aggressive instinct represents the major threat to civilization. As he puts it, "I adopt the standpoint, therefore, that the inclination to aggressiveness is an original, self-subsisting instinctual disposition in man, and I return to my view that it constitutes the greatest impediment to civilization."[15] The aggressive instinct, once again, is a derivative of the more basic death instinct. And in viewing the life and death instincts as locked into a cosmic battle, Freud emphasizes an eternal dualism: "This struggle is what all life essentially consist of, and the evolution of civilization may therefore be simply described as the struggle for life of the human species. And it is the battle of the giants that our nurse-maids try to appease with their lullaby about heaven."[16]

Note here that Freud's ongoing fascination with dualism reaches a cosmic proportion. The life and death instincts apply to *all* biological life. These forces do not simply occupy the human mind; instead, they are built into and influence all of life. Thus Freud moves from psychology to metaphysics in a quick but subtle manner. This elevation of the life and death instincts to cosmic principles pushes Freud into a kind of quasi-religious outlook. Freud's "religion" may be a commitment to naturalism and positivism, but it involves a kind of faith in the ultimate nature of things. How does Freud "know" that there is nothing but the material world and nothing beyond his naturalistic ontology? Quite frankly, he doesn't. Thus Freud's dual-instinct theory becomes far more than a psychological hypothesis that enables him to observe clinical data. Instead, it becomes a larger worldview with two cosmological principles in conflict. Freud would surely deny that he is creating a new myth or religion; however, insofar as he states that the naturalistic realm is the only realm within the universe, and that his psychological claims can account for all of life, he is indeed speaking in a quasi-religious fashion.[17] This is Freudian *faith*. Freud, just like everyone else, is stuck with the epistemological problem of not knowing, in an empirical way, what is the ultimate context of human experience. Yet he claims to know, sometimes with a dogma as pronounced as any religious perspective. I don't fault him for moving his perspective beyond a strict empiricism; however, he should not claim to be acting as a scientist when he does so.

It is also interesting to note how utterly at odds Freud's dualistic split is with the thought of Jung, whom we will consider in the next chapter. While Freud's earlier work set forth a dualism between ego instincts (self-preservation) and sexual instincts, he moved to a broader classification of a life instinct versus a death instinct. For Jung, Freud falls prey to an unhealed split in which the universe is left dangling in opposition without any final integrating possibility.

Freud, then, viewed humanity's evil inclinations as rooted in our biology. Because we are "born with" thanatos, as well as eros, we are engaged in a psychological civil war. While social and environmental factors contribute to human destructiveness, the primary reality is that we are instinctually dangerous to both ourselves and civilization. Eliminating negative social situations such as poverty and poor child care will hardly guarantee nondestructive children. The reason is that no amount of social reform can eliminate a biological tendency. Aggression and violence, for the seasoned Freud, are "natural." They do not represent some gross deformity of our original, positive-only inclinations. Indeed, we are a battleground and the stakes include the future of civilization.

FREUD, EVIL, AND RELIGION

Freud rejected any perspective on human destructiveness that moved beyond the natural sphere. He remained throughout his life a thoroughgoing materialist. All solutions to the human dilemma must come from the method of science, a method that rules out, from the outset, any possibility of a transcendent realm. While Freud greatly admired his ex-Jesuit philosophy professor, Franz Brentano—who advocated theism—Freud would end up being even more influenced by Ernest Bruke. This happened at the University of Vienna when Bruke encouraged the young Freud to commit himself to a physiological explanation of all things. For Bruke, we live only in a physical universe; there is no other realm. Along with Bruke's direct influence, Freud was indirectly influenced by the philosopher Ludwig Feuerbach. Feuerbach, especially in *The Essence of Christianity,* argued that the notion of "God" is a projection of the best part of humanity.[18] Unwittingly, human beings ignore their own internal goodness and instead project it onto an imaginary divine character. Humans rob themselves of their own positive assets by insisting that these strengths belong to God. The "left-over" characteristics, which are essentially negative, human beings then claim for themselves. This projection process greatly aids self-alienation. The remedy is a reclaiming of our own positive aspects and a dismissal of the delusional image of God. As long as God is powerful, humanity can never progress. We must "take back" these projected qualities and let go of all theological delusions. Theology is only a psychological tale, anyway. Theology tells us nothing about metaphysics; it only tells us what occurs in each individual's psyche.

As psychiatrist Armand Nicholi suggests, in many ways Freud simply worked on the implications of Feuerbach's thesis.[19] Freud argued that the notion of God as an idealized Superman is "so patently infantile and so foreign to reality, that . . . it is painful to think that the great majority of mortals will never rise above this view of life."[20] The notion of a Divine Being was born out of a primitive stage of humanity's development. Nicholi suggests that the two primary arguments Freud raised against religion were (*a*) the fact that religion could be explained psychologically and that there is nothing "supernatural" about its origins, and (*b*) the amount of human suffering in the world ruled out the possibility of divine providence. So, in a sense, it was Freud's struggle with suffering and evil that led, at least in part, to his atheism. Freud was, after all, no stranger to loss. His nanny, who interestingly enough took Freud to Catholic services when he was very young, died when Freud was three years old. He also lost a younger brother, his father, his beloved daughter Sophie, and Sophie's four-and-a-half-year-old son, a grandson with whom Freud was very close indeed. While the loss of Freud's father rather famously sent him into a psychological period of deep exploration, the loss of his beloved grandson pushed him into an emotional agony. Add to this personal loss the constant anti-Semitism that he endured, along with the severe pain connected to the cancer in his jaw.

And on top of all this, he was the personal partner of a multitude of people as they found the courage to explore their own suffering. He answered the theodicy question with a definite conviction: there is no God. We will see many parallels between Freud and Darwin here: just as Freud was excruciatingly aware of psychological suffering in the human condition, so Darwin was aware, at a level far deeper than most, of the cruelties and sufferings in the natural world. The issue of suffering, which inevitably involves the problem of evil, was a centerpiece in both their thought.

The other major Freudian argument is that religious faith can be explained naturally without any need to appeal to "revelation." We form the likeness of God after the likeness of our own father. In fact, God *is* the exalted Father. In the face of insecurity and uncertainty, it is often natural to crave a cosmic protection that shields us from the vicissitudes of life. In such a desperate context, the creation of a "cosmic daddy" often occurs. At base, it is a refusal to grow up and face the anxieties that are simply part of living. As self-conscious creatures, we cannot escape knowledge of our own mortality. While the illusion of God may offer us temporary (and false) comfort, it will not deliver us from our dilemma.

The fact that we wish for a divine providence, in Freud's mind, seems to negate its plausibility. Because we want it to be so, it probably isn't. This is strange logic. C. S. Lewis has frequently pointed out that in many areas of life, a strong wish for something may serve as evidence that it exists. We thirst, and there is water; we hunger, and there is food; we long for a partner, and we fall in love. Why does the desire for divine providence make it so unlikely?

Also, this attempt to explain the origin of faith as desire leaves no room for those religious individuals who at one time desired that God *not* exist. Some persons abhor the notion of God because they view this idea as a meddling interference with their own self-government. Freud seems to overlook the idea that some persons may *desire* atheism. Some feel that any acknowledgment of a divine reality inevitably impinges on their own private world. They prefer aloneness to a relationship with God.

Lewis also pointed out that the Freudian father projection can work the other way.[21] Freud clearly acknowledges that all relationships with the human father are ambiguous. Consequently, cannot disbelief in God be simply a psychological projection of the wish for the father's absence? Could atheism not express a wish to be free of the father? The point is that this psychological reduction of religion cuts both ways.

It might be easy to criticize Freud for moving too swiftly from his clinical observations of patients to his philosophical constructs about the nature of ultimate reality and religion. However, I would suggest that Freud enters his clinical work with a philosophical orientation already intact. As so often happens, Freud moves from a scientific method to scientism without fully acknowledging that he has switched an empirical hat for a metaphysical one. Freud obviously has every right to his philosophical outlook; however, he should not claim that he arrived there as a result of strict scientific research.

Nicholi makes a fairly strong case that Freud remained fascinated all his life with the idea of the devil. He loved Goethe's *Faust*, Milton's *Paradise Lost*, and the very last book he read before his death was Baleaki's *The Fatal Skin*, which also involves a pact with the devil. One can speculate on the reasons for this fascination: Satan as the ultimate rebel, and so forth. What is interesting, however, is Freud's speculations on the psychological origin of the idea of the devil. As I have already mentioned, Freud held that the ambivalence toward the father (which involved both love and hate) is projected onto God. Yet this ambivalence toward the Divine is not acceptable. So the love one feels is directed toward God and the resentment and hatred one feels is displaced onto the devil. The devil is the target of our unexpressed hatred of God. The devil is necessary because of our own negative feelings toward God, feelings that are far too frightening to us. We are free to hate the devil as much as we want. He becomes the necessary outlet for our real anger, which cannot be expressed directly. According to Freud, this is how the concept of the devil is psychologically born.

TILLICH, NIEBUHR, AND FREUD

Theologian and philosopher Paul Tillich was throughout his life deeply impressed with Freud's astute observations concerning the unconscious processes that underlie our official reasoning. Refusing to take human thought at face value, Freud challenged the notion that conscious reason is the all-important criteria of our behavior. Tillich understands Freud as primarily an "existentialist," in that he radically exposed the often irrational, self-avoiding, anxiety-producing features of the human condition.[22] Yet while Tillich believed Freud to be brilliant, he also believed that Freud consistently confused our "estranged" condition with our "essential" nature. For Tillich, it is important to understand that humanity is essentially good, even though all humans live in a distorted condition. In our essence, or the deepest level of our reality, we are not estranged, neurotic, or hopelessly self-destructive. Because Freud viewed the *essence* of humanity as the distorted image he observed, he ended up a very gloomy and pessimistic soul. As Tillich put it, "His dismay of culture shows that he is very consistent in his negative judgments about man as existentially distorted. Now if you see man only from the point of existence and not from the point of view of essence, only from the point of estrangement and not from the view of essential goodness, then this consequence is unavoidable. And it is true for Freud in this respect."[23]

This distinction between our essential and estranged condition can be observed when we consider the traditional Christian notion of "concupiscence," which is quite similar to the Freudian libido. For traditional Christian thought, concupiscence is not part of humanity's essential nature. Instead, it is an inordinate or highly exaggerated desire based on our own idolatry. We turn a limited value into a "god" without which we cannot live. But we experience concupiscence only after we have already lost our "center" and replaced our ultimate concern with limited, finite deities. Having lost our rootedness in the ultimate, we then frantically try to turn finite things into objects or experiences we worship. Because we have deified these limited goods, we then love them in highly distorted ways. Our desires are completely out of control and our lives are out of balance because we have invested all of ourselves into something finite. This is akin to addiction. In fact, for Tillich, this investment becomes "demonic," in that it possesses us and controls our lives.

Freud's description of libido is often helpful in understanding this estranged condition, but again, this does not describe our *essential* nature. There is nothing within our nature which demands that we act this way.

Instead, out of our anxiety and freedom, we seem to inevitably fall into this distorted awareness in which we are often dominated by tumultuous desires. Perhaps Tillich would say the following: "Look, the human condition of estranged existence is every bit as bad as Freud indicates. But we wouldn't even understand that human existence is estranged unless we had some grasp of our essence. We understand sickness only in reference to health."

Freud's understanding of estranged existence (though he fails to distinguish it from our essence) is for Tillich a gift to Christian theology.[24] Freud helps theologians further develop a dynamic, rather than a static, view of sin. In fact, Tillich draws some extremely interesting parallels between the thought of Freud and Martin Luther.[25] Tillich further believes that some of the neo-Freudians have lost this depth of Freudian analysis by minimizing the severity of the human condition and substituting a more optimistic, naturalistic hope for improvement. In describing these neo-Freudians, including his friends Karen Horney and Erich Fromm, Tillich says the following: "They have rejected the profound insight of Freud about existential libido and the death instinct, and in so doing they have reduced and cut off from Freud what made him and still makes him the most profound of all the depth psychologists. . . . But Freud, theologically speaking, saw more about human nature than all his followers who, when they lost the existential element in Freud, went more to an essentialist and optimistic view of man."[26]

These more optimistic neo-Freudians believe we can correct, on the basis of natural intervention, our fundamental problem of estrangement. These voices basically argue for an ultimate form of self-healing that Tillich finds deeply suspicious. For Tillich, better parenting, an improved environment, more education, or better distributions of wealth will not heal our fundamental problem of estrangement. This problem is much too deep for that.

> They try with their methods to overcome existential negativity,
> anxiety, estrangement, meaninglessness, and guilt. They deny that
> they are universal, that they are existential in that sense. They call all
> anxiety, all guilt, all emptiness, illnesses which can be overcome as any
> illness can be, and they try to remove them. But this is impossible.

The existentialist structure cannot be healed by the most refined techniques. They are objects of salvation. The analyst can be an instrument of salvation as every friend, every parent, every child can be an instrument of salvation. But as analyst he cannot bring salvation by means of his medical methods, for this requires the healing center of the personality.[27]

Stated another way, the huge existential issues of life cannot be "therapized" away. Psychotherapeutic technique, as important as it is, cannot eliminate the anxiety-producing questions of meaning, value, purpose. These issues are simply part of the package of being human.

Like Tillich, Reinhold Niebuhr finds a great deal to admire in the work of Freud, particularly his emphasis on the elaborate self-defenses and distortions of which the human mind is capable. Niebuhr believes that Freud holds a very realistic conception of the human psyche.[28] Niebuhr particularly likes the manner in which Freud challenges the pretentious claims of the Enlightenment, claims which insist that objective reason can deliver a final, uncontaminated truth about the world. For Niebuhr, Freud reconstructs an older, less optimistic view of the world. But he accomplishes this by using scientific language. Niebuhr, for instance, believes that Freud's rich discussion of the inevitability of egoistic corruption breathes new life into the traditional notion of sin. Niebuhr focuses on the intricate self-deceptions involved in pride in his classic *The Nature and Destiny of Man*.[29] Niebuhr indicates that ignorance is much less of a human problem than self-deception and self-absorption. Sin does not want to be exposed and the human mind has plenty of concealments and fog to keep our excessive self-concern hidden.

However, Niebuhr differs drastically with Freud in that he is not a materialist. For Freud, as we have seen, there is nothing outside the natural realm. It is our *natural instincts,* argues Freud, that can be so destructive. Similar to Tillich, Niebuhr does not believe that our essential nature or "natural instincts" are the problem. The problem is that our natural inclinations have been distorted and estranged. Niebuhr argues that it is wrong to view our so-called animal natures as the raw, instinctual, primitive urges and appetites of the id. We do not "naturally" yearn for inordinate pleasure, as Freud believed. Our appetites are not "by nature" excessive. Even our "lower nature" has some degree of regulation. Further, we are a combination of nature and spirit. And this spiritual dimension comes equipped with its own energies and vitalities. This dimension of our lives does not simply borrow all of its energies from the id. These energies can be seen in great works of art and other endeavors, which are more than the rechanneled energies of the id.

Thus the problems of human life do not simply result from inordinate expressions or excessive repressions of our libidinous desires. The "higher" dimension of our lives, the spiritual dimension, can also create its own problems. These "higher" problems of greed, pride, and ambition are, for Niebuhr, the most destructive of all. In describing Niebuhr's perspective, Don Browning and I put it as follows:

> Nature and spirit are distinguishable but never separate; for Niebuhr, they interpenetrate and mutually qualify one another. All of our natural impulses are qualified by spirit, by which he means the capacity for freedom, imagination, and self-transcendence. We never experience our sexuality or our hunger, our procreative impulses or our drive to survive, our fear of our natural aggressivity, as raw, mechanical, and totally determined by natural forces. They are always in humans qualified by freedom and imagination. We have alternatives and latitudes in expressing all our natural tendencies and needs in ways that animals do not. On the other hand, none of our expressions of freedom, imagination, and self-transcendence is disconnected from our biological life. Our freedom is only a freedom to orient our biology one way or the other but never to disconnect ourselves from it, totally repress it, or act forgetfully of it. This truth makes our human creativity quite complex indeed.[30]

This Niebuhrian sense of spirit refers to the human capacity for freedom, imagination, and self-transcendence. But this capacity is always an *embodied* capacity. Any spiritual attempt to eradicate the body, no matter how great the effort at self-denial, is doomed to fail. Besides, we do not need to run away from our bodies in order to be spiritual persons. We cannot abandon nature on our way to God.

Yet the opposite is equally true. No matter how much we indulge ourselves in the delights of nature, we can never eliminate our capacity for spiritual self-transcendence. Hedonism, no matter how extravagant, simply does not have the power to disconnect us from our capacity for self-transcendence. Body denial won't eliminate biology and spiritual denial won't eliminate self-transcendence. Like it or not, argues Niebuhr, we are a combination of nature and spirit.

For Niebuhr, all dualism is unacceptable, including a dualism that separates nature and mind or spirit in such a way that nature is perceived as chaotic, unregulated, irrational energy that desperately needs mind or spirit to give it form. This dualism gives "mind" the Herculean task of having to control the natural inclinations toward irrationality and destruction. Stated differently, Niebuhr does not think the "death wish" is automatically built into us. We are not inherently or biologically destructive or evil. We *become* destructive of ourselves and others as we mishandle anxiety and misuse our freedom. While anxiety is not itself sin, it is, as Søren Kierkegaard so frequently said, the *precondition* of sin. While ontological anxiety is built into our human situation, it is not *necessary* that we act in anxiously self-centered and destructive ways. We are not "doomed."

What is crucial to understand here is that *evil or destruction does not automatically occur as a result of our biological make-up*. Again, we are not "hard-wired" to sin. Destructiveness is not a necessary part of our condition. For Niebuhr, Freud provides a deep analysis of our distorted condition. Like Tillich, however, he claims that Freud was wrong to say that this destructive tendency arises directly from our basic nature. Thanatos is not a part of our inherent condition. Or stated more simply, we are not born to be destructive.

Psychoanalysis, since Freud, has generally moved away from the concept of innate aggressiveness and the death instinct, and instead argued that aggressiveness results from need deficiency. The work of Ronald Fairbairne, Donald Winnicott, and especially Heinz Kohut has highlighted the significance of relational attachment rather than drive release as the crucial motivating factor of human beings. Rather than viewing the infant as innately aggressive, some—but not all—psychoanalysts believe the object-seeking infant is much more concerned with human connection than Freud realized. Aggression is more a by-product of psychological need frustration than it is a biological urge driving us from birth. One psychoanalyst, Erich Fromm, spent a great deal of time analyzing the undercurrents of destructive behavior. It is to his theory that we now turn.

ERICH FROMM AND HUMAN DESTRUCTIVENESS

Erich Fromm is a profoundly interdisciplinary thinker and psychoanalyst. Fromm integrates psychoanalysis with Marxist social theory, philosophy, religion, anthropology, and other disciplines. His work is not only broad and comprehensive, but also quite readable. His writings have clearly been read and appreciated by a popular, as well as academic, market. Fromm is especially creative and insightful when he deals with the topic of evil. His book, *The Heart of Man: Its Genius for Good and Evil*, will be my main focus in investigating Fromm.[31] However, his *Anatomy of Human Destructiveness*, which has already been mentioned, will also be used as a resource for grasping his valuable contribution.

In *The Heart of Man*, Fromm wades into a question that he recognizes has been debated for centuries: Is humanity *essentially* good or evil? Having been raised Jewish and steeped in the Hebrew Bible, Fromm is convinced that Judaism does *not* teach that humanity is corrupt. While Adam and Eve clearly disobeyed God's law, this disobedience "is the condition for man's self-awareness, for his capacity to choose, and thus in the last analysis this first act of disobedience is man's first step toward freedom."[32] Disobedience, then, was a necessary part of developing as human beings.

For the Jewish tradition, what makes a person evil is *doing* evil. Evil is not a state into which we are born. By engaging in more and more destructive acts, persons can become "hardened" to their own evil, not unlike the manner in which Pharaoh's heart was hardened. Evil is a progressive problem brought on by the accumulation of more and more destructive acts. Thus, in the Jewish tradition, there are two inclinations, the *yester ha-rah* (inclination toward evil) and the *yester ha-tob* (inclination toward goodness), which reside within each person. Each person must decide between these two options. As Fromm states it, "Man is left alone with his 'two strivings,' that for good and for evil, and the decision is his alone."[33]

Christian thought, Fromm admits, moves in a different direction with its concepts of original sin and the bondage of the will. Christianity has emphasized a disposition toward sin, a universal potential that places all people in the same boat. Sin refers to more than behaviors; instead, it refers to the disposition of our fallen nature. Adam's disobedience tells *all* of our stories. Thus Adam's sin affected far more than Adam; it also affected all of his ancestors. The human *condition* is intricately bound up with sin. This sin is primarily a relationship problem with our Source, God. Unless it is healed, we are quite incapable of fulfilling God's purposes through our own free will.

While Fromm believes this line of thought in Christianity is far too pessimistic, he wants to emphasize that his own position is not naïvely optimistic: "As one whose views have often been misrepresented as underestimating the potential of evil within man, I want to emphasize that such sentimental optimism is not the mood of my thought. It would be difficult indeed for anyone who has a long clinical experience as a psychoanalyst to belittle the destructive forces within man."[34]

Yet for Fromm, the mere existence of destructive forces within humanity does not mean that they are *primary*. While they may be strong, this does not automatically mean that they are dominant. Instead, this human destructiveness may well represent a basic distortion of deeper, benign inclinations. Further, the acknowledgment of these destructive forces does not mean that humanity cannot eventually overcome them. There is no reason to believe that they are an eternal structure of the human condition. Thus we see important differences between Fromm and Freud. Freud believed our destructive tendencies are innate and biologically given; Fromm did not. And second, Freud indicated that we are "stuck" with the battle between individual happiness and civilization; Fromm believed we may eventually overcome it. Freud's final dualism is not shared by Fromm, who holds out utopian hopes for a better tomorrow. And also, Fromm argues that human beings engage in destructive behavior for social reasons, not just biological ones. The notion that our biological "death wish" leads to war is a clear case of psychological reductionism. Wars are fought for political, social, and economic reasons and not merely psychological ones.

Fromm also identifies several reasons for violence. He mentions *reactive violence*, which is done in the service of life. While it is based on fear, its aim is preservation, not destruction. This is defensive and necessary for survival. Then there is *revengeful violence*, which is not really defense because the violence has already been done and we want to restore our self-esteem before the insult or injury. "Psychoanalytic material demonstrates that the mature, productive person is less motivated by the desire for revenge than the neurotic person who has difficulties in living independently and fully, and who is often prone to stake his whole existence on the wish for revenge."[35] And other violence can be attributed to a *shattering of faith*. Sometimes this happens at a very early and delicate age. It is the collapse of faith in the love, goodness, and fairness of the world. It can involve a faith in mother, father, grandparents, or God. The death of a pet, for instance, can chip away at the "friendliness" of life. As Fromm indicates, "it does not make much difference whether it is faith in a person or in God which is shattered. It is always the faith in life, in the possibility of trusting it, of having confidence in it, which is broken."[36] In severe faith-shatterings, the person may react by hating life itself.

> If there is nothing or nobody to believe in, if one's faith in goodness and justice has all been a foolish illusion, if life is ruled by the Devil rather than by God—then, indeed, life becomes hateful; one can no longer bear the pain of disappointment. One wishes to prove that life is evil, that men are evil, that oneself is evil. The disappointed believer and lover of life thus will be turned into a cynic and a destroyer. This destructiveness is one of despair; disappointment in life has led to hate of life.[37]

Fromm also describes *compensatory violence*. In this form of violence, destructiveness is used as a compensation for one's own feelings of powerlessness. One has lost potency, the ability to direct one's will and energy toward the completion of a specific goal. Thus compensatory violence attempts to "make up for" one's feeling of impotence. For Fromm, the great

Colosseum of Rome represents this compensatory violence. Thousands of impotent people received great pleasure in seeing others destroyed by beasts or in killing each other. Compensatory violence results from "unlived life."[38] The solution to compensatory violence is living fully.

And finally, there is a deeply regressed form of violence Fromm calls *archaic bloodthirst*.[39] This involves an attempt to escape reason and return to brute animal existence. This person feels alive *by taking life*. Blood is the essence of life, so killing makes one feel strong and superior.

"LIFE LOVERS" AND "DEATH LOVERS"

Fromm is very straightforward in his conviction that there are persons who love life and persons who love death. Of course, the vast majority of us are a mixture. Nevertheless, Fromm identifies the life lovers as having a biophilous orientation and death lovers as having a necrophilous inclination. Fromm further believes that this distinction represents the greatest psychological and moral difference between people.

The question quickly becomes, "What is the relationship between Fromm's necrophilous person and Freud's death instinct?" Let's recall Freud's statement made in the *New Introductory Lectures* in 1933:

> If it is true that once in an inconceivably remote past, and in an unimaginable way, life rose out of inanimate matter, then, in accordance with our hypothesis, an instinct must have at that time come into being, whose aim it was to abolish life once more and to re-establish the inorganic state of things. If in this instinct we recognize the impulse to self-destruction in our hypotheses, then we can regard that impulse as the manifestation of a *death* instinct which can never be absent in any vital process.[40]

As the life instinct attempts to combine organic substance into larger units, the death instinct attempts to undue everything the life instinct endeavors. This is a kind of intrapsychic version of Zoroastrianism in which the forces of darkness engage in eternal battle with the forces of light. Again, the two instincts are rooted in biology and therefore inevitable.

Fromm is not willing to go as far as Freud in placing the death instinct within the biological realm. He believes, for instance, that the vast majority of organic life fights tenaciously for its survival. Because Fromm's objection to Freud is so pivotal, I will quote him at length.

> The contradiction between Eros and destruction, between the affinity to life and the affinity to death is, indeed, the most fundamental contradiction which exists in man. This duality, however, is not one of two biologically inherent instincts, relatively constant and always battling with each other until the final victory of the death instinct, but it is one between the primary and most fundamental tendency of life—to preserve in life—and its contradiction, which comes into being when man fails in his goal. In this view the "death instinct" is a *malignant* phenomenon which grows and takes over to the extent to which Eros does not unfold. The death instinct represents *psychopathology* and not, as in Freud's view, a part of *normal biology*. The life instinct thus constitutes the primary potentiality in man; the death instinct a secondary potentiality. The primary potentiality develops if the appropriate conditions for life are present, just as a seed grows only if the proper conditions of moisture, temperature, etc., are given. If the proper conditions are not present, the necrophilous tendencies will emerge and dominate the person.[41]

This comment, in my view, represents one of the most crucial statements of Fromm's entire work on human destructiveness. The death instinct is not a biological "equal" to the life instinct. In fact, though its potential is always present, it grows out of a frustration of the life instinct. Thus the death instinct is not a *natural*, ordinary development. Instead, it is pathological. The death instinct is not as *primary* as the life instinct. A biological drive does not push the death instinct into existence; instead, it is a distortion of the life instinct. When the right psychological conditions are not present and eros is frustrated, then, and only then, is thanatos born.

This seemingly small point of departure from Freud represents a major change in personality theory and development. Fromm's humanism overshadows the more pessimistic Freudian paradigm. He is saying that if the right psychological conditions are present, the life instinct will unfold naturally. This understanding places Fromm very close to the humanistic psychology positions of Carl Rogers and Abraham Maslow. Destructiveness is always a secondary problem stemming from the frustrations of self-actualization. The pivotal, non-Freudian point can thus be stated as follows: it is the social conditions of the child, and not the biological inclination toward destructiveness, that creates thanatos or the necrophilous person.

This is not to say, however, that Fromm is as cheery in his view of the human condition as are Rogers and Maslow. Clearly he is not. The biophilous tendency, or what humanistic psychologists call self-actualization, is certainly not an automatic, "blossoming forth" process if the right social conditions are present. It's more of a struggle than humanistic psychology often wants to admit. The temptations toward regression, resistance to growth, fear, and self-obsession are always with us. Rogers and Maslow come very close to suggesting that once the unidirectional self-actualizing tendency is biologically set in motion, it has no serious internal competitor. This view, in my mind, is a bit too dismissive of the anxiety and courage needed to move toward growth and productive living.[42]

So what are the conditions that help promote a biophilous person? Being around others who love life is the crucial factor. Warmth, affectionate contact, a nonthreatening atmosphere, guidance through example, kind words—all of these are important qualities for a child who tries to love life. Conversely, necrophilous people can be contagious. Excessive criticism, fear, a monotonous schedule, and mechanical orderliness are the enemies of biophilia.

FROMM'S SYNDROME OF DECAY

The first symptom of the syndrome of decay, then, is the necrophilous orientation. While it does not literally mean a sexual desire for corpses, as the word *necrophile* normally means, it does involve a sadistic desire to drain the life out of others. While corpses, sickness, and destruction are a preoccupation for some necrophilous persons, probably the majority are more preoccupied with psychological lifelessness. They want to control, dominate, and extinguish the liveliness in another. They want to transform a potentially lively partner into a dead, robotic person. The necrophile forbids anything to grow or expand. Joy comes from controlling and draining the lives from others. Like a vampire, the necrophile enjoys sucking the life-blood out of another. Gradually, his or her partner becomes lifeless. The extreme forms of this can be found among some serial killers who prefer being around corpses instead of people who are alive. Psychological necrophiliacs want others' spirits or vitality to be dead, even if their physical bodies are not.

Another ingredient in Fromm's syndrome of decay is what he calls "malignant narcissism." Note the word *malignant*. This is to suggest an aggressive, dominating form of narcissism that is more than the enlightened self-interest we all need in order to survive. It is also more than a simple desire for attention. "Benign" narcissism, as Fromm calls it, involves a pride in our own efforts and achievements. Benign narcissism, however, is capable of achieving a certain distance from our work or accomplishments. We are able, for instance, to compare our work with that of others realistically. This reality check helps keep our narcissism at bay.

Malignant narcissism, however, is a different matter. Here we perceive everything we do as wonderful *simply because we do it*. Because we are unique, special, and entitled, we do not have to produce. All forms of justification are unnecessary. Fromm describes it as follows:

> If I am "great" because of some quality I *have*, and not because
> of something I *achieve*, I do not need to be related to anybody or
> anything; I need not make any effort. In maintaining the picture of
> my greatness I remove myself more and more from reality and I have
> to increase the narcissistic charge in order to be better protected from
> the danger that my narcissistically inflated ego might be revealed as
> the product of empty imagination. Malignant narcissism, thus, is not
> self-limiting, and in consequence it is crudely solipsistic as well as
> xenophobic.[43]

For malignant narcissists, other people merely serve as an adoring audience. Others are there simply "for them," and they have extremely limited abilities to love and care for others. As the center of the universe, everyone revolves around them. This is not to say that they don't have a high opinion of those close to them. However, the reason for this high elevation of their partners, friends, or children is because all these people *are connected to them!* This is what gives others their value: they are connected to the narcissist. Because a narcissist sees everything in his or her life as inflated, his or her partner is the greatest partner in the world; his or her children are the most special children in the universe; and his or her friends are the cream of the crop. All these people have one glowing characteristic in common—they are each connected to the narcissist. Thus others are great because they are extensions of the narcissist.

Another key feature of malignant narcissism, according to Fromm, is a profoundly egocentrically biased reason. The exaggerated sense of self distorts and colors one's entire judgment of reality. The whole time, however, the narcissist will insist that he or she is being completely objective and unbiased. Anything that challenges the narcissist's elevated place is viewed with contempt. In fact, anything that differs from the way the narcissist sees it is viewed as deeply inadequate, if not dangerous. This creates enormous cognitive distortion. I view all of reality out of the lens of my cosmic specialness; therefore it is awful and dastardly if someone disagrees with my omniscient view of the world. Any alternative perspective is completely underestimated and dismissed as inadequate. Because the narcissist is the center of the universe, he or she also has the job of defining ultimate reality.

Individual narcissism tends to be easier to detect than what Fromm calls "social narcissism," which can be extremely destructive. The features of individual and social narcissism are much the same except that with social narcissism group members reinforce each other's sense of superiority and entitlement. Collective support strengthens the narcissistic portrait of reality: "The essence of this overestimation of one's own position and the hate for all who differ from it is narcissism. 'We' are admirable; 'they' are despicable. 'We' are good; 'they' are evil. Any criticism of one's own doctrine is a vicious and unbearable attack; criticism of the other's position is a well-meant attempt to help them return to the truth."[44]

Fromm notes that, ironically, religious groups often fall into this group narcissism. Why is it ironic? Because religious groups would seem to have their narcissism checked by the constant reminder that they are not the God they worship; instead, they are human creatures who recognize a Source much larger than themselves. One would think that this recognition would help minimize feelings of personal omnipotence. However, many religious people narcissistically identify with this Source of life. In other words, their narcissism is tied to the idea that they are "playing on the right team." By identifying with the absoluteness of God, their own narcissism is vicariously inflated.

The last ingredient of the syndrome of decay is what Fromm calls "incestuous fixation on mother."[45] Fromm psychologically expands the notion of incestuous fixation, a pre-Oedipal attachment to the mother. This attachment involves a deep desire for protection, certainty, and a freedom from responsibility. In the early days of life, of course, we need precisely this kind of caretaking. However, we should eventually develop beyond this preoccupation with motherly protection. If we don't, argues Fromm, we can look for the security, certainty, and unconditional love of "mother" everywhere. This search for perfect nurture involves a life without risks, shielded, safe world in which we refuse the burden of freedom. A symbiotic attachment to a mothering figure, be it an ideology, group, church, nation, and so on, reveals a desire to return to the womb.

> If I fail to cut the umbilical cord, if I insist on worshipping the idol
> of certainty and protection, then the idol becomes sacred. It must not
> be criticized. If "mother" cannot be wrong, how can I judge anyone
> else objectively if he is in conflict with "mother" or disapproved by
> her? This form of impairment is much less obvious when the object
> of fixation is not mother but the family, the nation, or the race. . . .
> The tendency to remain bound to the mothering person and her
> equivalents—to blood, family, and tribe—is inherent in all men and
> women. It is constantly in conflict with the opposite tendency—to
> be born, to progress, to grow. In the case of severe pathology, the
> regressive tendency for growth wins. In the case of severe pathology,
> the regressive tendency for symbiotic union wins, and it results in

the person's more or less total incapacitation. Freud's concept of the incestuous strivings to be found in any child is perfectly correct. Yet the significance of this concept transcends Freud's own assumption. Incestuous wishes are not primarily a result of sexual desires, but continue one of the most fundamental tendencies in man: the wish to remain tied to where he came from, the fear of being free, and the fear of being destroyed by the very figure toward whom he has made himself helpless, renouncing his independence.[46]

The Nazi preoccupation with the "motherland" is an obvious example of how a lust for a secure world can push people toward great evil. Personhood is lost in this frantic attempt to find absolute security.

Necrophilous tendencies, malignant narcissism, and symbiotic incestuous fixation, then, are Fromm's three primary elements of evil and human destructiveness. They represent a sadistic desire for lifelessness, an extreme self-centeredness, and a dehumanizing craving for security. They push the world into distortion and decay.

FROMM AND TILLICH ON ESTRANGEMENT AND HEALING

While Fromm writes a great deal about the human inclination toward evil, he differs from Freud in two important ways: (*a*) he does not believe this destructive inclination emerges from our biological nature, but is instead a secondary reaction to the frustration of our positive inclinations; and (*b*) he believes that it is indeed possible to heal this destructive inclination. Like Marx, Fromm has a vision of "unalienated humanity," an eschatological hope that he believes can be realized. The realization of this hope requires nothing beyond humanity's own efforts. Put another way, Fromm sees no need for appealing to the transcendent realm to heal our brokenness. Thus he is more optimistic than Freud in two respects. First, he believes that destructive tendencies are not biologically rooted. And second, he believes that humanity can eventually heal its estrangement problem. This "salvation" requires no appeal to God or the "ultimate Source" of reality.[47]

For Tillich, our alienation is *total*. All dimensions of our lives are estranged, and we cannot appeal to one dimension in order to rescue or heal the other dimensions. As religious studies professor Guy Hammond points out, Tillich referred to two types of existentialists: the "radical" and the "utopian."[48] The radical existentialists, which Tillich believes includes Freud, argue that complete reconciliation is never possible. Final healing or salvation is simply not going to happen. We must make the best of a very estranged world. The utopian existentialists, on the other hand, argue that alienation is certainly a *present* reality, but one that may eventually be overcome. Through psychological and social intervention, the "estrangement problem" can one day be rectified. Human existence is not necessarily tragic. There is some "unalienated" or "unestranged" part of ourselves to which we can appeal. This part will in turn help us heal and restore the alienated dimensions. This, for Fromm, is the way naturalistic redemption must work. Our healthy side must heal the sick side. Estranged existence cannot produce its own cure, but full human consciousness *can*. This potential within the human condition is called the "productive orientation," which is indeed similar to the concept of self-actualization in the humanistic psychologies we will observe in the next chapter. Humanity, again, must save itself. The entire notion of "God's grace," for Fromm, is simply a symbolic way of talking about what humanity actually does for itself. It is *our* love, not God's love, that is the healing reality. In fact, all theological statements can be reduced to anthropological ones. "God" does not refer to a power beyond humanity; instead, "God" refers to our own powers. God is the higher self.

As one might well guess, while Tillich appreciates many of Fromm's insights, he is also critical of what he considers to be Fromm's utopia. Put another way, while Tillich likes Fromm's *diagnosis*, he does not like his *prognosis*.[49] As Tillich puts it: "How can alienated man overcome alienation by himself? How can the 'dead' man of the 20th century revive himelf? Without an answer to these questions Fromm's description of communitarian humanism sounds utopian . . ."[50]

In describing Fromm, Hammond writes, "The main tenor of his work seems to imply that the regressive impulse (or the 'death wish') is not an ineradicable instinct in human nature. It can be overcome, and perhaps eliminated, through the power of consciousness, through a social and historical process."[51] The fuller our consciousness, the less our destructiveness. Fromm is convinced that we can use the human powers of reason, creativity, and love to minimize, and eventually eliminate, all human destructiveness. Granted, this will be gradual. However, we can supply our own healing.

Tillich strongly disagrees. Because estrangement involves *all* aspects of our being, we simply cannot offer ourselves redemption. There is no "unalienated part" to which we can appeal. The problem is that we are estranged not just from ourselves or each other; instead, we are also estranged from our Ground or Source. This separation and estrangement from our Source (God) must be healed before we can heal other dimensions of our estrangement. Because we are finite, limited creatures, we will never experience the type of full consciousness described by Fromm. There will always be a deep sense of ambiguity. The healing of our estrangement will, of necessity, be a "gift" of unconditional acceptance that we simply cannot offer ourselves.

Thus Tillich and Niebuhr both agree that Fromm is *right* in saying that our destructiveness has not occurred because of a Freudian biological necessity. However, they would say Fromm is *wrong* in his proclamation that humanity can heal itself from its estrangement problem. Only an acceptance that comes from a Source much larger than humanity can ultimately heal this separation.

ERNEST BECKER: EVIL AND THE DENIAL OF DEATH

Cultural anthropologist and psychoanalytic interpreter Ernest Becker won the Pulitzer Prize for his outstanding work, *The Denial of Death,*[52] a book that preceded his important and final work, *Escape from Evil.*[53] According to Becker, these two works are "companion volumes."[54] In order to understand the development of Becker's perspective on the issue of evil, I will explore the overlapping argument contained in each book.

In *The Denial of Death,* Becker makes a rather sweeping claim that can be easily enough understood from the book's title—namely, that we human beings spend our lives repressing our own mortality as we narcissistically attempt to play out a deep yearning to be heroic. This heroism denies our finitude, vulnerability, and inevitable encounter with death. Relying heavily on Kierkegaard, and at many times sounding very similar to Niebuhr, Becker argues that we human beings are a unique combination of nature and spirit, a condition that creates enormous anxiety. We are able to rise above our creatureliness and yet we are profoundly embedded in our decaying mortality. Our primary fight is with finitude itself, or more particularly, with the awareness of our own demise. We want to stand out, to fulfill our "ache of cosmic specialness."[55] One of the tasks of every culture is to provide individuals with ways of becoming heroic and transcending the limitations of finitude.

This desire to expand our own organism, to inflate ourselves, appears to be rooted in biology, a kind of natural and inevitable narcissism. At least through our imagination, we inflate ourselves to cosmic proportions as we deny the most terrifying thing of all—our necessary limitations and eventual demise. We want to be our own Creator, our own cause, the sustainer of our own life. In short, we long to be our own God. This divinity fantasy involves recreating the entire world in our own image. Following Adler, Becker believes this desire to be superior, to even be cosmically special, is the driving force in the human condition. It propels us into enormous lies about our own invincibility and invulnerability.

For Becker, the childhood experience of sibling rivalry expresses a deep and tragic truth about the human condition:

> Sibling rivalry is a critical problem that reflects the basic human condition: it is not that children are vicious, selfish, or domineering. It is that they so openly express man's tragic destiny: he must desperately justify himself as an object of primary value in the universe; he must stand out, be a hero, make the biggest possible contribution to world life; show that he *counts* more than anything or anyone else. . . . [T]o become conscious of what one is doing to earn his feeling of heroism is the main self-analytic problem of life. Everything painful and sobering in what psychoanalytic genius and religious genius have discovered about man revolves around the terror of admitting what one is doing to earn his self-esteem.[56]

The problem, of course, is that we are *not* omnipotent. Our own death is the ultimate reminder of this reality so we must engage in nearly constant repression concerning our demise. All forms of heroism, for Becker, are unconscious attempts to deny mortality. Becker enlists the support of psychoanalyst Gregory Zilboorg:

> For behind the sense of insecurity in the face of danger, behind the
> sense of discouragement and depression, there always lurks the basic
> fear of death, a fear which undergoes most complex elaborations
> and manifests itself in many indirect ways. . . . No one is free of
> the fear of death. . . . The anxiety neuroses, the various phobic
> states, even a considerable number of depressive suicidal states and
> many schizophrenias amply demonstrate the ever-present fear of
> death which becomes woven into the major conflicts of the given
> psychopathological conditions. . . . We may take for granted that the
> fear of death is always present in our mental functioning.[57]

This anxiety about death is the backdrop for other types of anxiety. This notion is also eloquently conveyed by Tillich, who argued that the anxiety about specific limitations in one's life emerges from the ultimate limitation—death. As he put it, "The anxiety of death is the permanent horizon within which the anxiety of fate is at work. . . . Certainly the anxiety of death overshadows all concrete anxieties and gives them their ultimate seriousness."[58] According to Becker, if this anxiety were continually conscious, we would not even be able to function.

For Becker, as for Kierkegaard, the human paradox is that we have the capacity for a symbolic identity *above* nature yet we are firmly grounded *in* nature: "Man is literally split in two: he has an awareness of his own splendid uniqueness in that he sticks out of nature with a towering majesty, and yet he goes back into the ground a few feet in order to blindly and dumbly to rot and disappear forever."[59] On the one hand, humans are lofty and magnificent; on the other hand, we are decaying, dying animals. Becker believes that we are reminded of our animal nature by our anality: regardless of how self-transcending we may appear, we all must defecate. "The anus and its incomprehensible, repulsive product represents not only physical determinism and boundness, but the fate as well of all that is physical: decay and death."[60] No matter what our pretensions may suggest, fallibility is all around us. Thus while we want desperately to be free of our anxiety about death so that we can live more fully, it is life itself that triggers our anxiety of dying.[61] Becker states this boldly: "It cannot be overstressed, one final time, that to see the world as it really is devastating and terrifying. It achieves the very result that the child has painfully built his character over the years in order to avoid: it *makes routine, automatic, secure, self-confident activity impossible.* It makes thoughtless living in the world of men an impossibility. It places a trembling animal at the mercy of the entire cosmos and the problem of the meaning of it."[62]

Becker, then, makes an important departure from Freud. The primary repression does not concern sexuality, but death. And instead of a death instinct, we instead have a death *fear.* Rather than saying that human beings have a biological urge toward death, they instead have an unconscious dread of death.

FEAR OF DEATH AND EVIL

But what, we may ask, does this discussion of death have to do with human evil? Becker's conviction is straightforward: out of our fear of death and our attempts to escape its reality, we engage in evil, destructive lives. Evil is a by-product of our fear of death and the refusal of our own finitude. Our viciousness is tied to our attempts to flee from our own plight.

Becker believes that most human beings see death itself as the greatest "evil." Mortality is wicked. And ironically, in our attempt to escape this greatest of all evils, we create much more evil. Our lust for self-perpetuation creates much destructiveness; our desire for continued experience eradicates the experience of others; our frantic need for more often means that others have less. Our desire to transcend our mortal lives leads us toward immoral behavior. Others "pick up the tab" for the hatred we feel for our own mortality. "Each person nourishes his immortality in the ideology of self-perpetuation to which he gives his allegiance; this gives his life the only abiding significance he can have. No wonder men go into a rage over fine points of belief: if your adversary wins the argument about truth, *you die. Your immortality system has been shown to be fallible.*"[63]

A basic source of evil, then, is human beings trying to be different than what they are. This fight with finitude has devastating consequences on our neighbors. The refusal to accept our true condition sets up an ongoing pattern of destructiveness: "The thing that makes man the most devastating animal that ever stuck his neck up into the sky is that he wants a stature and a destiny that is impossible for an animal; he wants an earth that is not an earth but a heaven, and the price for this kind of fantastic ambition is to make the earth an even more eager graveyard than it naturally is."[64]

Killing others, then, becomes a way of defying our own death. It is *they*, not *we*, who are dying. By witnessing the death of others, we perpetuate the illusion that we are escaping it. Becker believes this attitude was a key factor in the popularity of the Roman arenas. The arena games staged a triumph over death by watching others face it while attendees avoided it. "For man, maximum excitement is the confrontation of death and the skillful defiance of it by watching others fed to it as he survives transfixed with rapture."[65] Also, when the fate of others is held in one's own hands, it produces a feeling of mastery of death. This is a factor in sadism—it gives people a sense of power over others, and indirectly, over death. We are able to focus externally on the death of another as we avoid the awareness of our own demise. Stated more strongly, the killing of others serves as a means of killing our own self-contempt, our mortality. We attempt to "prove" our own immortality by exposing the mortality of others. This could also explain our culture's frequent preoccupations with murder, hazardous car accidents, and other forms of violent death. It is not uncommon to watch traffic nearly stop to observe a hazardous accident. This is frequently understood as a mere curiosity or even a "concern." Yet one wonders if it doesn't provide the opportunity to come face-to-face with death, then pass on by relieved that one is still alive. We have won over death one more time.

The attempt to escape the greatest evil for every individual—his or her own demise—thus becomes the source of the evil we inflict on others. Perhaps the most direct and powerful statement Becker makes on evil is this:

The paradox is that *evil comes from man's urge to heroic victory over evil*. The evil that troubles man most is his vulnerability; he seems impotent to guarantee the absolute meaning of his life, its significance in the cosmos. He assures a plentitude of evil, then, by trying to make closure on his cosmic heroism *in this life and this world*. . . . [A]ll the intolerable sufferings of mankind result from man's attempt to make the whole world of nature reflect *his* reality, his heroic victory; he thus tries to achieve a perfection on earth, a visual testimonial to his cosmic importance; but this testimonial can only be given conclusively by the beyond, by the source of creation itself which alone knows man's value because it knows his task, the meaning of his life; man has confused two spheres, the visible and whatever is beyond, and this blindness has permitted him to undertake the impossible—to extend the values of his limited visible sphere over all the rest of creation, whatever forms it may take. The tragic evils of history, then, are a commensurate result of a blindness and impossibility of such magnitude.[66]

Thus human beings cause evil in their very attempts to triumph over it. Evil is a byproduct of a Godlike narcissism. Becker quotes Alfred Adler: "All neurosis is vanity."[67]

DOES BECKER EXAGGERATE OUR NARCISSISM?

Philosopher Donald Evans has offered a very thoughtful critique of Becker's central thesis.[68] Before he critiques Becker, however, he offers a summary of Becker's position that provides an excellent overview of Becker's thought:

First, every human being is mainly motivated by an inbuilt narcissism, a megalomaniac fantasy of self as god, self-sufficient and self-creative. Second, this proud project is radically undermined by our impotence in relation to an overwhelming, terrifying universe and an inevitable death, so we disguise our impotence in projects which have divine pretensions and which help us to repress our terror concerning life and our anxiety concerning death. Third, we also nevertheless yearn to yield ourselves up in surrender, becoming like infants in total dependence on a power which transcends us. Fourth, we all try to cope with the first three elements in our nature by idolizing a person or society or God. Idolatry focused on God is best because it enables us to combine the most godlike creativity with the most complete yielding while most successfully disguising our impotence against nature and death as we identify with the Creator of nature, the invulnerable Immortal. Fifth, the ideal form of creativity is one which acknowledges the inescapable spirit/body dualism in human beings and identifies with the spirit, bypassing the body and all that is associated with the body, including heterosexual involvement.[69]

Evans argues that Becker's claims concerning the universality and intensity of narcissism are exaggerated. Tendencies toward narcissism vary greatly from person to person. In some, of course, it is very strong. However, this should not be generalized to the entire population. The variation of narcissistic inclinations can be explained by examining parent-child interaction, and not by postulating a universal, inbuilt tendency. We need not resort to biological explanations to account for narcissism.

Also, adults are at least partially successful in their struggles with narcissism. In fact, many move away from self-obsession and toward a genuine sense of participation with others. Our desire to relate and to connect with others, argues Evans, is as strong as our desire to stand out. Stated even more strongly, our tendencies toward narcissistic self-sufficiency may well grow out of our childhood frustrations in trying to relate to others. This is a serious challenge to the Beckerian thesis: narcissism is a derivative of a frustrated desire to connect, love, and be loved, as Evans notes: "A narcissistic preoccupation with issues of status and power, self-esteem and 'heroism' is to a great extent an unconscious strategy for evading the pain of a frustrated urge to love and be loved. Far from being the most fundamental motive, narcissism is itself largely derivative. And to the extent that it is derivative it can be undermined."[70] As we repress a desire to connect, we become more and more self-absorbed. A tension between narcissism and participation is present in everyone. While one inclination may dominate over the other, both are present. Human beings are more varied than

Becker's mono-motivational theory suggests.[71]

As we have seen, Becker believes that almost all of our activities are an outgrowth of our fear of death and nature. We all want to pursue our heroism in spite of our smallness in the overall scheme of things. Yet for Evans, the intensity of this denial of death depends upon the extent of one's narcissism. The more narcissistic we are, the more death seems intolerable as it "mocks our pretension to omnipotence and ridicules our attempts to upstage the universe."[72] Death certainly interferes with a "God-complex." Yet again, some have a God-complex far more than others. Becker's thesis assumes that we are all dominated by narcissism, and hence death is intensely feared. For Evans, again, this universalizing of extreme narcissism is the problem. Some people are much more participative and connected to others than the narcissists Becker describes. In fact, they are less concerned with their fear of death than they are with a celebration of life.

Evans goes on to suggest that this participation of life and connection with others *helps decrease the fear of death:* "Death is still unwelcome and the pains of dying are still abhorred: there may still be an Agony in the Garden. But daily life is not unconsciously or consciously dominated by an awareness of death which is intensely anxious, defiant and obsessive. The inevitability of death can be faced with assurance and acceptance as a fact on the periphery of life."[73]

Thus Evans's critique of Becker argues that (*a*) Becker has exaggerated the intensity and universality of narcissism, (*b*) this exaggeration of narcissism brings on an equally inflated thesis that the fear of death is the primary preoccupation of life, and (*c*) human evil can be primarily explained by our attempts to outmaneuver our own mortality. But if his theory of evil rests on a miscalculation concerning the extent of narcissism and its corresponding flight from death, then his understanding of human destruction is itself called into question.

One wonders, however, whether Evans works with a limited understanding of self-obsession. For instance, self-absorption does not always convey itself in inflated, condescending, highly conceited ways. It may even appear as "humble" or other-centered. The issue, however, is whether one's own sense of security becomes the dominant issue in one's life. We can devote ourselves to others as if they were gods, and yet beneath this devotion, we may have a radical preoccupation with our own sense of security and well-being. Self-absorption does not always appear in ugly, self-centered ways. We can even sacrifice a great deal as a way of trying to gain the security of another's acceptance. The help we offer may be less concerned with benefiting another than with our own sense of acceptance and approval from another. Put another way, pride can take many forms, if by pride we mean some form of self-preoccupation in which the self replaces God as the center of existence. Puffed up pride is indeed narcissistic, but there are many milder forms as well. Many of us build our lives around our insecurities, or more accurately, in an attempt to hide and disguise our insecurities.

SUMMARY

In this chapter, I have investigated the important psychoanalytic perspectives of Freud, Fromm, and Becker. I have indicated how Freud gradually developed his conviction that human destructiveness is an essential part of the human condition. This innate aggressiveness doesn't emerge simply from need frustration; instead, it is basic to the human condition. I then examined the theological response of Tillich and Niebuhr, who both appreciate Freud's rich analysis, but believe Freud describes only our *estranged,* and not our *essential,* condition.

I then turned to Erich Fromm in an effort to see how he departed from Freud's view of human destructiveness. Fromm is particularly astute in the development of his "syndrome of decay," which I attempted to outline. I then examined Tillich's challenge to Fromm's utopian vision.

And finally, I looked at Ernest Becker's provocative thesis that evil stems primarily from our own denial of death, and our narcissistic need to attain immortality. While his diagnosis of universal narcissism may be somewhat overstated, Becker's passionate argument is very instructive.

The psychoanalytic perspective does not have a monopoly on the "human interpretation" enterprise. Other psychological theories have contributions to make concerning human evil. I will now turn to cognitive-behavioral, Jungian, and humanistic psychological portraits of the human condition in an effort to find further clues about human destructiveness and evil.

CHAPTER FOUR

HUMAN POTENTIAL AND HUMAN DESTRUCTIVENESS

THE PSYCHOLOGY OF HATE

You always become the thing you fight the most.
—*Carl Jung*

If anything seems apparent in the scope of human history, it is that we human beings are quite capable of hating. This is not necessarily a pessimistic, gloomy view of the human condition; instead, it is a *realistic* one. Some argue that we come into this world with a biological inclination toward hatred. Others argue that we have to be taught to hate and that it is not inherent within our nature. Some believe that we hate only when we feel threatened. Others believe we hate when our desire for love has been frustrated. Some believe the goal of life is to eliminate our hatred. These individuals see hatred as incompatible with love. Others believe that it is impossible to love if we do not also have the capacity to hate. Some believe that our inclinations toward hatred can never be eradicated, but merely curbed. Still others believe that the goal of life is to hate the appropriate things, such as injustice and anything that dehumanizes us.

Regardless of the perspective, hatred is often related to evil. Destruction is frequently an outgrowth of human hatred. Yet in spite of hate's widespread appearance, many deny their own capacity to hate. Other, "friendlier" or more civilized words are used to replace the rather crude word *hatred.* Yet perhaps one of the reasons that hatred so rampantly exists is that we often deny its presence, pretend to be above it, and consequently, allow it to roam unchallenged.

In this chapter, I will examine three interpretations of hatred, perspectives that may greatly aid our overall grasp of human destructivenesss. The first perspective is a cognitive-behavioral one. In other words, it sees the primary problem of hatred as mental distortion and reactive thinking. The work of psychiatrist Aaron Beck, particularly in his important book, *Prisoners of Hate: The Cognitive Basis of Anger, Hostility, and Violence,* will be explored.[1] The underlying question here concerns the role of the thinking process in the formation of hatred. The second perspective comes out of the work of Carl Jung and is well represented by John Sanford.[2] This approach is concerned with the role of the unconscious in hating, and particularly with what is often called "the shadow." It connects the hatred of others to our own self-hatred, which is then projected outward. By failing to acknowledge our own shadow, we put others in the unfortunate position of having to carry it for us. We hate *them* in order to avoid *ourselves.*

And the third major perspective I will examine is that of David Augsburger in his 2004 book, *Hate-Work: Working Through the Pain and Pleasures of Hate.*[3] Augsburger argues that we have not clearly identified the various types and varieties of hate, and therefore our thinking about it has been confused. While appreciating and using the shadow's role in hatred, Augsburger believes that a multidimensional model of hatred is needed. He argues that we need to move through a developmental process that often starts with dualistic, us-and-them thinking and moves into an ability to separate the offender from the offense. While Augsburger believes that no single model is capable of explaining the range of our hatreds, he *does* believe that through the transforming power of love and grace we can learn to hate the right thing, which is injustice itself. In a sense, the goal is to "hate hatred," or to direct our energies toward that which dehumanizes us.

I will explore each of these perspectives in an attempt to identify their central contributions. After this exposition, I will conclude with an evaluation and critique of these perspectives.

THREAT, ANXIETY, AND REACTIVE THINKING

What role does distorted thinking play in the experience of hate? According to cognitive-behavioral psychiatrist Aaron Beck, it plays a very significant one. Beck, who along with Albert Ellis helped develop a cognitive revolution in the helping professions, has written a major statement on the underlying thought processes that lead to hatred.[4] Cognitive-behavioral therapy, like rational-emotional behavioral therapy, argues that disturbed feelings emerge from distorted thinking. Rather than focusing merely on particular affective states, cognitive therapists are interested in the underlying mental processes that produce those feelings. Irrational, exaggerated, or distorted thinking always precedes emotional disturbance. So, the cognitive therapist plays the role of mental detective as he or she tries to track down and identify the thought distortion beneath troublesome emotions. Feelings should be acknowledged, but not given the status of the final reality of the psyche. They should be seen as the consequences of particular cognitive activity. Beck's associate, David Burns, states the cognitive-behavioral conviction well:

> What is the key to releasing yourself from your emotional prison? Simply this: your thoughts create your emotions; therefore, your emotions cannot prove that your thoughts are accurate. Unpleasant feelings merely indicate that you are thinking something negative and believing it. Your emotions *follow* your thoughts as surely as baby ducks follow their mother. But the fact that the baby ducks follow faithfully along doesn't prove that the mother knows where she is going![5]

The internal explanation we assign events in our lives is therefore crucial. Beck explains this through the example of a young child who is about to receive a shot from a doctor.[6] The child may scream, fight, feel anxious, and become angry at the shot giver and those who insist upon the shot. To the young child, the doctor is simply overpowering him to inflict pain and the bystanders in the room are going along with the torture. Yet this same experience can occur with an adult who is also anxious about needles, and there will be a complete lack of anger accompanying the patient's nervousness. What's the difference? Obviously the adult interprets the event differently. A different meaning is assigned to the shot. Rather than arbitrary torture, the unpleasant experience is meant to help the patient. The *interpretation* of the shot, not the shot itself, causes the anger: "The crucial element is the *explanation* of the other person's action, and whether that explanation makes the other person's behavior acceptable to us. If it does not, we become angry and want to punish the offender. For the most part we regard the behavior that offends us as intentional rather than accidental, as malicious rather than benign. Inconveniences and frustrations come and go, but the sense of being wronged persists."[7]

The shift from hurt to anger is often a quick one. We feel that our self-esteem has been damaged and quickly move to the unfairness of the critic who "caused" this feeling. We hate those who make us feel badly. Often, the source of our own feeling of inferiority is attributed to some monstrously unfair critic. For instance, our boss points out some things about our work performance that need improvement. She may also point out some positive things. But we focus on the negative comments, feel inferior, and then ruminate on how we cannot possibly please her. The next step is often a focus on her hypercritical, unreasonable expectations and her "nerve" to criticize our performance. Previous feelings of inferiority are transformed into anger at the unfairness of the boss. Who does she think she is? Lowered self-esteem often produces a conviction that we are being judged unfairly.[8] Our boss must deliberately want to make us feel badly. And as Beck puts it, "the more one regards the distressing act as intentional or due to the negligence, indifference, or deficiency of the offender, the stronger the reaction."[9]

THE ROLE OF EGOCENTRICITY

One of the most salient features of distorted thinking is egocentricity. While self-interest is obviously important for survival, our evolutionary history has been marked by an egocentric bias in which we evaluate everything in terms of how it affects *us*. We frequently "overinterpret" situations from our own framework. Our neighbor is making a lot of noise in order to ruin our afternoon nap; the student who falls asleep must think my lecture is boring; and the driver going so slowly ahead of me somehow knows that I'm running late! As Beck notes, "We all have the tendency to perceive ourselves as the lead actor of a play and to judge other people's behavior exclusively in reference to ourselves. We take the role of the protagonist and the other players are our supporters or antagonists. The motivations and actions of the other players revolve around us in some way. As in an old-fashioned morality play, we are innocent and good; our adversaries are villainous and bad."[10] Beck adds that our egocentricity pushes us to believe that other people interpret the situation in the same manner that we interpret it. Therefore, they "know" what they are doing but apparently don't care. The offender is more culpable because we project intention into his or her behavior. Their actions are deliberately designed for our displeasure!

Beck believes that these individual biases, which can be easily observed in psychotherapy, are also true of group processes. "Groupism," says Beck, "is the collective counterpart of egoism."[11] Individual interests are transferred to group interests. Group members reinforce each other's "us-and-them" thinking and add gasoline to the fires of individual prejudice. A collective bias may be especially difficult to see because it is reinforced by other group members. A hunger for belonging, attachment, and bonding may push an individual into the perils of "groupthink" where dualistic thinking is reinforced. This stereotyping "erases the unique characteristics of outgroup members."[12] Also, a paranoia about the hostile intensions of others is often encouraged: "The development of a paranoid perspective would seem to be almost inevitable in a group that has a collective self-image of vulnerability. . . . The paranoid perspective leads to interpretations and expectations of malicious behavior that go far beyond the objective evidence. This perspective imposes hidden malevolent meanings and motives on relatively innocuous events."[13]

Prehistoric life probably necessitated all-or-nothing survival thinking that divided the world between "us" and "them." A quick assessment of whether someone was a friend or foe may have made a difference between life and death. An instant reaction was crucial for survival. Snap judgments were essential for maintaining life. Dualistic thinking was adaptive. In the face of threat, "sizing up" a situation prepares us for immediate "fight or flight." In such situations, thought processes are very simple and involve rapid, absolute categories of good and bad. Certainly in circumstances that threaten us, this so-called primitive way of thinking still occurs. We are on "red alert." As Beck says, ambiguous stimuli must be processed rapidly. Dichotomous judgments are inevitable.

So this is primitive thinking. It evaluates the world egocentrically. It is typical of both early-childhood development as well as earlier stages of human evolutionary development. Life is perceived as too dangerous to think "creatively." If we believe our vital interests are at stake, whether individually or collectively, primal thinking is an automatic response.

> The efficient features of primal thinking are also its disadvantages. The selective reduction of data into a few crude categories wastes much available information. Certain features of the situation are highlighted or exaggerated, and others are minimized or excluded from processing. Personally relevant details are taken out of context, the meanings tending to be excessively egocentric and the conclusions too broad. Consequently, the thinking is unbalanced: it may be satisfactory for true life-or-death emergencies, but it is disruptive to the smooth functioning of everyday life and to the solution of normal interpersonal problems.[14]

Unfortunately, when we feel emotionally challenged or psychologically threatened, we tend to fall back into this old dualistic pattern. Even though there is no *physical* threat, we feel a *psychological* one. Anxiety therefore prompts defensive, uncreative survival thinking. We are not capable of thinking about alternatives or options to the conflict. Excessive anxiety has produced a hostile reaction. But for Beck, this excessive anxiety has itself emerged from exaggerated, distorted thinking. The anxiety does not *cause* us to think crookedly. Instead, an exaggerated, crooked thinking creates our anxiety. Beck denies the existential emphasis on objectless anxiety, or the Freudian understanding of "free-floating anxiety." If we look carefully enough, we will find that anxiety is always based on a subtle and distorted interpretation of life.

So Beck's theory can be fairly easily stated: anxiety and threat push us toward biased, egocentric, primitive thinking, which at one time was necessary for our evolutionary survival, but which now serves as more of a detriment than a help. Just as Freud believed that the defense mechanisms were essential for our childhood but later become an obstacle for our self-discovery, so our dualistic, primitive thinking in the early periods of our collective history may have been necessary to survive, but are now more problematic than useful.

Beck is very aware that both self-protection and self-promotion are important for our survival. However, egocentricity creates difficulty when it is cut off from important social traits such as love, empathy, and even altruism. In the face of threat, the human species can easily forget these social traits and instead narrow the focus to self-protection.[15]

Beck believes that his theory of hate is transcultural. He claims that a series of cognitive distortions is universally present in all hate:

> No matter what the external causes of antagonistic behavior, the same internal or psychological mechanisms are generally involved in its arousal and expression. And as with destructive interpersonal action, cognitive distortions incite anger and prompt the hostile behavior. Thus, unwarranted personal attacks that arise from prejudice, bigotry, ethnocentrism, or military invasion involve the primal thinking apparatus; absolute categorical cognition, on the one hand, and obliviousness to the human identity of the victim, on the other.[16]

An understanding of these common cognitive habits provides the possibility of a psychotherapeutic treatment of hatred. Thus one can develop a universal formula for hate reduction regardless of the particular social, historical, gender, and racial location of the patient. While Beck recognizes the difference between what he calls "cold, calculated violence" and "hot reactive violence," he believes that an underlying cognitive distortion occurs in each. Granted, the cold violence may not involve the kind of anxious reaction and obvious display of exaggerated thinking typical of reactionary violence. The primary issue in cold violence may seem to be a lack of morality rather than a lack of clear thinking. Beck believes that hot, reactive violence is much more common.

> As part of our survival heritage, we are very much aware of events that could have a detrimental effect on our own well-being and personal interests. We are sensitive to actions that suggest a put-down, imposition, or interference. . . . The tendency to over-interpret situations in terms of our own frame of reference is an expression of the "egocentric perspective." When we are under stress or feel threatened, our self-centered thinking becomes accentuated, and at the same time the area of our concern expands to irrelevant or remotely relevant events. Out of the tapestry of the multiple patterns contributing to another person's behavior, we select a single strand that may affect us personally.[17]

Hate, for Beck, is largely a breakdown of information processing brought on by a bias. These biases can begin at a very early, unconscious stage. Our hatred is thus always related to a cognitive distortion.

REACTIVE OFFENDERS AND PSYCHOPATHS

While there are differences between individual offenders and their types of violent behavior, Beck believes certain common psychological factors can be identified in all forms of antisocial behavior. "The common psychological problem lies in the offender's perception—or misperception—of himself and other people."[18] There are, in fact, a particular cluster of antisocial concepts and beliefs. These beliefs, argues Beck, shape the interpretation of other people's words and actions. The offender sees himself or herself primarily as a victim. This thinking may be dominated by the following rigid beliefs: "authorities are controlling, disparaging, and punitive; spouses are manipulative, deceitful, and rejecting; outsiders are treacherous, self-serving and hostile; nobody can be trusted."[19] Because of these beliefs and a fragile self-esteem, the offender frequently interprets others' behavior as hostile and antagonistic. Any outside control must mean that the offender is vulnerable. In order to cope with this threat from outsiders, the offender creates another cluster of beliefs: "To maintain my freedom/pride/security, I need to fight back; physical force is the only way to get people to respond to you; if you don't get even, people will run you over."[20]

Beck parallels this attitude with that of a boxer. As a boxer steps into the ring, he focuses all his attention on the movements of his opponent. Every move is a threat he must counter. He must not let down his guard or he could get punched, and perhaps even knocked out. The goal is to get his opponent before his opponent gets him. For the offender, life is an ongoing battle. Others are continually perceived as belligerent so he must be belligerent first. This process is especially compounded when an event triggers the offender's most vulnerable self-perception. Then, almost any amount of hostility is warranted. In cases of spousal abuse, for instance, the abusive male often views himself as vulnerable to his partner's words or actions. The twisted thinking pushes him to fight against being a victim, which leads to the unfortunate consequence of physically abusing his wife. The threat of insecurity or being hurt is quickly masked by violent attack.

These reactive offenders must be separated from what Beck calls primary psychopaths, who are actually quite rare. While there are some similarities between the two groups, there are huge differences. The reactive offenders feel vulnerable and fragile; the psychopath feels invulnerable and superior. The reactive offender sees others as hostile enemies; the psychopath condescendingly views others as inferior, weak, and stupid. The violence of the reactive offender is a defensive violence; the violence of the psychopath is simply malicious. The psychopath perverts empathy by using his or her understanding of others to manipulate them. The psychopath has a deficiency in his or her information processing. Whereas nonpsychopaths are able to process clues that would cause them to pause and reflect on their behavior, the psychopath lacks this cognitive ability. This conveys the appearance of fearlessness. While psychopaths are aware of the rules, they believe they are above them. The reactive offender is much easier to work with in therapy because his or her beliefs about the world and others can be modified over time. Psychopaths, on the other hand, present a far greater challenge.

MENTAL DISTORTION AND ENEMY MAKING

Influenced by the work of Sam Keen,[21] Beck believes that a group's collective, dualistic judgment can be expressed in the following: "Our cause is sacred; theirs is evil. We are righteous; they are wicked. We are innocent; they are guilty. We are the victims; they are the victimizers."[22] Following Keen, we can identify several cognitive distortions involved in enemy making. First, we lump all members of the opposition together so that they lose their identities as unique individuals. They are "all the same." Second, because they are all the same, they are interchangeable and hence disposable. Since they are "all alike," there is no unique loss in destroying one of them. Third, we strip the opposition of any human qualities for which we might have empathy or compassion. The opposition becomes an inanimate object rather than a person. Fourth, we "demonize" the opposition by viewing "it" as the very embodiment of evil. The enemy *must* be exterminated. Fifth, we connect every abstract notion of evil to the enemy so that we can continue to hate and destroy "it." Sixth, we focus constantly on how the enemy threatens to destroy us. And finally, we attack the evil image but kill real people.

Perhaps the backbone of Keen's theory of enemy making, however, is something Beck does not acknowledge. For Keen, the enemy is the projected shadow. It is our own unresolved intrapsychic junkyard that is projected onto the enemy. As a strict cognitive-behavioral therapist, Beck has little interest in the supposedly repressed, dark elements of the unconscious, much less the collective unconscious. He would prefer to connect evil with unfortunate cognitive processes and not with the malevolent impulses of the unconscious. We will later examine whether this strict cognitive view of hate and evil is adequate for a full account of the human condition, as well as further explore the role of the shadow in hatred.

THE OTHER SIDE OF HATE

Beck believes that we live in a world preoccupied with the dark side of human nature. He also believes it is important to correct this understanding with a focus on the lighter side of the human condition. Human beings, argues Beck, have the capacity for altruistic behavior that can balance out, and even override, their hostile inclination.[23] Further, we have great capacities for rational thinking, tendencies that can challenge and change our more distorted and primal thinking. Qualities such as empathy, cooperation, and rationality are just as intrinsic to human nature as qualities of anger and violence. By using our positive traits in an effective manner, we can build a stronger society. This will necessitate an ongoing willingness to challenge our mental construction of both others and ourselves with questions such as these: "Is it possible that I have misconstrued the apparently offensive behavior of another person (or groups)? Are my interpretations based on real evidence or on my preconceptions? Am I distorting my image of the other person or group because of my own vulnerabilities or fears?"[24]

These questions will challenge a purely egocentric mode of thinking. And again, Beck reminds us that cooperative social behavior is as much a part of our essential makeup as egocentric bias. A realistic portrait of the human condition must recognize both tendencies. "Thus, we manifest our basic ambivalence—self-indulgence, self-adulation, and selfishness in one situation, and self-sacrifice, humility, and generosity in another."[25] Prosocial tendencies are "wired into" us as much as antisocial tendencies. By scrutinizing our own cognitive distortions, we can move toward our positive potential.

So let's summarize Beck's cognitive approach to hate and evil. First, we perceive a threat to ourselves or the values we hold sacred. Second, we move into a primal mode of all-or-nothing thinking. Third, we automatically prepare for attack to protect ourselves or our sacred values. Fourth, our hostile mode of primal thinking crowds out other human qualities such as empathy or perspective-taking. Anxiety eliminates creative thinking. Fifth, unless interrupted, we move from the perception of a transgression to a preparation for an attack to an actual attack. By challenging these dominant thought patterns we can develop benevolence, empathy, compassion, and end hatred. Beck is optimistic about the salvific role of reason in ending human violence and hatred.

At the end of this chapter, I will examine whether Beck's optimism about humanity ending its own hatred and violence through reason is realistic. But for now, let's turn toward another perspective on the nature of hatred and evil, a perspective that emphasizes the role of the shadow.

HATE AND THE SHADOW

Jungian analyst and Episcopal priest John Sanford has devoted much of his impressive scholarship to the issues of evil, the shadow, hatred, and Jung's understanding of religion. I will examine two of his books, *Evil: The Shadow Side of Reality*[26] and *The Strange Trial of Mr. Hyde: A New Look at the Nature of Human Evil*.[27] Sanford describes his work as "more philosophical than pastoral,"[28] and a glance at his writing clearly indicates a formidable background in analytic psychology. While Sanford is quite aware that some persons view evil only from an egocentric viewpoint (how it affects them personally), he believes this leads to a radical relativism in which a substantive discussion of evil is impossible. He rejects the notion that what is good and evil is simply the view of the human observer: "For if this is so, then there is no fundamental moral basis to life and the universe, nor is there any moral order to curb mankind from its egocentric and destructively self-serving ambitions.[29] Sanford also believes that evil cannot be reduced to the negative effects of sociopolitical conditioning: "Modern man prefers to believe that the evils of our time somehow do not exist in the human soul or spiritual sphere, but have political or economic causes, and could be eliminated by a different political system, more education, the correct psychological conditioning or one more war to wipe out the enemy, for he does not want to see that the enemy is to found in the devils and the demons in himself."[30] Thus Sanford is interested in more than our changing personal conceptions of evil. As a Jungian, he wants to explore the archetypal foundation of evil. Evil, he believes, is more than what the human ego "decides" to label malevolent or destructive toward personal interest. Evil is a part of reality, an ontological fact.

In order to understand how Sanford and Jung offer insight into the relationship between evil and hate, it will be necessary to examine quickly some key Jungian concepts concerning human personhood. The first important distinction is between what Jung calls the "ego" and the "self." The *ego* refers to the center of conscious life, the "I" part of the personality that consciously chooses and wills certain things. The ego has continuity through memory. The *self*, on the other hand, is the center of the entire personality, both conscious and unconscious. The ego is concerned with its own advancement, so it evaluates good and evil according to how it is personally affected. In order for the ego to function in society, it must put forth a positive image, a mask or persona, which enables the ego to carry out its daily functioning. The word *persona* comes from the masks worn by actors in ancient Greece and Rome, masks that depicted the characters they were playing.

For Jung and Sanford, this persona is necessary but problematic. It is necessary in order to function in the public sphere, yet it always tempts us to equate our entire personality with it. We overidentify with our positive image and repress, deny, and disown that which does not match our ego ideal. All of the feelings, thoughts, desires, and fantasies that do not live up to the rigid standards of the ego ideal are shoved away from consciousness and placed in a closet of the unconscious. The more robustly we attempt to identify with the purity and goodness of our public image, the more material we have to store in this dark place in the unconscious. Thus a major psychological dilemma revolves around trying to be better than we are. This divides us and estranges the conscious ego from what Jung called "the shadow," which is that part of us deemed unacceptable by the ego. Jung described the shadow as "the negative side of the personality, the sum of all those unpleasant qualities we like to hide, together with the insufficiently developed functions and the content of the personal unconscious."[31] The shadow represents the junkyard of the psyche, the place where rejected aspects are repressed into the darkness. The shadow is the antithesis of the conscious ego. Yet when the ego steps forward, the rejected parts of its portrait are not far behind. Hatred is, of course, one of the first things to be split off from the self and placed within a shadowy subterfuge. Few of us want to readily admit that we feel hatred. This admission is uncomfortable for the moral presentation of self we want to make. Also, the admission of hatred is somewhat humbling—namely, we are saying that something external is "controlling" our feelings.

One of the clearest indications of the presence of our shadow is the extent to which we disproportionately react to something. This excessive reaction may be a telltale that something external to us is actually provoking an internal battle. But admitting the inner demon with which we are doing battle is too frightening so we must fight an outer enemy. This external target serves the classic scapegoat function. It keeps our awareness away from ourselves by focusing on the external reality. We "need" others to avoid ourselves. This is why self-avoidance and enemy-formation are two sides of the same coin. Jung believed that both intense fascination and intense repulsion were indications of the shadow's presence. This may involve literary figures, persons in film, and any number of sources. Normally, the shadow is of the same sex as the ego that denies it. Again, shadow casting is a survival maneuver for the daytime ego. The nocturnal impulses do not have to be faced within oneself as long as one can find a culprit "out there."

When we cast our shadow onto others, we normally see nothing other than the shadow. The person on whom our shadow is cast ceases to be a person and is instead a simple vessel of our shadow. We create them in our own *denied* image. Again, they serve a valuable function in perpetuating self-denial. Their humanity is lost as they are reduced to our own feared image. Perspective taking or empathy is impossible because that would sabotage the very purpose of shadow casting. We need "the other" to be our caricature of them, our created image. In order for us to expel our demons, the other has to become that demon. Our sense of salvation therefore necessitates the demonizing of others.

JESUS, PAUL, AND THE SHADOW

Sanford believes that the Christian tradition offers both an opportunity to integrate the shadow and to repress it. He further believes there are two views of evil expressed in the New Testament. One view, represented by the Gospels and later by Origen, emphasizes wholeness, nonduality, and an integration of the "light" elements of the ego with the "dark" elements of the shadow. The teachings of Jesus emphasize shadow integration. The other view, which can be seen in Paul and epitomized in the book of Revelation, promotes both an intrapsychic and cosmic dualism that never finds integration, wholeness, or redemptive healing. This view is as influenced by the cosmic dualism of Zoroastrianism as it is the teachings of Jesus. Instead of integrating the shadow into wholeness, it encourages the repression of the shadow. This preoccupation with the ego-ideal leads to self-righteousness and an ignorance concerning the darker side of one's "pure" motives. Without a regular recognition of the shadow, we lose humility and become quite judgmental. For Sanford, this is precisely the attitude Jesus frequently exposed: "Jesus was quite tolerant of most human frailties, but he was indignant at this identification with the persona, and concealing the shadow, because it was psychologically dishonest, and led to self-righteousness, lack of compassion, and spiritual rigidity."[32]

For Sanford, there is a huge difference between Jesus and Paul. Jesus was aware of what we are calling the persona and shadow. Paul, however, was not. While Paul himself exhibited a great deal of psychological insight into his own condition, he did not encourage others to wrestle with their own inner struggles between the shadow and he persona. Instead, argues Sanford, he encouraged the repression of the shadow and the complete identification with the goodness, light, and love in the persona. Sanford is blunt about the differences between Jesus and Paul: "So while Jesus called for a growth in psychological consciousness, and for the spiritual courage to struggle with the problem of our dual nature, Paul called for just the opposite, that is, for repression."[33] Sanford points toward Paul's well-known description of himself in Romans 7:15-26.

> I do not understand my own actions. For I do not do what I want,
> but I do the very thing I hate. Now if I do what I do not want, I agree
> that the law is good. But in fact it is no longer I that do it, but sin that
> dwells within me. For I know that nothing good dwells within me,
> that is, in my flesh. I can will what is right, but I cannot do it. For I
> do not do the good I want, but the evil I do not want is what I do.
> Now if I do what I do not want, it is no longer I that do it, but sin

that dwells within me. So I find it to be a law that when I want to do what is good, evil lies close at hand. For I delight in the law of God in my inmost self, but I see in my members another law at war with the law of my mind, making me captive to the law of sin that dwells in my members. Wretched man that I am! Who will rescue me from this body of death? Thanks be to God through Jesus Christ our Lord! So then, with my mind I am a slave to the law of God, but with my flesh I am a slave to the law of sin. (NRSV)

For Sanford, Paul is describing the duality of his nature. He is identifying the differences between the ego ideal and his shadow. But Sanford believes that Paul refuses to accept this contradiction within himself. He declares that it is not "himself" who acts this way but instead the "sin which lives within him." Sanford believes this reveals a refusal to acknowledge and accept his shadow. This further rejects and pushes the shadow away. The problem is that without acceptance, the shadow will simply get stronger. This doesn't resolve the problem; instead it merely represses it.

Sanford further points out that in other passages Paul seems to show little awareness of his dual inclinations. For instance, in Galatians 5:12, he warns about Judaizing Christians who claim to follow him, yet insist upon traditional Jewish practices such as circumcision. Paul is angry at these individuals who seem to undermine his work. He says: "I wish those who unsettle you would castrate themselves!" (NRSV). In other words, Paul is having a fantasy that circumcision would "accidentally" turn into castration, thus teaching the Judaizing Christians a lesson. For Sanford, this rather "nasty" fantasy is quite forgiveable. But Paul's admonition to other people is less so: "What is not so forgivable is Paul's failure to see the contrast between this vindictive fantasy on the one hand and his frequent admonitions to others in the Christian community that they should never be angry but show forth and practice only love, patience, and forgiveness. Paul acts toward his Christian converts like a parent often does toward his children: anger is reserved as the prerogative of the parent, while the children are expected to be models of perfect behavior."[34] Sanford believes that Paul encourages his congregations to live only out of their "light" side, thus repressing those things about themselves that are deemed bad. Love, patience, reasonableness, gentleness, and humility are praised while hatred, anger, sexual desires, fantasies, and strong emotions are denied.[35] For Sanford, Paul is completely appropriate in telling his congregations to not act out all of their impulses. But Paul's solution is repression, and that is not appropriate for psychological health. Further, Paul is "almost always antagonistic to emotion."[36] Anger and sexual desire, for instance, are typically viewed as evil. And to have bad emotions and fantasies, even when we refuse to act them out, is to be evil: "The fantasies and emotions that we fear in ourselves belong to the dark, shadowy background of the unconscious. If we cannot face and accept them, we become divided people. In saying that it is not the deed, but the thought itself that is sinful, Paul's ethic puts mankind in an intolerable position."[37] Sanford then indicates that he does not want to be "too hard" on Paul, because clearly this was the attitude of the early church in general. "The problem is not that Paul is such a bad person, but that he was an historically conditioned personality who, however inspired he might have been in certain respects, did not go beyond the prevailing collective opinions with regard to the psychological problem of the persona and the Shadow."[38]

Unfortunately, argues Sanford, the church followed the example of Paul rather than of Jesus. A great deal of the "psychological damage" in the Christian tradition could have been avoided if we had followed the words of Jesus:

> So the essential difference between the teachings of Paul and those of Jesus can be said to be this: Paul urges us into a one-sided expression of "goodness"; Jesus urges us to become complete or whole. Paul's psychological ethic can only be accomplished by repression, that is, by a systematic unconsciousness of the Shadow. Jesus' ethic can only be fulfilled by becoming conscious of the developmental process that can proceed only when consciousness of the Shadow has been reached. Paul's attitude, as we have seen, is expressive of the general attitude of his times. Throughout the centuries the Church has not departed significantly from it. In this regard, the Church has not lived up to the higher consciousness of Jesus but has remained on a lower psychological level. The result has been a perpetuation of man's split

and the aggravation, rather than resolution, of the problem of he Shadow.[39]

This Pauline dualism ends with the book of Revelation, whose author proclaims a cosmic split, an ultimate dualism. The eternal conflict between God and Satan reflects the unresolved split in the human psyche. This division is between the ego ideal and the shadow. In the book of Revelation, says Sanford, we do not witness God's nature; instead, we see the unresolved human condition. By refusing the shadow, we inevitably *set ourselves up to hate*. Hate is mandatory because we refuse to embrace ourselves.

This charge against Paul is no small one. Again, Sanford unequivocally states that a great deal of psychological damage has been done by writings that the Christian church has deemed canonical and inspired. Obviously a host of New Testament scholars would dispute Sanford's claim concerning this large discontinuity between the teachings of Paul and Jesus. Further, many would perhaps argue that Sanford strains a little too hard to turn Jesus into a first-century Jungian. But that debate is beyond the parameters of this book. What is crucial for us is to understand the dynamics of the shadow and shadow projection in the process of hate. To accomplish this further, we need to turn to a classic tale of the shadow in Western culture, a tale to which Sanford devotes much attention, Robert Louis Stevenson's story of Dr. Jekyll and Mr. Hyde.

THE JEKYLL AND HYDE STORY

One of the most colorful and brilliant descriptions of an internal split between the ego and the shadow is Robert Louis Stevenson's classic, *Dr. Jekyll and Mr. Hyde*.[40] When Stevenson wrote his Gothic tale in 1886, he had little idea that his dichotomized creature would have such influence. Written before the impact of Freud's ideas about personality, Stevenson poetically describes the housing of contradictory selves within the same flesh, two forces warring for the governing control of the psyche. Sanford has spent considerable time interpreting this classic because he believes it expresses an archetypal pattern, a universal struggle between the conscious ego and its nearby shadow.

A quick recap: Henry Jekyll is a highly respected physician with a strong desire to separate his noble aspirations from his darker side. To accomplish this division and be once-and-for-all rid of his uncivilized inclinations, Jekyll creates a potion. He drinks the concoction with great eagerness, thinking he has found the solution to his inner tensions. Much to his shock, Mr. Hyde, a sensual, selfish, aggressive madman emerges on the other side of the potion. While Hyde created enormous problems for Jekyll, and was quite repulsive, the good doctor was perpetually fascinated with him.

Mr. Hyde is the example of the shadow *par excellence*. He is the exiled, ridiculed, alienated part of Henry Jekyll. Mr. Hyde does not fit into the self-portrait Jekyll felt compelled to exhibit, so Hyde is pushed underground. Recognition and acceptance might have redeemed the shadowy creature, but Jekyll refused to embrace Hyde. By rejecting Hyde, Jekyll actually helped the grotesque creature grow stronger. The cure for the Hyde problem would have been ownership and acceptance of the total self. But Jekyll, representing the narrow confines of the ego, would not allow Hyde to emerge in the daylight of consciousness. Consequently, Hyde roamed through the darkness of the unconscious, building strength for the day when he would take Jekyll over.

Jekyll reflects all the restrictions of Victorian conscience. In reality, however, he was tired of chasing his perfectionism. He was quite vulnerable to the excitement and energy of Edward Hyde. Jekyll's own mundane rules set him up for an enchantment with Mr. Hyde. The humdrum world of his excessively ordered life naturally gave rise to the wandering thoughts and outrageous pleasures of Hyde. Jekyll was censoring himself right into exhibitionism.

Hyde, disowned by Jekyll's sober control, was ambitious, wildly impulsive, reckless, and self-seeking. Hyde was unburdened by obligations or restraint. He burned pictures of Jekyll's father and scribbled blasphemies in Jekyll's books. All of Hyde's energies were directed toward self-seeking and he had no interest in reflecting on, or assessing, his inner life. He hated the phony display of Jekyll's hypocritical world. Restrictions, pretense, and inhibition were his primary enemies.

In Stevenson's tale, Henry Jekyll dies from a lack of self-acceptance.

Jekyll kills himself. Even at the very end of his life, Jekyll will not own Mr. Hyde as part of his psyche. Hyde was perceived as a hideous creature quite separate from the good doctor. Yet Jekyll's dual existence could go no further. The division was too painful. The split could no longer be fueled by denial.

This tale clearly suggests that when we refuse to acknowledge the conflicting voices within, we cut off part of ourselves we deem unacceptable. The cut-off, dismembered, hated part of ourselves *hates back*. Unrecognized, it roams with growing hunger to control our lives. The more quarantined we make this region of ourselves, the more diabolical and less human it becomes. Exposure, recognition, and acceptance would offer the possibility of integration and balance. The stranger within longs for attention, and if he or she cannot get this attention directly, the stranger will act out in disturbed ways. Cut-off feelings can develop a vicious tenacity.

There is a very important principle here that directly relates to the discussion of hatred. *Hatred of others may very well begin with a hatred of ourselves*. The ego first hates part of its experience, rejects it, and pushes it underground. The hated dimension of the psyche grows. Soon, it does what might well be expected: *it hates back*. It hates all the pretense, all the rejection, all the condescending posturing that is typical of the ego ideal. The shadow becomes more and more rebellious and self-sabotaging. Sheldon Kopp states this as follows.

> Every acknowledged attitude has as its counterpart an equally
> substantial polar opposite. The more extreme the attitude, the
> more exaggerated, undifferentiated, and out of touch is its hidden
> equivalent. Unless we become acceptingly aware of those unconscious
> *shadow* sides of who we are, we are certain to find ourselves at the
> mercy of their primitive demands. . . . Remaining unconscious of these
> disowned parts of ourselves is both costly and dangerous. No matter
> how much we limit our experience in the service of protecting their
> inner constraints, we can never fully eliminate the risk of episodic
> outbreak of the forbidden impulses.[41]

Jekyll attempted to deal with his spiritual malady through a chemical solution. The potion was to be the salvific agent, the all-important ingredient in what seemed like a hopeless battle. The fear of self-acceptance was so great that Jekyll instead waged an intrapsychic civil war. The courage required to embrace his shadow was too much. Instead, Jekyll needed an easier way. His chemical's significance, then, moved from the physical to the metaphysical realm. It offered a redemptive promise. Jekyll was drunk on the idea of eliminating his shadow. He had no idea of his shadow's hidden strength.

It must again be emphasized, however, that simply "giving into" the full inclinations of the shadow is also destructive. Giving oneself over completely to one's shadow is a form of possession: "This is why living out the darkest impulses of the Shadow cannot be a solution to the shadow problem, for we can easily become possessed by or absorbed into evil if we try such a thing. This attests to the archetypal nature of evil, for it is one of the qualities of the archetypes that they possess the ego, which is like being devoured by or made identical with the archetype."[42] Complete identification with the shadow is as dangerous as excessive repression of it. Both are imbalanced and destructive. As Jung put it, "For it is just as sinful from the standpoint of nature and truth to be above oneself as to be below oneself."[43]

Thus Sanford and Jung offer an interesting and provocative theory of how and why we hate others. First, we refuse to acknowledge, accept, and own our shadow. Second, the behavior or attitudes in another reminds us of our shadow. Third, since we are unwilling to acknowledge that our anxiety arises from within ourselves, we continue to deny our shadow by projecting it onto others. "They," not us, are the ones who need to be judged. Fourth, having dodged the source of our anxiety, we "need" the outsider to help keep the heat off of ourselves. They are necessary in order for us to avoid ourselves. All of our deepest inner fears are cast onto another. We don't see them as they are; instead, we see them clothed in our shadow. We are therefore free to attack external reality without a fear that the real enemy is within us.

Karen Horney also describes this process as the externalization of our own self-hate.[44] We need others to keep from hating ourselves. Conversely, greater acceptance of the shadow would mean less necessity to hate an enemy.

VARIETIES AND TRANSFORMATIONS OF HATE

David Augsburger's comprehensive book, *Hate-Work: Working Through the Pain and Pleasures of Hate*, begins with the important recognition that in our discussions of hate, we have frequently not understood the *varieties* or *types* of hate.[45] By reducing hate to a singular experience we have missed the various colors and shapes of it, and have therefore limited our abilities to resolve hate issues. While hate may *appear* to emerge from a single motive, a closer look will reveal that hatred is far more complex and nuanced than any single-minded approach can describe:

> Hate is not a single, simple emotion or motivation—no matter
> how single-minded or simpleminded it often appears to us. Hatred
> is composed of a wide spectrum of reactions, from emotion, to
> sentiment, to behavior, to prejudice, to commitment to values.
> It may be intense, focused, and direct; or it may be impersonal,
> detached, instrumental, and indirect. Hate is a complex series of
> negative feelings-attitudes-sets of behaviors. Yet a single word is largely
> employed to cover the whole set.[46]

Our "hate language" does not adequately convey the varieties of the emotion. Just as we have the one word, "snow," to describe falling white flakes in winter while Eskimos have a multitude of words to differentiate various types of snow, so we need a broader vocabulary for grasping the multiplicity of hates within human experience.[47] Augsburger thus describes hate as a "family" of emotions, rather than a singular feeling.

In Augsburger's spectrum of hates, he offers a type of developmental scheme that charts the nature of hate and indicates a person's growing ability to deal with ambiguity, mixed feelings, and less clear-cut answers. The movement throughout this spectrum is largely a cognitive shift from strict dualistic, either/or thinking to a tolerance for ambiguity to an empathic ability to see the humanness in those we hate. At one end of the spectrum, the hated act and the hated person are completely married. Here, we have no ability to differentiate the actor from the act. With maturity and greater developmental achievement, we eventually begin to experience moments of empathy in which the hated object does not seem utterly alien to ourselves. This breakthrough of compassion, however, is more than a self-willed achievement. Instead, it is a transforming gift of grace. If we hope to move to the point of compassion for the enemy, of caring for the person while hating the dehumanizing act that has been done, we must be open to transcendent help. Here Augsburger clearly moves beyond Beck. Loving our enemies is hardly a Pelagian, self-willed achievement; instead, it is a consequence of being receptive to the gift of compassion.

While there is value in the old adage that we should "hate the sin and love the sinner," it is notoriously difficult. This is especially true because a person's particular, destructive act easily snowballs into a damaging pattern of behavior that seems cemented to the structure of the personality, which in turn, appears to express the full range of personhood. When patterns of behavior find such deep rootage in the personality, it is nearly impossible to separate act from person. This is particularly true if the primary orientation or mission of a person's life has served destruction and chaos. We need only consider the difficulty for post 9/11 Americans to separate the person of Osama Bin Laden from that dreadful day in 2001.

Augsburger makes a strong case that hate is both inevitable and essential. This may at first sound strange, particularly coming from a pastoral counselor firmly rooted in a pacificist stance. Yet the issue is not getting rid of our hate; instead, it is hating the right things. In other words, what *deserves* our hate? The answer, as we shall see, is that mature hate is directed at injustice itself. Or to put it differently, healthy hate is a hatred against evil, that is, those things that destroy the sanctity of life. We are therefore "called" to hate as well as to love. In fact, we cannot love without also experiencing hate. A concern for social justice presupposes a hatred of injustice; a love of fairness assumes a disdain for unfairness; and a deep commitment to hearing another involves a hatred of the estranged loneliness that plagues so many people's lives.

Yet moving through the pain and pleasure of hate is a tedious, spiritual journey. Some hate begins in highly dualistic, black-or-white categories. Again, at this stage, there is little tolerance for ambiguity. Reality is clear-cut and one-way. From this less developed end of the spectrum, our hatred is targeted at specific persons or groups. The focus is not upon unjust actions; instead, we hate the people themselves. Life is fairly easily divided between "us" and "them." Evil can be both named and separated from our own personhood or group. *They* are one hundred percent evil; *we* are good. There is very little self-examination in this framework. Also, dualistic haters do not acknowledge the personhood of the hated object. The other person is instead a "thing." Again, there is a complete identification of the person with the vile act.

Augsburger identifies three types of hate as operative within this dualistic framework. The first is *simple* hatred in which we merely feel a strong dislike for something. This could range all the way from mosquitoes to rude drivers. The second type of hatred is *spiteful* hatred. This refers to a deep resentment toward someone who has hurt us. Here we may replay over and over in our mind's theatre an injustice done to us. The third form of hatred within the black-or-white category is *malicious* hatred, which involves a lust for revenge. This moves beyond mere resentment and longs for revenge for the hurt. According to Augsburger, all three of these forms of hatred, forms that everyone inevitably experiences, are built upon an inability to distinguish the perpetrator from the injury. The rude driver is nothing but a jerk; the sexual offender is nothing but a pervert; and the person to the left of me politically is nothing but a damn liberal. While all of these hatreds can be understandable, the common denominator is the tendency to force life's complexities into neat packages or clear categories. And it is important to note that these tendencies can come from the right or the left. "Liberals" are no more immune from dichotomous thinking than are "conservatives." It is, in fact, the people who smugly believe they have transcended these categories who may be the most dangerous. Augsburger quotes G. K. Chesterton: "There are two kind of people in the world: the conscious dogmatists and the unconscious dogmatists. I have always found myself that the unconscious dogmatists were by far the most dogmatic."[48] Dualistic thinking can insidiously creep into mentalities that think they have transcended the black-or-white thinking of more "primitive" groups.

Augsburger recognizes that stereotypes are universal and unavoidable. Yet the most dangerous minds are those which deny that they have *any* stereotypes whatsoever. A healthy attitude recognizes that mental schema inevitably get formed as a necessary part of cognitive development. However, these generalizations need to be open to revision. By contrast, negative stereotypes view every individual through the derogatory lens aimed at the entire group. There are no exceptions because my prearranged generalization about "you people" says so! Negative stereotypes are unwilling to be modified by new data or contradictory evidence. The security of the stereotype is tenaciously guarded even if it means clobbering people with generalizations. It's safer that way. The map of the world will not allow variation if security is to be kept intact. These categories of thought in rigid stereotypes are emotionally charged rather than intellectually guided. In short, they are held because they make life more convenient by turning complexity into easy-to-identify categories.

The next two forms of hate are retributive hate or retaliation, and "principled" hate, which seeks a rationale or justification for its hated object. Retaliation is somewhat different than revenge because it seeks a kind of justice in which the other person gets what he or she "deserves." The retribution should be proportional to the wrongdoing, something that pure revenge often surpasses. Retributive hate is closely linked with principled hate, which seeks reasonable justification for another's punishment: "It arises in the construction, by the individual or group, of a legitimate case for loathing, a prejudicial platform for despising the other that becomes a chronic disposition or a communal mindset toward the outgroup, or a national policy of opposing some political entity or enemy."[49] In principled hate, a more sophisticated set of beliefs and justifications are attached to the act of hating.

The final forms of hatred, "moral" and "just" hate, begin to disconnect offender from offense, not in the sense of exoneration or excuse making, but in the sense of seeing the person as more than the destructive behavior. Moral hatred focuses primarily on the immoral act committed by the person but still is not always ready to separate person from deed. It frequently involves an outrage. Further, moral hatred believes that *not* to be outraged at the person who committed the act is to be morally indifferent or uncommitted to a high standard of justice.

> Moral hatred may at first seem essentially impersonal since it focuses primarily on the lack of morality in the other's actions. But the person's evil behavior, public acts, and private choices get enmeshed in

beliefs, personhood, and character like cancer cells invading healthy tissue. Hating the malignant but respecting the benign is difficult; distinguishing growth from the grower is a delicate demarcation. Tumor and tumorous organ sometimes eventually become one and the same. . . . The preeminent danger of moral hatred is that it may blind us to the humane and decent elements within another. The temptation to ascend a righteous throne and pronounce absolute sentence lurks in all moral judgment. Our entitlement to the high ground seems self-evident when passion fires the mind. Truly moral thought can never dismiss the question "Is the person no more than the worst act committed, or is every individual more than the most noxious act?"[50]

"Just" hatred, the last hate on Augsburger's continuum, affirms moral hatred and seeks to defend the rights of the victim, but also wants a justice that respects the personhood of *everyone* involved, including the perpetrator. Just hatred is grounded in a passion for universal fairness. The target of just hate is injustice itself, such as discrimination, abuse, inequality, and violence. One can almost say that in just hatred we *hate* hate. Just hatred, again, is synonymous with love. Just hatred acknowledges the limitations of human finitude in its assessments. It understands the complexity of evil. It feels a deep sadness, along with anger, concerning injustice. It hates what distorts and handicaps personhood.

In just hatred, one has discovered that no person can be so decayed that the person loses the last trace of some decency, loyalty, or integrity, or so "rotted" as to have no remaining trace of goodness or residue of worth. The hated injustice is, although often painfully difficult to do, differentiated from the perpetrator(s) of the evil. Just hatred seeks an end to the evil and works diligently at inviting and facilitating appropriate repentance and restitution, so that justice may be seen to be done. Just hate recognizes that we must face not only the other group's evil but our own as well. It realizes that there is no reconciliation between groups until people talk about their own ethnic group's crimes as honestly as they point out those of others.[51]

As Ausgburger suggests, the problem is that we all too easily see our own actions through the lens of our intentions. We *meant* well, so therefore our actions are not so bad. Yet we rarely extend to others this same courtesy. We do not see their actions through the doorway of their intentions; instead, we see them as arbitrary, or worse still, deliberately malicious.[52] Our own actions are based on the higher ground of good intentions. No such good intentions are attributed to the "evil" actions of others. "They hurt us and they meant to—period!"

It is, of course, possible to experience several "levels" of hate simultaneously. One does not always exclude another. But Augsburger's suggestion is twofold: (*a*) hate is inevitable, and therefore (*b*) the point is not to get rid of it but to hate the right things.

REASONS FOR HATE

Once we admit that we hate, perhaps the next question is *why* we hate. What reasons account for our hatred. Augsburger briefly surveys some suggestions while acknowledging that we will probably never arrive at an all-convincing explanation for this human inclination. One explanation is that we are simply biologically "wired" to hate. Hating is an essential part of our humanness. Hostility is a built-in, necessary aspect of our evolutionary survival. Prejudice is an inevitable outgrowth of self-interest. We are "natural-born bigots." Perhaps these tendencies are genetically passed on to future generations as a way of guaranteeing survival.

Another explanation is that we are simply socialized to hate. After all, every social and historical location carries a highly conditioned picture of reality and, like it or not, we are prisoners of our time and place. While we may come to recognize and rise above some of our prejudice, we may also operate, at least in part, out of ignorance concerning our socially determined attitudes.

Perhaps we simply have a deep need to classify and categorize life for the purposes of our own survival. We could not make it without these conceptual schemes. Augsburger describes what he calls a social-interactional view:

Our world is confusingly diverse, and one must learn labels and construct stereotypes in order to pattern and manage our interactions and relationships. Our need to simplify the complexity of human community leads us to construct prejudices as manageable patterns of perception, definition, and interaction. Although these offer the desired efficiency, they have an inevitable and unfortunate dark side. They create bigotry and multiply negative prejudices, which alienate us from each other.[53]

Or, perhaps our hatred is rooted in a moral or religious flaw. As we have felt the anxiety of threat, we turn toward a radical self-interest and react with hostility toward any threat to our security. In short, perhaps we hate because of original sin.

Again, Augsburger doesn't think we're likely to find agreement on the *reasons* we hate. However, he doesn't think this is essential, anyway. The point is *that* we hate, regardless of hate's origins. Just as theologians can speculate endlessly on the source and origin of sin, so social scientists can theorize eternally about the causes of hate. Our time would be better served by describing *how* we hate and what we can do about it.

THE FIRST EXPERIENCE OF HATE

While Augsburger does not claim to find the universal *cause* of hate, he believes neo-Freudian thinkers such as Melanie Klein, Margaret Mahler, Michael Balint, and Donald Winnicott have accurately described our *first experience* with hate. In order to understand this experience, we must go back to infancy. As developmental psychologists frequently point out, the infant's first experience is a hopeful one—hope for the warmth, regularity, and consistent care from the primary caretaker. The central "hoped-for" experience is that of being fed. While warmth, touch, and sound are also important, the primary inclination within the infant, according to Melanie Klein, is to associate the mother with the breast.[54] In fact, according to Klein's carefully observed mother-infant interactions, the mother *is* the breast for the infant. The infant's first relationship, then, is to a body part, not a whole person. Anything that blocks the relationship between baby and breast the baby perceives as severely alarming. Yet regardless of how consistent, patient, and loving the parent tries to be, the infant's expectations (demands?) will not be satisfied. The inability to locate the breast will be met with an energetic search followed by distress, screaming, and anger. Even when the mother reappears, clinical observation has shown that the baby may reject the mother or attack her out of anger.

For Klein and other neo-Freudians, this experience leads to the first dualism encountered in the baby's world—the "good" and "bad" mother. The good mother is the one who feeds and comforts the baby, while the bad mother is a "no-show" who abandons the baby in its need. The baby has no clue whatsoever as to how to reconcile these strong feelings associated with each of these mothers. So the baby, out of survival necessity, must split off its experience of good and bad. The baby must separate and compartmentalize these positive and negative feelings toward the mother. The bad mother, who is hated, must be severed from the good mother, who provides the ingredients necessary for the child's physical and emotional survival. Thus hate feelings are disconnected from needy, loving feelings.

During this experience, however, the baby separates more than two "external" mothers. The baby has not developed a separate sense of self, and so the baby and mother are merged together in a single unity. Therefore, when the baby divides the mother, it also divides itself. Hating the "bad" breast that doesn't report for duty threatens the experience of the "good" breast who is there to serve. As these two breast objects are separated, so is the baby's inner experience also separated. Hating the breast means hating part of one's own experience. The primary object is thus internalized and split between good and bad. In order to maintain psychic equilibrium, the baby must expel the "bad" elements, along with the frustration and rage that accompany it. Necessarily preoccupied with its own needs, the infant divides the world into two categories of experience: those that are pleasurable or provide gratification, and those that are painful and frustrating. With the baby driven by what Christopher Monte calls a "rudimentary hedonism," the mother, or more particularly the mother's breast, becomes the first object of both love and hate.[55] Melanie Klein describes this well:

The baby's first object of love and hate—his mother—is both desired and hated with all the intensity and strength that is characteristic of the early urges of he baby. In the very beginning he loves his mother at the time that she is satisfying his needs for nourishment, alleviating his feelings of hunger, and giving him the sensual pleasure which he experiences when his mouth is stimulated by sucking at her breast. This gratification is an essential part of the child's sexuality, and is indeed its initial expression. But when the baby is hungry and his desires are not gratified, or when he is feeling bodily pain or discomfort, then the whole situation suddenly alters. Hatred and aggressive feelings are aroused and he becomes dominated by the impulses to destroy the very person who is the object of all his desires and who in his mind is linked up with everything he experiences—good and bad alike.[56]

The "split-off" parts are expelled. The baby becomes an exorcist of his or her own experience. After the baby has cast out these threatening feelings, they will later be projected onto others. Augsburger provides a useful summary of this experience: "So hate is born. The sequence is most likely like this: The mother/breast inevitably frustrates the baby. If there are good reparative experiences to intervene, the frustration is expressed as anger and comforted. If the mother is cold or punitive to the angry infant, the frustration turns to anger and then to hate. This part of the self is then expelled and projected onto others."[57] As the "bad mother" becomes the monster, the baby adds a great deal of fantasy to how awful she really is. Her image becomes pure evil. But the baby's good experiences with the mother eventually outweigh the bad experiences, and so the good mother is internalized.

The mother-child relationship becomes the primary pattern for the withdrawal and return that exist in all relationships. This is the inner picture of what relationships are like. What Winnicott has frequently called "good enough parenting" allows a child to maintain hope in spite of some inevitable disappointments. Detached, inconsistent, or abusive parenting provokes feelings of estrangement and isolation. Because our needs keep making us vulnerable and pushing us into disappointing hurts, we eventually may learn to hate our own needs and prefer to act as if those needs don't exist. Chief among those needs, of course, is the need for love. Hating our need for love and hating our disappointments become one and the same.

> Love requires a response for its completion, is fulfilled only when it is reciprocated. When a response is refused, love's motive and action are frustrated, mutuality is refused, personal existence is threatened in an absolute fashion, and the child fears for its own personal existence, resents negation, and the resentment becomes hatred. Hatred, as an original motive, is inevitable in personal relations. It is impossible that any parent or partner should always be able to respond to all needs according to all expectations. Hatred, as a component of complex motivations, is always present, though not necessarily dominant.[58]

Another psychoanalytic voice Augsburger employs is that of Richard Galston.[59] Galston describes three groups of people with differing capacities to hate. The first group is those who can't hate; the second is those who can hate but who cannot "get over" their hatred; and the third is those who are able to both hate and move beyond that hatred. Those who cannot seem to "tap" their hatred normally live very dependent, passive lives. Often their early emotional environment was so fragile that if they experienced hate, they were threatened with immediate abandonment. If they told a parent, during a frustrating experience, "I hate you!" that feeling was met with an immediate threat of complete rejection. The indirect message was that one can never feel hatred and then get over it; instead, one must never feel it *period!* The feeling of hatred so radically threatened the security of the person's world that the hatred simply "had to go." Especially in childhood, when honesty and security are locked in a battle, security always wins. Therefore the hatred becomes *repressed* instead of *suppressed*. While repression is an unconscious denial mechanism, suppression is able to recognize feelings without necessarily acting on them. This is an enormously important skill to develop. When we cultivate the ability to suppress feelings, we are able to embrace them without shame while not necessarily letting those feelings have the "final word" in how we behave. Repression, on the other hand, operates with the assumption that even recognizing unpleasant feelings is too dangerous, so they are shoved outside of awareness. Repression doesn't understand the difference between acknowledging one's feelings and allowing them to dictate one's response.

If we are passively unable to hate, we are usually incapacitated to fight against injustice. As Augsburger suggests, we often forget that there is a positive side to resentments.[60] Granted, the toxic, ruminating, negative side of resentments can place people in psychological trouble, but do we really want to be completely *without* resentments? Along with the toxic nature of resentment can be a demand for justice, a spunky fight for equality and fairness. James McClendon even calls resentment "God's good gift, protecting us in an injurious world from greater harm and inciting us to secure a justice we might otherwise be too placid or to compassionate to enforce.[61] The inability to resent reflects an equal inability to respect ourselves as persons of worth and dignity. It is injustice toward ourselves, and hence, unethical. Contrary to popular opinion, the process of forgiveness necessitates an accurate memory of the injustice done.

While resentments are probably inevitable, they are also often dangerous. The reason for this is that "memory has a special tendency to retain experiences of pain, so it is uniquely hospitable to hatred."[62] The human ego is very selective in its recall. It will even revise history to suit its purposes. Further, where pain has been done, there is a tendency to both harbor and elaborate the damage done.

> Memory is not a camera that takes intricate and objective photographs, or a computer that creates accurate files for future use or reproduces past events unaltered or unretouched. Memory is not a mirror of reality, an accurate historian, or a safe storage vault. Rather it is a novelist, constantly refining the events of the past into a narrative acceptable and accessible to the self. At its most subjective, memory functions like a kaleidoscope, recalling past events dynamically, partially, in edited form, creating a mythology of one's own life to protect an ideal self or to protest on behalf of an angry self. Since our memory can hold only a miniscule part of our experience, we must constantly forget in order to remember, and the reality we recall is made up of bits and pieces, fragments of conversations and

fractured narratives that are accidental, unreliable, always evolving, forever shifting beneath our mental feet. But this kaleidoscope is what constitutes the 'self' that I bring to the moment.[63]

Thus the past is always being refined and changed as it is observed from a new location. This "past" consists less of what actually occurred and more of what we *believe* took place. Yesterday is always interpreted through today's reality.

Augsburger, like Sanford and Jung, believes that the casting of the disowned aspects of ourselves onto others is a major contributing factor in hatred. Projecting our shadow onto others becomes an important tool of self-avoidance.

Projection requires a great deal of energy—the psychic energy of defensiveness, hypervigilance, suspicion—to maintain a dissociated state of nonreflective unawareness. Each of us employs a significant measure of mental and emotional energy policing our shadow storehouse, screening the windows to awareness, the doors to self-reflection, and the gates to the public arena of relationships. A clear picture of the person we dislike offers a revealing portrait of the shadow we repress.[64]

While it is unnecessary to repeat what I have already said about the significance of the shadow, I should acknowledge that this concept plays an important role in Augsburger's understanding of hatred. In fact, he spends an entire chapter dealing with it and concludes that the primary way to reduce shadow-projection is cultivating the important skill of empathy.

HATRED, ABSOLUTES, AND THE "EVIL IMAGINATION"

Augsburger notes that it is initially essential and developmentally inevitable that persons think in all-or-nothing categories. Either/or thinking is simply part of the cognitive development roadmap. This ability to quickly divide the world between good and bad is a capacity we never lose, particularly during stress. Age regressions, as most of us can attest, are regular features of our anger patterns. This infantile, good-or-bad schema prevents us from seeing that others can be simultaneously good *and* bad. During calmer moments, even slight self-reflection quickly reveals that we are not "all good," a recognition that may help us consider that the enemy is not "all bad."[65]

Any finite belief that is raised to the standard of an all-inclusive Absolute pushes us into idolatry and is potentially "demonic." By "demonic," Augsburger seems to follow Tillich's view that an inflated, finite reality can "possess" us in a very destructive way.[66]

Augsburger uses the work of H. Richard Niebuhr to illustrate the manner in which absolutistic thinking creates such havoc in life.[67] In his excellent little book, *The Meaning of Revelation*, Niebuhr lays this out. He reminds us that "self-defense is the most prevalent source of error in all thinking," and that "the great source of evil in life is the absolutizing of the relative."[68] He further states that there are three primary characteristics of the "evil imagination." The first characteristic is the tendency to think that the specific truth we have found is the *only* truth there is. This perspective confuses limited theological ideas, for instance, with God. The particular experiences or beliefs of one group are elevated to ultimate significance for everyone else. We "own" the Absolute and it is camped out in our own backyard. Closely related to this is the second characteristic—making self-preservation the ultimate concern of life. This self-preservation, of course, goes beyond physical existence and also includes our emotional preservation and cognitive claims. It has to do with worldview survival. And the third characteristic is an outgrowth of undue focus on self-security— namely, glorifying the self or group as the center of life. Augsburger insightfully identifies two assumptions beneath Niebuhr's notion of the evil imagination.

> For Niebuhr, two interrelated assumptions are at the heart of this tendency: (1) all human knowledge in general and revelation in particular are neither eternal nor unchanging—the human images and symbols of God may change and die, but God does not. Evil imagination confuses one's symbols and images of God with Godself. (2) All history is partial and relative—one among many—and follows

the course of all other histories: change and death. In evil imagination one's personal, social, or religious history is elevated as absolute and all else is relative. In contrast, Niebuhr called us to embrace the reality of God while confessing the ambiguity of human history and knowledge.[69]

As we attempt to defy finitude cognitively by stepping outside the boundaries of a specific social and historical location, we grow firm in the belief that the Absolute has been completely "trapped" within our own vision of the world. Having identified, clarified, and championed absolute truth, we are then justified to do whatever it takes to protect this truth and punish any who threaten it. Put simply, "true believers" easily become violent.

To help combat this "evil imagination," Augsburger challenges readers with a group of tough questions:

> Do I suppress awareness of my own ultimate powerlessness and absolute dependence by absolutizing and glorifying my images and symbols of God? Am I sometimes tempted to defend these with stubborn insistence on their total accuracy and their finality? If I think for a moment that I possess the ultimate truth of the Eternal, then *I* need not fear my finitude, frailty, contingency? Do fears of my own impermanence tempt me to cling to certain symbols, images, and propositions? Has the thought troubled me that if one of my images of God dies, I too will die; if my symbols for God are not maintained, I will not be sustained?[70]

When we feel that we are totally right, others, unfortunately, become completely wrong. The truth of our own position insists on the complete falsehood of other positions. A certainty of conviction that blinds itself to its own finitude is a dangerous thing. This conviction of absolute, authoritarian certainty reached its climax in what is probably the most demonic moment in human history, the Holocaust.

Augsburger essentially agrees with the process of enemy making we saw earlier in Sam Keen. Keen describes this process as follows.

> The enemy system (a shared delusional system) involves a process of

two or more enemies dumping their (unconscious) wastes in each other's backyards. All we despise in ourselves we attribute to them. And vice versa. Since this process of unconscious projection of the shadow is universal, enemies "need" each other to dispose of their accumulated, disowned, psychological toxins. We form a hate bond, an "adversarial symbiosis," an integrated system that guarantees that neither of us will be faced with our own shadow.[71]

Using propaganda posters, various sketches, and cartoons, Keen illustrates thirteen different archetypes of the enemy. These archetypes, or universal images from the collective unconscious, include the enemy as stranger, aggressor, faceless, enemy of God, barbarian, epitome of greed, criminal, torturer, rapist, beast (including reptile or vermin), death, worthy opponent (who allows us to be heroic in battle), and abstraction. A primary purpose of the enemy's face, whatever its form, is to dehumanize it so that it can be eliminated without guilt.

Augsburger points out that a primary value of enemy formation is the reduction of anxiety. Any personal culpability is transferred to the enemy, so shame and guilt are also greatly reduced. Fear, however, accelerates along with our imaginations. The inevitable by-product of making the enemy "so monstrous" is that we deeply scare ourselves. This fear quickly leads to violence. We can no longer distinguish real and imaginary danger. Our defenses are driven by paranoia. Threatened by feelings of powerlessness in the face of the "awful" enemy, we fight ferociously. Our terror justifies our violence. This is all part of a reactive hatred in which our behavior is controlled by external realities. Full of a tormenting anxiety, we react to the enemy in our minds. And then we tell ourselves that they "made" us do it. As our minds increasingly accelerate, the possibility of seeing the enemy as a person begins to vanish. In this situation, enemy empathy is perceived as foolish, naïve, and even self-destructive.

PURIFYING OUR HATRED

The goal of maturity, which Augsburger admits is no easy task and is never fully achieved, is to move from destructive hate through the process of empathy and compassion to just hate, which sees the previous enemy as a person not completely unlike ourselves. The goal is not to eliminate hate but to direct it at injustice itself. The solution is not to "quit hating" but to hate the right thing—namely, that which dehumanizes all of us. Just hate is simultaneously passionate about evil and compassionate toward the evildoer. "From hate of others, to hate of those who hate us, we can grow until we hate *hate* itself."[72] For Augsburger, we can only prepare the way for a breakthrough into empathic compassion; we do not "work the miracle." This is part of a transforming moment perceived as God's gift. It transcends Pelagian will power and is instead a grace-filled moment.

Simply prohibiting hate will never work. Instead, we must engage the more tedious task of understanding what prompts and drives our hatred. Also, we can model nonretaliatory ways of dealing with conflict as we reframe our resentments and become more familiar with the regions of our own inner darkness rather than simply projecting them onto others. We can quit pretending to have found and claimed the Absolute for ourselves. Such grandiose claims are frequently connected with the justification of violence toward those who differ. We can reverently and humbly recall the hideous examples of hate from the past, especially the nightmare of the Holocaust, and recommit ourselves to never letting that happen again. And we can turn away from the notion that violence is somehow redemptive, an idea that is so epidemic in our culture.

EVALUATING THESE THREE THEORIES OF HATE

While the topic of hate is broad enough to cover several volumes rather than one chapter, I have examined three significant thinkers and their particular profiles of the phenomenon of hate. Any discussion of evil would be remiss without an investigation into the dynamics of hatred. Aaron Beck, the first thinker explored, offers a rich understanding of the cognitive processes that underlie strong feelings of hatred. As a cognitive-behavioral psychiatrist, Beck, as we have seen, identifies crooked thinking as humanity's greatest culprit. Egocentric, biased, distorted thinking drives us to violence, destructiveness, and hatred. Clearly Beck's approach offers a substantial contribution to the dilemma of hate.

We may be left, however, with several questions concerning this cognitive-behavioral model. One question is a rather straightforward one and is especially important for individuals coming out of a depth psychology background—namely, does Beck minimize the significance of unconscious processes and conversely overestimate the capacity of conscious reason to rescue us from our hate problems? Beck places enormous stock in human reason. Unhealthy thinking is the *cause* of psychological disturbance and healthy thinking is the *cure* for what distresses us. But the question is whether or not reason can function in an autonomous, healthy manner while unconscious processes tug, pull, and threaten to "distort" it. Beck seems to indicate that the transition from a highly anxious or angry state to a calm and deliberate one can be accomplished fairly easily if we simply think differently. But does he make this process appear a little too easy? He assumes that conscious reason has the ability to name and smoke out our "automatic" or unconscious thoughts that create our feeling states. Is this confidence in reason's capacity warranted? Are there some injuries to the psyche that are "deeper" than reason itself can heal? Are there emotional wounds that need more than cognitive reframing? Are there unconscious conflicts below the surface of reason's investigatory power, conflicts that drive our hatred? Again, Beck's model is based on the assumption that these deeper regions of the psyche either do not exist or they can be reached by conscious reason. We must ask if this strictly cognitive approach does justice to the complexities of the human psyche. Stated differently, is healing strictly a cerebral process?

By reducing hatred, along with what the Western tradition has previously understood as "sin," to faulty thinking, Beck seems to minimize the role of the will, or what has been referred to as "the heart" in evildoing. His implication is that if we clear up unhealthy thinking, highly moral individuals will flourish. He further suggests that it is in the face of exaggerated anxiety, threat, or intense anger that our destructive tendencies come forth. The assumption, again, seems to be that as long as reason is calm and unruffled, destructive behavior will not occur. But don't people do spiteful, destructive things even when they are quite calm? Beck admits that psychopaths are capable of this, but one wonders if other parts of the population are not equally capable. Calm rationality is no guarantee of morality.

Beck assumes that reason is completely capable of taming anxiety. Granted, challenging and changing our thinking *is* often capable of helping us deal with everyday anxieties. But Beck refuses to acknowledge the anxiety that the existentialists describe, an anxiety that is simply built into human finitude. This anxiety, argues existentialists such as Rollo May and Paul Tillich, arises because we realize that we are limited creatures, that our choices define us, and that we are going to die.[73] A realization of mortality itself produces this type of anxiety.[74] This feeling of dread does not have a specific object, but instead is fueled by a generic uneasiness. Beck denies this and claims that there is not only a specific, identifiable fear underlying all anxiety, but that this fear can be recognized and tamed by the voice of reason. In short, Beck does not take into consideration the issue of existential anxiety. But for individuals such as Kierkegaard and Reinhold Niebuhr, reason is simply incapable of controlling and sedating this level of anxiety. What is needed more than "correct thinking" is a trust in the larger processes of life or God. Without this elementary form of faith, anxiety overwhelms us. Working with what appears to be a naturalistic ontology, Beck claims that human reason can rise above this existential anxiety and stake out a secure future for itself. Many believe this to be a highly optimistic, and even naïve, view of reason's capacity. Beck implies that human thinking can somehow step outside of our estrangement problem, and that we can find a neutral, objective place where biases no longer affect our cognitions. While we can indeed distance ourselves from our orienting assumptions about life, Beck's call to a completely unbiased place where reason is no longer affected by the distortions of finitude seems quite unrealistic.

Related to this, Beck and other cognitive therapists such as Albert Ellis frequently speak as if there is a unified sense of rationality to the cosmos. In other words, they sometimes sound like Stoics in the ancient world who believed that one of the tasks of life is to live in accordance with this universal reason or comic rationality they called the Logos. Yet Beck and Ellis make no such ontological claims about the reasonableness of ultimate reality. Theirs is a Stoicism without the Logos. Believing that life is undergirded by a cosmic rationality would push them in the direction of theistic metaphors that Beck does not mention, and Ellis flatly denies.[75]

Beck also seems to suggest that egocentric thinking, a fundamental contributor to hatred, guides us only when we are anxious or threatened. But I would suggest that there are times in which, even though we are not thinking in exaggerated, anxious ways, egocentric thinking still guides us. In the same way that the humanistic psychologists assume that we will act ethically once our basic needs are met, Beck seems to believe that we will always act ethically once we think correctly. This makes morality a purely cerebral concern.

I also wonder if Beck adequately appreciates the manner in which our thinking process is supported and reinforced by our conversational partners and reference groups. In other words, does he have an excessively individualized understanding of human cognition? Changing our conceptions of the world, as Peter Berger has pointed out so well, normally requires an entry into a new "plausibility structure" that supports and reinforces our new cognitions.[76] A new sense of reality does not usually last long if it is does not find others who share its framework and meaning. While there are a few mavericks who can buck an alien plausibility structure, most of us require an ongoing community to keep our new views of the world alive. Human cognition is too fragile to exist in isolation from a network of support.

These questions and objections in no way disregard Beck's important contribution. Surely he can help us deal with hatred more constructively. And clearly he can help us with everyday, neurotic forms of anxiety. But when we try to extend his perspective into an all-encompassing theory, problems emerge. When the ultimate questions of life appear—questions about the meaning of existence itself—calm reason cannot always ride the horse of anxiety. Reason is not strong enough or "pure" enough to resist our tendencies, in the face of this kind of anxiety, to deceive ourselves. And hatred is often related to this level of ontological anxiety, an anxiety rooted in the question of life's ultimate meaning. When our entire sense of meaning, purpose, and values are questioned, it is perhaps more difficult than Beck imagines to remain in cognitive control. Of course we can make improvements, but this hardly guarantees the kind of nonanxious world that would eliminate our hatred.

The next perspective we considered was the work of John Sanford and Carl Jung. Again, this understanding of hate's origin offers valuable insight into the human condition. The invitation to introspect when we feel hatred toward another, to ask ourselves what we may be secretly hating in ourselves and therefore projecting onto others, is a deeply important exercise. Individuals with intrapsychic awareness can often see that much of their protest and hatred of others' behavior is in fact a protest and hatred of their own shadow. This idea of enemy formation as the projection of our own shadow, so well developed by Sam Keen, should be a regular reminder to look within.[77]

While viewing hatred as shadowboxing is an important insight, I suspect that it, too, does not explain all of our experiences with hate. For instance, to hate someone who purposely injures one of our children may not be reducible to our own repressed desire to hurt our child. The hatred we feel for the drunk driver who killed our friend may have little to do with the denied hatred we have for our own shadow and its capacity to act recklessly. One problem with this view of hatred is that it tends to reduce all interpersonal issues to intrapsychic ones. In Jungian thought, for instance, "Loving my enemy," may be understood as a purely individual need to embrace my own shadow. While shadow ownership and self-acceptance may be crucial in the act of reaching out toward others, the interpersonal issue of acceptance is larger than self-acceptance. Loving my enemy is more than loving my shadow. Classic stories such as the parable of the prodigal son in the New Testament become far less significant when they are changed from a father's love of his son to our own love for our wandering ways.

Another issue with "shadow language" may appear quite ironic. While the purpose of identifying the shadow is greater self-awareness and self-acceptance, the sheer act of dividing up our psyche into separate components, even for the purpose of clarification and ownership, can unwittingly leave us feeling as if the shadow is autonomous and somehow not really "us." In other words, it may be possible to move from the self-exoneration in the phrase "The devil made me do it," to the phrase "The shadow made me do it." This, as Alfred Adler so frequently pointed out, is always the danger of dividing the psyche into various "components" or "parts."[78]

Sanford's indictment of Paul as a primary shadow repressor, and consequently, as a contributor to Western hatred, is a very weighty charge. As we have seen, Sanford believes the Christian church has been wrongheaded to follow the teachings of Paul, teachings that he believes are quite inconsistent with the teachings of Jesus. Considering the fact that Paul wrote most of the New Testament, Sanford is essentially saying that the early church's psychology cannot be trusted. If he wants to make such a claim, he needs to further support it by demonstrating that Jesus' teaching was void of all dualism and instead emphasized a nondualistic wholeness similar to Jung's. He needs to show further a radical discontinuity between the teachings of Jesus and Paul. I'm not sure he can do that. While Sanford is quite right that Jesus seemed particularly outraged at those who only presented their self-righteous persona while denying their shadow, a much stronger case needs to be made that Jesus' teaching was free of this "Pauline dualism."

Nevertheless, Sanford's work on evil, and indirectly on the topic of hatred, is well worth pursuing and offers some sophisticated insights concerning shadow projection. Sanford's fascination with and exploration of the Dr. Jekyll and Mr. Hyde story have especially been important for an increased understanding of the relationship of hatred and the dark side. My caution, again, is not that the Sanford/Jung perspective offers little. In fact, I think it offers much, so much in fact that one may be tempted to believe it tells the "whole story" of human hatred. That, however, is something I do not think it is able to do.

Of the perspectives considered in this chapter, David Augsburger's approach to hatred is the most comprehensive and multifaceted. He does not rely on a singular theory of hatred. While he does not mention Beck's work—a surprising omission considering the amount of research he has done—Augsburger *does* incorporate cognitive distortions within his developmental model. Also, his discussion of the "demon of the absolute," so deeply influenced by H. Richard Niebuhr, points toward the dangers of exaggerated thinking.

Perhaps the most controversial thesis in Augsburger's approach is that the elimination of hatred should not be the goal of human struggle. Instead, we should come to hate injustice or that which dehumanizes us. This he calls "just hatred." Without this hatred of injustice, love is weak and sentimental. In fact, Augsburger believes that a love of justice *demands* a hatred of injustice. The difficult factor, however, is sifting out the hatred of oppression from the hatred of the oppressor. It is clear that Augsburger does not embrace a calm, detached, Stoic attitude that downplays passion, and hence eliminates hatred. Instead, he sees hatred as an inevitable and necessary emotion that can be used in the service of social justice. In fact, as we shall see in the next chapter, any form of therapy that attempts to alleviate the anger and hatred against social injustice by telling clients that "all their problems are really intrapsychic struggles" merely reinforces the status quo.[79] Our hatred needs to undergo spiritual development and maturity; it does not need to be eliminated.

Augsburger's position is controversial because some schools of thought encourage a place "beyond" hatred, a tranquil world that embraces all of reality exactly as it is and refuses to make any sort of judgments. This view moves beyond an acceptance of reality; instead, it is an endorsement of the way things are. It sees that all is necessary and that the universe is moving along "exactly as it is supposed to." We cannot call some things "unjust" or "evil" because we do not have the vision of a cosmic perspective to do so. If we had such a vision, we would in fact see that it is all necessary. Or, as the popular slogan would have it, "It's all good."

Yet this view, often associated with a mystical embrace of reality, can easily promote passivity by insisting that all hate should be eliminated. In this monistic framework, we simply cannot divide the good from the bad, the moral from the immoral, and hence there is nothing *to* hate. Yet for Augsburger, I suspect, it is impossible to sustain an ethical outlook from this perspective. The call to detach and "let the world be" in the face of dehumanizing injustice is indeed a call to bystander apathy, an invitation to a passionless, ethically neutral life. Such a life is hardly worth living. Augsburger is very aware of hatred's destructive potential. But this is all the more reason to *transform* it rather than *repress* it.

SUMMARY

In this chapter, I have attempted to review carefully the cognitive-behavioral contribution to the issue of hatred, the Jungian perspective on the relationship between hatred and the shadow, and the eclectic perspective of leading pastoral counselor David Augsburger. While attempting to glean insight from each angle, I have also indicated its limitations, especially the cognitive-behavioral and Jungian approaches. This analysis of hatred has been placed in the larger context of evil and human destructiveness.

Many feel that if we want to grasp fully the dynamics of human evil, we must move beyond an individual, psychological analysis toward a more expanded view of larger social realities. The next two chapters will examine this larger social context of evil. It will investigate contributions made by social psychologists, sociologists, feminists, and liberation theologians. The focus will move from individual evil to systemic evil, from private concerns to the social injustices that surround us.

CHAPTER FIVE

Ordinary People and Malevolent Circumstances

The Social Context of Evil

It is not so much the kind of person one is, but the kind of situation one is in, that determines our actions.
—*Stanley Milgram*

It is not so much what life brings to us, but what life finds in us that makes the difference. —*Victor Frankl*

It might not be too much of a stretch to say that the subdiscipline of psychology, social psychology, emerged, to a large degree, as an attempt to understand "evil." More specifically, it grew out of an effort to grasp how the widespread conformity of Nazi Germany could possibly occur. How could people "go along with" such atrocities? Did this say something about the German "character"? Were they an especially vile people? After what seemed like a great deal of progress in previous generations, how could humanity take such a downward slide? Thus social psychology had an intimate relationship to the issue of anthropodicy—the question of how human beings can do such dastardly things to each other. This was the social-science version of the philosophical and theological problem of theodicy—how a loving and powerful God could allow such evil and human suffering in God's creation. This time, however, not God, but the human condition itself, was on trial.

Thus, while social psychology is obviously much larger than the question of evil, it originated out of a deep concern with it. The horrors of the twentieth century continue to prompt social psychologists to ponder how a social situation can turn normally rational, even ethical persons, into vicious puppets who will carry out sadistic orders. Kurt Lewin, who himself fled Nazi Germany, began to argue that it is possible to translate socially significant issues such as the authority of powerful leaders into hypotheses that could be empirically tested in controlled experiments. Again, much of this interest grew out of researching how dictators could establish such power over people.

Most of this research led to a rather unnerving conclusion. Perhaps it wasn't that these individuals who participated in such horrific war crimes were internally evil or innately "bad." Perhaps it had nothing to do with the "German character" or the particular character of any social group. Perhaps, instead, the social situations themselves brought out this malicious behavior. In other words, perhaps any of us could have engaged in such behavior if the right circumstantial factors presented themselves. This is an enormously significant claim: *a social situation can be so powerful that it overshadows genetics, previous ethical standards, a history of reinforcement, prior learning, or any dispositional factors.* Put simply, the social context can pressure people into doing a lot of things they normally wouldn't do. Evil is not performed by "monsters" from whom we can feel safely disconnected; instead, evil more often results from a growing erosion of ordinary people no different than you and me.

This discovery is related to one of the most important concepts in social psychology, the "fundamental attribution error." This refers to the mental distortion frequently made when we believe that all of someone's behavior comes from within them rather than being triggered by outside factors. The fundamental attribution error assumes that all behavior is "endogenous" (arising from within) rather than situationally provoked. The fundamental attribution error overly "psychologizes" situations that are in fact social. It sees evil as a strictly inside-out maneuver. Again, we humans, say social psychologists, have a natural tendency to attribute all destructive acts to internal dispositions. These malicious impulses from within are what get us in trouble. But this perspective, argues social psychology, minimizes our social context. Stated simply, it is a naïve belief that only "bad" people do bad things.

Thus social psychology argues that evil is far more subtle than instinctivist or dispositional theories have thought. It is often an outside-in affair in which people are corrupted by a social context that pushes them toward greater and greater malevolence. This position does not necessarily argue for social and environmental determinism. Instead, "influence" is the key factor. If the environment completely determines human choices, as in radical Skinnerian behaviorism, then personal ethics is meaningless anyway. Many social psychologists point out that evil occurs in incremental advances, a slow diminishing process brought on largely by social pressures.

A social-psychology investigation of evil will look much different than the psychoanalytic investigation of chapter 3. While some psychoanalytic perspectives have clearly moved toward a greater interest in social and cultural factors, the main thrust of the psychoanalytic paradigm has been toward understanding the unconscious conflicts that perpetuate human destructiveness. Clearly for Freud, "the demon is within." These hidden conflicts do not easily present themselves; they are instead concealed. Stated bluntly, it is not safe to take a self-report at face value. There is normally a great deal of unconscious activity behind even a flattering self-report. Deeper conflicts and hidden meanings must be discovered.

Most of the research in social psychology, on the other hand, takes self-report at face value and does not look at underlying factors. We will especially see this in the area of self-esteem and its relationship to destructive behavior. The majority of social psychologists consistently report that inflated and excessive self-esteem is a part of most destructive people. Why do they believe this? Because this is what these individuals consciously say to researchers as they respond to questionnaires. This, of course, completely minimizes the significance of unconscious factors and instead takes all self-flattery at face value. If a person suggests that he or she is "great," many social psychologists see no need to investigate whether this sense of greatness is in fact based on a deeper sense of insecurity and inadequacy. Self-reports are convenient for research, so they are accepted. For psychoanalysts, these conscious reports ignore a wealth of clinical insight surrounding the issues of low self-esteem and narcissism.

In this chapter, I wish to examine two of the most important studies in the social sciences, the work of Stanley Milgram and Philip Zimbardo. Both of these social psychologists argue strongly in favor of a "situationist" rather than a "dispositional" perspective on human destructiveness. I will raise the question concerning how much their work can help us understand the radical evil of the Holocaust. I will then investigate Roy Baumeister's social psychology of evil, noting especially his conviction that the "myth of pure evil" keeps us from a deeper understanding of human destructiveness. And I will then look at social critiques of individualism in psychology and psychotherapy, examining the central claim that an individual focus on the human condition has kept us self-preoccupied and blind to the real source of our maladies—the social and political realm. This chapter is closely linked with the next one, which will highlight the differences between a social and individual focus on sin. The question guiding both these chapters concerns whether we should primarily target the individual or the social realm in our quest to understand human destructiveness.

DESTRUCTIVE OBEDIENCE

Stanley Milgram, of Yale University, wanted to examine the role of conformity and obedience in humanity's capacity for destructive behavior. As a Jewish researcher, Milgram was especially interested in understanding how the Germans were willing to obey the orders of Hitler. Again, he wanted to know if this was a character flaw of the German people or whether this inclination also exists in others.

Milgram placed an advertisement in a New Haven newspaper asking for volunteers for a learning experiment. The ad indicated that the volunteers would be paid. Milgram did not have much money for this project, so he built his own "electric shock generator" with a range of fifteen to 450 volts.

The intensity of the voltage ranged from "Slight Shock" to "Intense Shock" to "Danger: Severe Shock."

The experimenter told the subjects that they were participating in a study concerning learning and memory. The volunteer would take on the role of "teacher" and administer shocks to "learners" who made errors on the exam. In reality, the experiment had nothing to do with learning and memory. It was instead concerned with the extent to which the volunteers would go in punishing the learner. The learner did not really receive an electric shock, but the teacher did not know this. From another room, the learner would yell, moan, and scream when the shock was administered. Thus the teacher was convinced that the shock was really occurring. As the learner made errors, the shock would increase and the learner's screams would become more pronounced. If the teacher hesitated about sending the shock, the experimenter would remind him about the importance of the study and the fact that he had volunteered.

Two-thirds of the subjects obeyed the experimenter and pushed the current all the way up to 450 volts. This happened in spite of the learner's screams and protests. The teacher was in no way threatened or forced. He certainly wasn't offered a large sum of money. Sometimes the teacher would complain after the learner screamed, but after the experimenter said that this test needed to be done, the teacher typically obeyed the experimenter's authority. In some cases, the experimenter would say to the teacher that he had no choice. Roy Baumeister, whose work will be explored later, offers an interesting reflection on this issue:

> The comment "You have no choice" was literally and patently absurd, because the subject obviously did have a choice, and indeed the whole point of the experiment was to learn about what choices people made in that situation. But hearing the authority figure say that you have no choice was enough to conceal the fact of choice and to get people to continue giving shocks. The reason, presumably, is that the subjects in the experiment did not want to believe they had a choice. They wanted to complete their assigned tasks without getting into an argument with the experimenter who was supervising them. To believe that they were responsible for their own decisions would have forced them to make

moral calculations and difficult decisions on very short notice. It was better to accept the authority figure's word that they had no choice.[1]

Milgram himself was surprised by his findings. Obedience was much easier to elicit than he thought it would be. Conversely, disobedience did not come easily. Again, by the end of the experiment, 65 percent of the learners had used the full 450 volts. Milgram stated, "ordinary people, simply doing their jobs, and without any particular hostility in their past, can become agents in a terrible destructive process."[2] And on another occasion he concluded, "If a system of death camps were set up in the United States of the sort we had in Nazi Germany, one would be able to find sufficient personnel for those camps in any medium-sized American town."[3] Israel W. Charny, the executive director of the 1982 International Conference on the Holocaust and Genocide agrees: "The assaulting quality of the Milgram experiment is really a valuable attack on the denial and indifference of all of us. Whatever upset follows facing the truth, we must eventually face up to the fact that so many of us are, in fact, available to be genociders or their assistants."[4]

Another famous study introduced to every psychology student is Philip Zimbardo's Stanford prison experiment, conducted in the early 1970s. Before engaging in the experiment, Zimbardo had each volunteer screened for psychological or physical health issues. These student volunteers were then randomly selected to play the role of guard or prisoner in the created prison. To make things even more realistic, after the role of each student had been identified, Zimbardo had those individuals who were designated as "prisoners" to be arrested in their dorms and homes. At the jail, uniforms and various other status symbols clearly distinguished the guards from the prisoners. Prisoners went through a series of rituals to establish their "lowly" status. They were placed in very small cells for twenty-four hours per day. While the prisoners were cut off from their original surroundings all the time, the guards only worked eight-hour shifts and were then free to go back home and resume their normal activities.

As the experiment developed, everyone, including Zimbardo himself, was quite shocked. The boundary between the actual volunteer and the role he was playing became erased. Polite young men became rather brutal guards. And extroverted young prisoners became passive and resigned. The situation became so intense that many prisoners developed stress reactions and had to be released from the experiment. In fact the entire experiment, which was supposed to last for two weeks, was shut down after a mere six days.

In Zimbardo's study, as in Milgram's, the situation seemed to pull individuals into a pattern of doing things they would normally not do. Ordinary students became brutal guards. They were overwhelmed by their role in the circumstance. The power of the context triggered destructive, hostile behavior. Thus Zimbardo clearly believes that a "situationist" approach to antisocial and destructive behavior has more explanatory power than a "dispositional" approach. Yet he realizes this is counterintuitive. Most of us have been schooled to believe in the notion that the cause of destructive behavior is a *destructive person* beneath the behavior. In other words, inward dispositions or character traits determine violent behavior. Evil is located within the psyche, a view that perhaps found its most extreme expression in Freud's notion of thanatos, which we have already investigated. The end result of the dispositional approach, for Zimbardo, is the false attribution of all destructive behavior to internal psychological processes. The problem with this approach is that it simplistically reduces complex social pressures to internal states, thus failing to consider how coercive situations can make any of us do destructive things. This approach ignores the environment and decontextualizes human behavior. While it may leave us self-congratulatory that we are not like other "evil" individuals, it is not good social science. As Zimbardo puts it, "the situationist perspective propels external determinants of behavior to the foreground, well beyond the status as merely background circumstance."[5] Thus we are able to see how ordinarily good people can be gradually seduced into highly destructive behavior.

> Locating evil within selected individuals or groups carries with it
> the "social virtue" of taking society "off the hook" as blameworthy;
> social structures and political decision making are exonerated from
> bearing any burden of the more fundamental circumstances that
> create racism, sexism, elitism, poverty, and marginal existence for some
> citizens. Furthermore, this dispositional orientation to understanding

evil implies a simplistic, binary world of good people, like us, and bad people, like them. That clear-cut dichotomy is divided by a manufactured line that separates good and evil. We then take comfort in the illusion that such a line constrains crossovers in either direction. We could never imagine being like *them*, of doing their unthinkable dirty deeds, and do not admit them into our company because they are so essentially different as to be unchangeable. This extreme position also means we forfeit the motivation to understand how they came to engage in what we view as evil behavior. I find it helpful to remind myself of the geopolitical analysis of the Russian novelist Alexander Solzhenitsyn, a victim of persecution by the Soviet KGB, that the line between good and evil lies in the center of every human heart.[6]

Even though Zimbardo sometimes uses the language of "good people doing bad things," he avoids positing a fundamental human motivation toward either "good" or "bad" behavior.

> We are not born with tendencies toward good or evil but with mental templates to do *either*. What I mean is that we have the potential to be better or worse than anyone who has existed in the past, to be more creative or more destructive, to make the world a better place or a worse place than before. It is only through the recognition that no one of us is an island, that we all share the human condition, that humility takes precedence over unfounded pride in acknowledging our vulnerability to situational forces.[7]

A psychoanalytic framework seeks to account for destructive behavior in terms of pathological origins. Yet Zimbardo points out that murderers, for instance, hardly share the same pathological background. Other factors must be involved. Social circumstances must be scrutinized to help us understand how individuals are seduced into such vile behavior.

Zimbardo's perspective is helpful in highlighting contextual factors that can easily be overlooked. He does indeed help us move away from an "us" and "them" approach that radically separates "good" and "evil" people. Yet my concerns with his findings are more philosophical than scientific. Stated differently, it is the conclusion he draws from the findings that raise concerns. Zimbardo moves back and forth from a deterministic to a nondeterministic paradigm in a rather confusing manner. He makes an exceptionally strong case for environmental influences, then turns right around and uses the language of determinism. On the one hand, he tells us that individuals are not completely exonerated by his situationist analysis, yet he then describes the situational factors as a "causal network" or "situational determinants of behavior."[8] He also introduces what he calls the "Zimbardo homily": "'While a few bad apples might spoil the barrel (filled with good fruit/people), a barrel filled with vinegar will *always* transform sweet cucumbers into sour pickles—regardless of the best intentions, resilience, and genetic nature of those cucumbers.' So does it make more sense to spend our resources on attempts to identify, isolate, and destroy the few bad apples or to learn how vinegar works so that we can teach cucumbers how to avoid undesirable vinegar barrels?"[9] While Zimbardo wants to maintain a sense of one's personal responsibility in theory, an analogy such as this one seems to eliminate such responsibility and put excessive weight on situational determinants. Where is the language of freedom?

Zimbardo has moved quickly from situational influence to situational "determinants." He wants to move away from dispositional factors as we consider the malevolent circumstances that contribute to evil. Yet he turns right around and wants to know how certain individuals have been able to "rise above" such pressures. As he puts it:

> [T]he situationist redefines heroism. When the majority of ordinary people can be overcome by such pressures toward compliance and conformity, the minority who resist should be considered *heroic*. Acknowledging the special nature of this resistance means that we should learn from their example by studying *how* they have been able to rise above such compelling pressures. That suggestion is coupled with another that encourages the development of an essential but ignored domain of psychology—heroes and heroism.[10]

Surely these factors of resistance that Zimbardo wants to study are dispositional. Thus he wants to reintroduce the realm of internal dispositions or traits as he examines those individuals who "heroically" rise above situational evil. Yet why would we want to study the dispositional factors or traits of individuals after he has announced that they are not a primary factor in behavior? If they are not a part of destructive behavior, then how can they be a part of "heroic" behavior? The language of causality and determinism seems inconsistently fused to a language of personal freedom. Some might argue that this is nitpicking over semantics. But I would suggest instead that this inconsistency points toward fundamentally incompatible philosophical assumptions about the human condition. Zimbardo, in his flight away from dispositional approaches, overstates the influencing power of the situation in such a way that it ends up determininistic. Then he wants to smuggle freedom back into an assumptive world that has already kicked it out. The point could perhaps be stated this way: Zimbardo's highly influential and excellent work on understanding how "ordinary people" can do destructive things makes a very important psychological contribution. Yet when his notion of influencing factors spills over into causal determinants of behavior, he becomes dangerously close to B. F. Skinner or other radical behaviorists who see freedom as ultimately an illusion. If our interiority is a key factor in why we *don't* choose evil, it is also a factor in why we *do*.

HOW MUCH DO SOCIAL-PSYCHOLOGY EXPERIMENTS TELL US ABOUT EVIL?

How much can the experiments of Milgram and Zimbardo explain concerning human destructiveness? How far should we push their theories? Clearly they are two of the most famous studies in the history of the social sciences. In fact, they are often presented, especially in social psychology classes, as the *primary* explanation for human evil, even the radical evil of the Holocaust. This connection, first introduced by Milgram himself, is undoubtedly related to his study's widespread interest. But the question is a very pointed and powerful one: Can laboratory experiments in New Haven actually account for the vicious, repugnant activities of the Holocaust? Opinion on this issue is hardly unified.

Milgram's research has been linked to Hannah Arendt's famous study of Adolf Eichmann, often called Hitler's killing machine. More specifically, Arendt's emphasis on the nonsensationalistic "banality" of evil was related to the idea that quite ordinary people can do extraordinarily brutal things if enough social pressure is placed on them. Arendt describes Eichmann: "The trouble with Eichmann is that so many were like him, and that the many were neither perverted nor sadistic, that they were, and still are, terribly and terrifyingly normal. From the viewpoint of our legal institutions, and of our moral standards of judgment, this normality was much more terrifying than all the atrocities put together."[11] By claiming they are "just following orders," individuals can engage in almost unimaginable destructive obedience. Together, this profile of Eichmann and Milgram's study seemed like a powerful refutation of the older idea that evil resides within human beings as a basic disposition. In other words, it seemed to minimize the power of personality in destructive behavior. One's disposition is overshadowed by one's circumstances. Destructive obedience results not from destructive personality tendencies, sadism, or other intrapsychic features. Instead, it emerges as a result of powerful coercive forces that propel human choice. Perhaps there is an "Eichmann in all of us" waiting for the right situational factors to release its destructive potential.

This issue points toward a century of debate in the social sciences. Does the central responsibility for individual behavior lie at the doorstep of personal choice or social influence? What is the relationship between individual choice and social context? What is the connection between human autonomy and circumstantial influence? Does human destructiveness emerge from powers within us or from contaminating influences outside of us? As we shall see in the next chapter, these questions have also emerged in theological debates about the origins of sin.

Milgram's work reminds us that even when participants felt very distressed about what they were doing, they nevertheless continued. Perhaps most disturbing of all, many of the shockers continued even when the "learners" on the other side of the wall quit responding altogether, thus suggesting that they were either unconscious or even dead. Describing two of the participants, Milgram reports the following: "At one point he pushed his fist into his forehead and muttered: 'Oh God, let's stop it.' And yet he continued to respond to every word of the experimenter, and obeyed to the end. . . . I observed a mature and initially poised businessman enter the laboratory smiling and confident. Within 20 minutes, he was reduced to a twitching, stuttering wreck, who was rapidly approaching a nervous collapse."[12] In other words, the participants were distressed as they considered what they were doing and yet they were asked to continue. This dissonance and stress is an important element in what may separate Milgram's study from certain Nazi activities. Indeed, in many of the situations with Nazis, they believed they were performing a "good" task by relieving the world of "Jewish vermin." In other words, the Nazi willingness to unflinchingly eradicate Jewish people may need an explanation beyond that of Milgram's disturbed, but obedient, shockers.

There has not been adequate clarification of the reasons that 35 percent of the participants did *not* go all they way in their shock infliction. Such intense focus has been placed on the majority who used maximum force that little attention has been focused on those who refused such an order. Could it be that the reasons were primarily "dispositional" in nature, a matter of character? The study is ethically problematic and thus hard to replicate. Some have suggested that the failure to clarify these individual differences casts a shadow on the study's ability to generalize about the human condition. Why were some more able to disengage from the experiment?

It is important to keep in mind that the subjects in the Milgram experiment did not *want* to harm their victims. This does not apply to the Holocaust. The SS officers were not under any pretense that Hitler was making his requests "for the best interest of the Jewish people," as Milgram's subjects thought about their obedience to the learning rules. The Jewish victims were not social peers, but extreme victims of dehumanization. In Milgram's study, by contrast, there was some degree of concern for the learner expressed when the subjects expressed such ambivalent feelings about continuing.

The link between the Milgram study and the Holocaust also tends to minimize the dehumanizing anti-Jewish element that clearly propelled the Nazi killings. Some believe that the Holocaust represents a unique and unrepeatable event that cannot be duplicated in a lab. Again, surely a key factor was the radical dehumanization of the Jewish people. Clearly the

Nazis did not see the Jews as persons. This reduction of personhood allowed them to smash the heads of babies into walls and throw Jewish infants into the air for "target practice." The level of sadism was nearly unthinkable. And perhaps the deepest perversion is that many of the Nazi soldiers were distressed not because they were viciously taking human life, but because parts of the bodies of Jewish victims were being slung on them after these bodies had been shot. Their "disgust" was not related to the appallingly immoral acts they were performing, but instead related to the fact that their uniforms were getting bloody. It is the utter vulgarity of such killing that has prompted Allan Fenigstein to disconnect the Holocaust from Milgram's empirical study.

> In general, the historical evidence on the spontaneity, initiative, enthusiasm, and pride with which the Nazis degraded, tortured, and killed their victims, is utterly incompatible with the concept of obedience, and simply has no counterpart in the behavior that Milgram observed in his laboratory studies. . . . The terms that are routinely used to describe the horrors of the Holocaust—e.g., atrocity, inhumanity, hatefulness, wickedness—are simply preposterous in the context of Milgram's studies.[13]

Thus some are concerned that the social psychological emphasis on situational power can move us away from the recognition that human beings were making choices throughout this entire massacre. Worse still, they are afraid that the underlying conviction of situationism is ultimately to exonerate the behavior of the Nazi killers. This seems outrageously insulting and offensive to both victims and survivors of the Holocaust. For them, there is no obedience "excuse" whatsoever, and to suggest such a notion is to trivialize some of the most despicable actions in humanity's history. D. R. Mandel, for instance, argues that the Nazi perpetrators and the situationist argument have definite similarities: "Holocaust perpetrators have asserted the obedience alibi as an assurance of their innocence. Social scientists have asserted the obedience alibi as an ostensibly situationist explanation of the Holocaust. Though the intent of one group has differed from the other, the message conveyed has been strikingly similar."[14] Similarly, other social psychologists believe that this preoccupation with situations and the ignoring of dispositions has the effect of "letting perpetrators off the hook." As psychology professors John Sabini, Michael Siepmann, and Julia Stein put it, "If claiming that situations are more important than dispositions lets the innocent off the hook, it does so by a blanket denial of human responsibility, and that is dehumanizing, not humanizing."[15]

This "condoning" quality embedded in a situationist perspective, though clearly denied by Zimbardo, provokes many to believe that social psychology is guilty of trivializing evil. While Zimbardo emphatically insists that he is merely explaining the power of situational forces, many believe that this emphasis nevertheless chips away at personal responsibility. Leonard Berkowitz is quite direct about this.

> Social psychology's relative inattention to the great atrocities
> committed during the extermination program reflects the field's failure
> to establish a conception of evil that differentiates among categories
> of wrongdoing. In so doing, there is a danger of trivializing terrible
> actions. In not distinguishing conceptually between truly egregious
> injustices such as the Nazi's Final Solution and somewhat lesser
> misdeeds . . . we basically place all of these behaviors in the same
> psychological category and thus run the risk of regarding all of them as
> equally bad.[16]

Others agree. Mandel argues that situationist accounts may "erroneously portray evildoers as good-intentioned souls who are swept along by the power of bad situations."[17] Further, they may argue that social psychologists have "made too much" of Arendt's phrase "the banality of evil." It was, after all, Eichmann who also said: "I will jump into my grave laughing, because the fact that I have the death of five million Jews on my conscience gives me extraordinary satisfaction."[18]

Psychologist Arthur Miller brings a sobering realism concerning the conclusions we reach about this situationist versus dispositional view of destructiveness.[19] He says, quite simply, that we often find what we are looking for. As he puts it, "Social psychologists who adopt a strongly situationist view of behavior invariably endorse the obedience experiments, whereas social psychologists taking a more dispositional or personality-oriented view of behavior are more critical, particularly in terms of their generalizability to the Holocaust."[20] In fact, just as Freud often suggested that those who opposed his ideas were in denial, so social psychologists suggest that those who differ with their situationist views are simply committing the fundamental attribution error. But simply calling the disposition-inclined thinker an "erroneous attributer" is not an argument.[21] To move adequately beyond the confines of disposition thinking, they must advance reasons about the limits and inadequacies of this way of thinking. Otherwise, it's the equivalent of calling someone irrational but not telling them why.

THE BREAKDOWN OF SELF-REGULATION

One of the most comprehensive statements on the issue of evil by a social psychologist is Roy Baumeister's previously mentioned book, *Evil: Inside Human Violence and Cruelty*. Baumeister is convinced that the primary reason for human evil is the breakdown of inner controls and self-regulation, a breakdown that is often justified by cultural beliefs. The two primary components of evil are an infliction of harm and the unleashing of chaos.[22] For Baumeister, if we are to understand evil adequately, we must examine it not just from the perspective of the victim, but also from the angle of the perpetrator as well. Baumeister is convinced that this is the only way to grasp a genuine understanding of the roots of evil. As he puts it:

> The main goal of this book is psychological understanding, not moral analysis. It will be necessary for me to tune out the overwhelmingly powerful victim's perspective to understand the perpetrators, and it will be necessary for you, the reader, as well. This is a technique to aid understanding, and we must now allow it to lead to a moral insensitivity. I do not want to make apologies or offer excuses for people who commit terrible actions. I do want to understand them, however, and it is necessary to understand the excuses, rationalizations, minimizations, and ambiguities that mark their state of mind.[23]

In other words, Baumeister, as a social psychologist, is attempting much the same thing that a psychotherapist would do—namely, temporarily bracketing moral judgments for the sake of psychological understanding. This does not mean that the world of morality is permanently abandoned. Instead, it is a commitment to descriptive understanding before one resumes a moral attitude toward the behavior.

Why is this so important? Because perpetrators are often seen only through the eyes of the victim. From the victim's perspective, the perpetrator's acts look completely purposeful and intentionally vicious. In fact, the victim may even "read into" the motives of the perpetrator characteristics that are not really present. For instance, if someone holds me up at gunpoint, I may say that they enjoyed intimidating me and felt a rush from the fact that I was scared. In reality, however, the robber may simply want the money. The gun, along with the fear it induced, is simply a necessary or instrumental part of the robbery. If he could have robbed me without my noticing it, that may have been what he preferred. Thus victims understandably interpret an event in terms of its impact on them.

Perpetrators, on the other hand, often believe they are completely justified in their actions. A deliberately sadistic act based on a lust for destruction, says Baumeister, is very rare. Granted, it happens, but not that often. Evil is much more subtle than that.

Baumeister suggests that we often like to view evil in this obvious black-or-white manner because it allows us to separate ourselves completely from foul, destructive individuals. They are totally unlike us in every way. We don't want evil to be ordinary. And we want evil to immediately announce itself as evil. The idea that evil could often come clothed as a "good thing" unnerves us: "The perpetrators of evil are often ordinary, well-meaning human beings with their own motives, reasons, and rationalization for what they are doing. Although victims deserve to be heard, their views cannot be taken as the definitive account of why the perpetrators acted as they did. To reach an understanding, it is necessary to hear what perpetrators have to say."[24] Listening to perpetrators is not an easy task. They often see themselves as victims. Batterers, for instance, often identify themselves as the victims of spouse abuse in cases of domestic violence. These perpetrators are often hypersensitive to any outside criticism.

For Baumeister, then, a genuine understanding of human destructiveness must risk a position that is often condemned—namely, sympathizing with the victim but not taking the victim's account as the total, objective truth, particularly when it comes to understanding the motives and thinking process of the perpetrators. "It is true that perpetrators have reasons for shading and altering the truth, but victims appear to have their own wants and needs that alter the way they describe what happened. One cannot rely on either the victim's story or the perpetrator's; the reality may lie somewhere in between."[25]

All of this is a way of saying that to understand human destructiveness, we must counter what Baumeister calls the "myth of pure evil." This myth suggests that evil is 100 percent impure, malicious, vile, and destructive. There are "good" people and there are "bad" people. In every human altercation, the point is to find out who is the villain. And the villain always has completely malicious motives. This image is greatly reinforced in our culture by movies that present the antagonist as evil through and through, while the victim is the epitome of innocence. This myth of pure evil, in spite of its lack of empirical support, continues to dominate images in popular culture.

Yet Baumeister is aware that this is very politically incorrect to admit. For instance, take the example of domestic violence. There is no doubt about the fact that it is completely inappropriate for a man to hit a woman (or vice versa). But the myth of pure evil can easily interpret the situation in a manner that denies the mutual provocation and aggression which are a part of most domestic fights. One person is evil and the other is a completely innocent victim. The evil abuser simply decides, out of his or her own maliciousness, to wreak havoc on the rest of the innocent family. Sometimes this does indeed happen and it is dreadful. But most of the time, there is a mutual, escalating violence that culminates in the sad conclusion of physical abuse. "Researchers who study marital violence are quite familiar with these cycles of mutual, escalating violence."[26] But most of us would rather see violence in black-or-white terms. Who's innocent and who's guilty? This is the question we bring to conflict.

Most people wish to see violence in morally clear terms with innocent, virtuous victims and evil, malicious perpetrators. In fact, however, most people become violent only when they think they have been attacked in some way. . . . It is far more likely that in a marriage full of mutual resentment, hostility, power struggles, and occasional exchanges of ugly and cruel remarks, one person may cross the line into physical violence when he or she feels the spouse's actions were unfair and unacceptable.[27]

This in no way excuses physical abuse. It is always inappropriate. Yet Baumeister insists that we must understand the context in which violence occurs if we are to grasp its full dynamic adequately.

It is important, according to Baumeister, to move away from this "myth of pure evil." But what are the characteristics of this myth? Baumeister lists several. First is the notion that evil always involves intentional harm and is therefore deliberately destructive. Second is the idea that evil wishes to inflict pain primarily for the pleasure it experiences while doing so. Stated differently, all evil is sadistic. Third, victims are completely innocent and good. Victims are always simply going about their own business when they are suddenly ambushed by evil. The evil one is always repulsive. Fourth, evil is "the other," the "enemy," the "outsider." Evil is always foreign and not "us." Fifth, evil is unchanging. Evil people have always been bad even in the earliest days of their childhoods. Sixth, evil is the antithesis of peace, order, and stability. It is chaotic and irrational and intrudes upon the normal routines of life. Seventh, evil characters are always egocentric, arrogant, and full of themselves. They never lack self-esteem; instead, they overestimate their own worth. And finally, evil people cannot maintain control over their feelings, especially their rage and anger. Baumeister admits, however, that the last two characteristics, which concern egocentricity and self-control, conform to reality far more than the others.

So the myth of pure evil remains popular even though there is a mountain of evidence against it. Baumeister says it is more convenient to believe in it. One's own group remains without blemish. Evil is always "over there," not "here." "It is more comfortable to believe that the world contains evil, malicious people who attack innocent victims for no reason than to believe that one's sufferings are the result of one's own poor judgment and ill-advised actions that provoked a violent response from someone else."[28]

But if Baumeister wants to demythologize the notion of "pure evil," then how does he account for destructive behavior? He suggests four roots of evil. The first of these is *greed, lust, and ambition.* This motivation involves instrumental violence, and not violence for its own sake. In this situation, perpetrators actually prefer avoiding violence if they can get the same results without it. The goal is material gain, not terrorizing people. The perpetrator is willing to go to unfortunate ends to get what he or she wants, but not to commit evil for evil's sake. For instance, criminals may not believe that it is plausible to get what they want by using legitimate means. Therefore, violence becomes a way of getting it. Evil is a shortcut. It's much easier to steal something than to work for it. Evil focuses very narrowly on the present.

A second root of evil, according to Baumeister, is *egotism and revenge.* Threats to self-esteem provoke a need for aggression and revenge. Baumeister is very aware of the fact that this characteristic of evil runs counter to much of self-help literature in psychology:

> My conclusion that violent people tend to have highly favorable opinions of themselves runs directly contrary to a well-entrenched view that *low self-esteem* is a major cause of violence. The argument runs something like this. Those who commit crimes and other acts of violence suffer from an inner sense of worthlessness. They believe that the world fails to appreciate them. By striking out, they are trying to gain esteem and prove their positive worth to a doubting world. If society could only provide these unfortunates with a good feeling about themselves, they would not act violently, and crime would be vastly reduced or even ended. . . . Think of the obnoxious, hostile, or bullying people you have known—were they humble, modest, and self-effacing? (That's mainly what low self-esteem looks like). Most of the aggressive people I have known were the opposite: conceited, arrogant, and often consumed with thoughts about how they were superior to everyone else.[29]

For Baumeister, we should dismiss the notion that low self-esteem leads to violence or destructive behavior. It doesn't match the evidence. Yet the issue for Baumeister is more nuanced than this. It is not just people with high self-esteem who are dangerous; instead, the most dangerous people are those with high, but shaky self-esteem. When people have a high opinion of themselves and they regularly receive confirmation of that opinion, they are not prone to violence. However, people who have a high opinion of themselves and do not have this view confirmed by outsiders are much more inclined to become violent. As Baumeister puts it, "the roots of violence lie in the gap between a highly favorable self-appraisal and a bad appraisal by somebody else."[30] Individuals with inflated, but unrealistic self-esteem are naturally going to encounter more threats to their egos. Grandiosity based on one's own misguided assessment will constantly run the risk of being challenged. Thus it is an *unstable* egotism that is the most dangerous. For Baumeister, a person with a genuinely unshakable sense of self-esteem will not normally be violent because he or she will be immune to ego threats. The work of Michel Kernis has also confirmed Baumeister's thesis. In his research, Kernis found that individuals with high and stable self-esteem were the least prone to exaggerated reactivity. On the other hand, people with high but unstable self-esteem were indeed reactionary.[31] Thus Baumeister concludes that hostile people do not really have low self-esteem. Instead, they have a high view of themselves that fluctuates based on daily circumstances.[32] "A fragile ego is another term for a favorable but vulnerable self-opinion."[33]

Many psychotherapists would no doubt respond that this "fragile ego" that seeks to flatter itself is hardly "high" self-esteem. It is instead an attempt to cover up feelings of inadequacy and insecurity. Yet Baumeister is convinced that there are not "deeper" feelings of low self-esteem lurking beneath this posturing. For instance, social-psychological studies of bullies have consistently revealed an *absence* of low self-esteem. By low self-esteem, Baumeister means a weak, passive, self-doubting attitude. Thus there were no signs of secret feelings of low self-esteem.[34] Researcher Dan Olweus, after several years of studying bullies concluded, "In contrast to a fairly common assumption among psychologists and psychiatrists, we have found no indication that the aggressive bullies (boys) are anxious and insecure under a tough surface."[35]

Also, argues Baumeister, if low self-esteem causes violence, then why are there so many people with obvious, nonhidden forms of low self-esteem who are not violent?

> Thus, anyone who wants to salvage the low self-esteem theory has to argue, oddly, that *overt* low self-esteem is nonviolent and only *covert* low self-esteem is violent. In other words, they have to say that low self-esteem is bad only when you can't see it. Aside from the theoretical vacuousness and apparent absurdity of that argument, it begs the question. If low self-esteem is only linked to violence when it is hidden, then one must look at the hiddenness itself as the decisive cause. What is hiding the low self-esteem is, of course, the veneer of egotism and pride. Low self-esteem is only violent when it is combined with a surface pattern of arrogance, confidence, or egotism. Thus we are back to where this argument began. The favorable opinions about the self are the decisive ones in causing violence.[36]

As we have previously seen, this issue of self-esteem frequently involves a battle between social psychologists and clinicians. Just as social psychologists argue that clinicians often overlook the clear research on high self-esteem, clinicians argue that social psychologists miss the underlying dynamics of low self-esteem. What social psychologists call "high, but fragile self-esteem," argue clinicians, is not self-esteem at all. When a self-report of high self-esteem is carefully explored in a clinical setting, the so-called "high self-esteem" is exposed as a defense for underlying feelings of inadequacy. Many psychoanalytic theorists would argue that Baumeister's view on self-esteem is as naïve as he accuses them of being. I doubt seriously that this issue will go away soon.

Another root of evil identified by Baumeister has to do with "true believers and idealists." These are people who believe they are "doing good" the entire time they are actually committing evil. "If you think that you are doing something that is strongly on the side of good, then whoever oppresses you or blocks your work must be against the good—hence, evil."[37] Groups are very crucial for this "idealistic" evil. Passionate convictions reinforced by a group become even more passionate. Groups can be much nastier than individuals, and groups who cling to an absolute can often produce much destruction.

The final root of evil identified by Baumeister is sadism. He states the importance of the issue of sadism: "The question of whether people enjoy harming others—and if they do, the question of how much evil can be explained by this pleasure—is the single most elusive and vexing problem in the entire topic of evil."[38] Baumeister's own conclusion is that sadistic pleasure is genuine, unusual, and gradually acquired. Sadism is rare but real. It appears to be somewhat similar to the dynamics of addiction. Sadism develops a "tolerance" for a certain level of pain infliction and needs more and more to produce the desired effect on the sadist.

So Baumeister wants to move away from any single-cause theory of evil. In attempting to provide a comprehensive view of human destructiveness, he will be accused by some of blaming the victim. His point, as we have seen, is to move away from black-and-white thinking and toward a more adequate grasp of the variables involved in evil behavior. In order to accomplish this, it is necessary to listen to perpetrators (however difficult that may be) as well as victims.

As we have seen, social psychology, and certainly sociology, can often be quite critical of an individualist, dispositional view of human destructiveness. This has been especially prominent in the criticism against an excessively individual focus in psychotherapy. By concentrating on inner issues as the source of pathology and destructiveness, some believe we are ignoring the much more significant world of social influence.

SOCIAL CRITIQUES OF EXCESSIVE INDIVIDUALISM

Throughout the past few decades, social scientists, ethicists, psychotherapists, philosophers, and theologians have been in conflict over whether to privilege individual or social reality in understanding the human condition. In order to locate evil or destructive behavior, should we focus primarily on the inner world of a person or should we see a person as a reflection of sociopolitical and economic structural problems that need repair? Should a psychotherapist, for example, find his or her primary identity as a caretaker of the psyche or a social reformer? Many social critics have proclaimed that psychology has led us down a self-indulgent path of "awareness" intoxication. Worse still, this narrowly individual focus has kept us ignorant about how the private "self" is actually shaped by social and political realities.[39] These ahistorical, asocial, apolitical, psychological perspectives have promoted a naïve notion of the self disconnected from the network of relationships that provides its identity. Critics argue that this model has been consumed with the inner realities of the self while neglecting the systems that mold that self. They encourage us to move from an individual to a systemic focus. These critiques especially accuse psychotherapy of turning attention away from social and political change and toward an extreme self-centeredness void of social responsibility. Christopher Lasch, with his *Culture of Narcissism* in 1978, was a widely-read critic of self-indulgence. But before that, in 1976, Edwin Schur claimed that counselors and psychotherapists have blocked the possibilities for genuine social change by convincing their clients that all of their problems are rooted in their own psyches. This has had the effect of decreasing anger over injustice and turning attention inward. Therapists have been inviting their clients to ask themselves why they are "making themselves angry" rather than doing something about social injustice. Attention is thus moved from the social dimension to the intrapsychic dimension, a move that clearly allows for the continuation of the status quo. This encourages an isolated autonomy that snuffs out the possibility of social change. Put simply, it says we "oppress" ourselves. Thus we interiorize socioeconomic problems and look for magical solutions within. The intrapsychic world is an escape from the actual roots of our problem—the social and political sphere. We can attempt to control our lives by "choosing" not to be upset by things. Thus a new brand of Stoicism allows destructive social structures to continue uninterrupted.

Schur therefore brings the same critique to psychotherapy that Karl Marx brought to religion.[40] Marx postulated that religion, as the opiate of the people, was so preoccupied with an afterlife that it led people to an indifference toward *this* life. It is very hard to stimulate social change in this world when groups of people are obsessed with their rewards in the next world. Similarly, Schur accuses psychotherapy of cultivating a preoccupation with the "inner life" rather than religion's "afterlife." The result, however, is the same. Attention is turned away from social transformation as persons escape into the private, inner world. Therapists therefore serve the priestly function of helping their clients find internal salvation—an intrapsychic healing divorced from the larger context of our lives.

Lasch, in ways similar to Schur, claims that the shift to psychic self-improvement, so typical of the 1970s, grows out of deep pessimism concerning the possibilities for social advancement and transformation that had been a part of the 1960s. The 1970s represent a disenchantment with the possibilities of social change. Therefore, attention is turned toward the ever-expanding personal-growth industry. What is lacking in this inward turn, however, is a sense of historical rootedness in a process larger than ourselves. As isolated, separated individuals, we are cut off from the past and unconcerned with the future. It is as if we are implicitly saying, "The universe begins with me." Our own private, personal experience is elevated as the only standard for truth. The "self" serves as a sanctuary from sociopolitical involvement. Further, a healthy life is associated with an overthrow of all inhibitions and the indulgence of all desires. Lasch believes this attitude is far different from Freud's more modest goal of therapy—to love and to work.[41]

Lasch distinguishes this new brand of narcissism from the rugged individualism of the nineteenth-century transcendentalists such as Emerson and Thoreau. The primary difference is that the narcissist, unlike the rugged individualist who stood on his or her own, craves an audience who will reflect back an exaggerated self. The narcissist relies on others for his or her self-validation. The rugged individualist, on the other hand, is interested in exploring the wilderness, which is clearly outside the self. And he or she doesn't need anyone to watch while this is done.

Therapy, then, has become a new form of religion. This transformation of therapy into religion has been made possible by the decline of religious commitment in the nineteenth and twentieth centuries, and by the inflation of post-Freudian therapeutic claims. These new claims have involved joy, self-actualization, and the fulfillment of human potential. Lasch indicts these pop therapies for sacrificing a far greater realism present in Freud's more modest vision. For Lasch, this conversion of therapy into religion also misses a very important point—namely, that the pop therapies are actually antireligious. Religion attempts to bring us into the larger context of our meaning in the overall scheme of things. In other words, religion raises questions about how we fit into a puzzle much larger than the isolated "self." It seeks an all-encompassing interpretation of reality. Therapy, by contrast, typically attempts to reduce reality to individual awareness. Therapy is therefore unequipped to handle questions about ultimate meaning and purpose.[42]

While applauding much of Schur's argument, Lasch takes issue with Schur on a very important point.[43] While Lasch agrees with Schur that individuals can run away from their social and political responsibilities by a flight into the self, he also thinks that individuals can run away from their inner lives by a preoccupation with social and political issues. Stated differently, compulsive social action can involve a retreat from the frightening inner world of the self.

Paul Vitz also offers a critique of psychology as a new form of religion.[44] In fact, Vitz argues that "selfist" psychology has become a secularized religion of self-adoration. Similar to Lasch, Vitz argues that a radical preoccupation with individual rights has led our culture to believe that concepts such as "duty," "denial," or "inhibition," reflect a "primitive" way of thinking. Vitz goes for the jugular of "selfist" psychology—namely, the belief in the actualizing tendency. He uses biological evolution to argue against a unidirectional growth tendency. In fact, he believes we have a tendency toward selfishness that often obscures the collective moral wisdom of the past.[45] For Vitz, individualistic psychology tries to reify the social order into a "monster" that sabotages individual expansion. Sounding much like Jean-Jacques Rousseau, individualist psychologists portray society as the culprit which contaminates basic individual goodness. How easily we forget that the social order is humanly constructed and maintained.

Another critique of self-centered psychology comes from the pen of Martin Gross in his book *The Psychological Society*.[46] Gross believes that a new psychology has made messianic promises it could never keep. It has proclaimed that we would have no failure, no unhappiness, no crime, and no malevolence if we could simply "adjust" our psyches. But rather than providing security, this preoccupation with self has increased, not decreased, our anxiety and insecurity. Like other critics, Gross also indicts psychology for taking on a religious demeanor. Psychological parishioners are devotees of the religion of buried psyche as they continually search for the "hidden" or "true" person who peeks through the unconscious from time to time. The unconscious becomes clear when we speak to a therapist-priest who helps us with our intrapsychic "revelation." In this religion of the unconscious, our conscious mind becomes a "second-class being" or puppet controlled by the unconscious.[47] We can control our lives only if we learn the mysteries of psychology, a contemporary form of Gnosticism. Like a witch doctor, the therapist will help us if we give him or her power and money. Gross is especially fond of Jerome Frank's comment that the mental-health industry creates its own customers.[48] Gross differs from Lasch in that he includes Freud and the psychoanalytic tradition in his indictment. Also, he thinks that instead of excessive individualism, this self-worship actually leads to conformism. We give ourselves over too easily to the latest self-help guru.

However they may state their objections, these critics all share a central concern: psychology and the psychotherapy it has produced has led our culture toward narcissistic self-indulgence. Individual issues are at the forefront and social responsibility remains in the shadows. Therapies in the last half of the twentieth century have been driven by an underlying ethical egoism. One's own sense of self-actualization is the standard for one's life. Little attention is paid to the dilemma of *my* self-actualization running into *your* self-actualization. But if it does, the underlying premise seems to be that my own fulfillment is the most significant criteria for all ethical decision making. As Don Browning and I have suggested in a previous publication, most of the humanistic psychologies have assumed a preestablished state of harmony in which all persons can self-actualize without bumping into each other.[49] But simultaneous self-actualization may not be possible in many of life's circumstances. Many couples, for instance, know the struggle of maintaining an equal regard relationship as they each take times sacrificing for each other. An example from my own experience quickly comes to mind.

One of my undergraduate professors received a fellowship to study at Yale for one year. His wife, a very bright woman who was applying to law school anyway, decided that since they were going to New Haven, she might as well take her chances on getting into Yale Law School. She was accepted and did very well during her first year there. As the end of the year approached, however, my professor was left with the cold reality that if he did not return to his position at a midwestern university, he would lose his teaching post. He felt that he had no right to ask his wife to return with him and he fully expected that she would finish law school at Yale. To complicate matters, they had two children whom they deeply loved. They decided to go back to the midwestern university where she would finish her law studies and he would resume his teaching. Many would say that she "sold out" and sacrificed her own actualization for the sake of her family. But as I talked with her about it, it was quite clear why she made this decision. Her husband was very willing to go back to the Midwest and either take the kids or leave them with her, depending on what would be most helpful to her. But neither of them wanted to be away from each other or their children. Thus she turned down an opportunity to graduate from Yale because having her family together was a higher priority than the prestige of an Ivy League law degree. I had no doubt that he would have done the same thing had the situation been reversed. While she would have loved to have graduated from Yale, the self-actualization of various family members was in conflict. Later, it would be her husband's turn to sacrifice. It was a mutual relationship based on equal regard, but this was *not* an easy decision. The idea that we can all simply "blossom together" without struggles of negotiation and compromise is often quite naïve.

Another factor that has contributed to this lack of ethical focus in humanistic psychology, especially, is that therapists have assumed that if their clients reconnect with the organismic actualizing tendency, then moral decisions will simply come naturally. Just as there is a biological unfolding of growth, so there will be a natural inclination to know intuitively how to act morally. Thus the need for ethical principles or guidance has been downplayed. One will simply "know what to do" as issues come up. And the humanistic psychologists have not been alone in this assumption. Freud, for instance, also assumed that post-analyzed individuals will simply know how to be ethical.

Don Browning was one of the first to sound the alarm concerning the issue of ethics in psychotherapy with his 1976 book, *The Moral Context of Pastoral Care.*[50] While written primarily to pastoral counselors, this book served as an important wake-up call to all those working in the helping professions. Perhaps the heart of Browning's effort can be stated in this reflection:

> When pastoral care relinquishes the attempt to reestablish at the level
> of the individual, a sense of normative values that might be shared by
> a general public, it is furthering the process of privatism and pietism.
> An ethos which suggests that moral values are to be bracketed and
> relegated to the private tastes of individuals involved makes one more
> contribution to the general idea that there is no shared or public moral
> universe. In that case, secular individualism becomes the dominant
> style of the day.[51]

Browning knows quite well that, in the process of therapy, a therapist will temporarily bracket ethical concerns so that a client can explore internal conflicts. This psychological exploration demands an atmosphere free of moral judgment. Yet we can relax and temporarily suspend ethical considerations because the counselee already has a normative set of values and ethical commitments. The point is not to *live* in such suspension. Yet some individuals do not seem to emerge from a sense of ethical guidelines and moral obligation. What happens to those clients who enter a counseling relationship with very little regard for others or for ethical standards? Put simply, some clients seem to offer few ethical commitments *to suspend*! Yet psychotherapists should not encourage clients to *live* in that suspended state. When that happens, nonjudgmental acceptance becomes cheap grace. And cheap grace promotes a kind of thoughtless ethical egoism in which one's own dislikes or pleasures become the guiding principle in one's ethical life.

Almost twenty years after Browning's book, William Doherty wrote a well-received book on the connection between moral issues and psychotherapy.[52] Echoing some of the insights of Browning, Doherty states the central aim of his book:

> This book argues that therapists since the time of Freud have
> overemphasized individual self-interest, giving short shrift to family
> and community responsibilities. It calls for the inclusion of moral

discourse in the practice of psychotherapy and the cultivation in
therapists of the virtues and skills needed to be moral consultants to
their clients in a pluralistic and morally opaque world. I argue that
issues of moral responsibility and community well-being are always
present in therapy, and that carefully balanced attention to these
issues can greatly expand the contributions of psychotherapy to the
alleviation of human problems.[53]

Doherty argues that the absence of a moral vocabulary in psychotherapy
results from the belief that psychological explanations eliminate any
need for ethical discussion. Psychological science can replace older
moral language and show that the *only* reason that individuals engage in
destructive behavior is because of their own internal conflicts. Clear up the
psychological conflict and the "moral" issue will disappear. Immorality is a
by-product of psychological dysfunction. The idea that one might actually
do something destructive and *not* be conflicted about it seems impossible
to some therapists.

Doherty also argues that recent cultural changes have created an entirely
different moral context for counseling. He suggests that during Freud's life,
and through the next sixty years of psychotherapy's history, therapists could
safely assume that their clients came to their offices with an abundance of
guilt and self-condemnation. Having been oppressed by a strict morality
and self-condemnation, they needed a little therapeutic liberation. And
Doherty recognizes that some such individuals still appear in therapist's
offices. Yet has the trend not changed? Rather than excessive self-blame,
Doherty wonders if some client's blame themselves for *anything*.

By the 1990s, however, whatever served as the moral center of
mainstream culture seems not to be holding. Massive cheating in the
business world and in military academics, unprecedented levels of
crime and violence, shocking reports of physical and sexual abuse in
families, widespread abandonment of children by divorced as well
as never-married fathers followed by justifications based on personal
entitlement, doing one's own thing, or victimization—these are all
examples of trends that undermine any concern that contemporary

Americans have overlearned a rigidly conventional morality that they must be liberated from by an army of psychotherapists.[54]

Thus, to continue assuming that today's counselees suffer the pain and guilt of having been *overly* moralized rather than *under* moralized perpetuates a culture of social and communal disregard while it promotes narcissistic ethics. As Doherty states it very well, "Psychological language tends to be long on explanations and short on responsibility."[55]

SUMMARY

This chapter has been concerned with the relationship between an individual, dispositional approach to human destructiveness and a situationist approach that accents the social factors affecting those so-called individual actions. We began with a look at two very important social psychologists, Stanley Milgram and Philip Zimbardo. We raised the difficult question as to whether their studies adequately explain the destructive obedience evident in the Holocaust. We further looked at Roy Baumeister's attempt to both dispute the "myth of pure evil" and offer four sources of destructive behavior. We then returned to the question driving this chapter—namely, should an individual, psychotherapeutic approach be preferred over a social and systemic attempt to explain evil? We examined some rather biting criticisms of the excessive individualism in contemporary culture.

Yet we are hardly done with this question. In fact, it will propel the next chapter's concern with whether to privilege an individual or social perspective on the theological issue of sin. This controversy is quite lively in current discussion. It is to this issue that we turn.

CHAPTER SIX

INDIVIDUAL AND SYSTEMIC EVIL

SHOULD ONE BE PRIVILEGED OVER THE OTHER?

. . . women's problems are not individualistic but social
and corporate in origin and nature. Social structures create
individual ills. —*Marjorie Hewitt Suchocki*

In the long run, warped social structures are consequences not
causes of human greed, pride, insecurity, and self-concern which
in turn flow from the exercise of freedom, not its oppression.
—*Langdon Gilkey*

As we saw in the last chapter, psychologists are often divided over whether destructive behavior has primarily individual or social origins. While some look toward dispositional or internal explanations for evil behavior, many social psychologists point toward the surrounding situation that pressures ordinary people to do quite destructive things. Both sides accuse the other of reductionism: psychologically oriented thinkers argue that we must not reduce the "self" to a sociopolitical construction; socially oriented thinkers insist that we must not reduce sociopolitical processes to intrapsychic issues.

This tension concerning whether to privilege an individual or a social understanding of human destructiveness has also deeply affected theological conceptions of sin. At the risk of oversimplifying things a bit, we could perhaps say that Christian thought has moved in the following direction over the past century: at the turn of the twentieth century, liberal theology, having been heavily influenced by nineteenth-century progressive optimism, focused a great deal on the social causes of evil and destructiveness. This involved a common assumption that humanity could usher in the kingdom of God through social transformation. Put simply, our individual woes were in reality social, economic, and political in nature. If we could clean up our social world, become more educated, and provide greater opportunities for people, we could surely flourish. The notion of personal sin took a backseat to social evil. Our problems revolved around ignorance, poverty, and lack of opportunities. The human heart was essentially good, but stuck in a world with unfortunate social structures. The concept of original sin, if it had any meaning at all, simply pointed to the social transmission of injustice.

Later in the twentieth century, however, the whistle would be blown on both nineteenth-century optimism and the early twentieth-century focus on social sin. The writings of Karl Barth, Emil Brunner, Rudolf Bultmann, Karl Rahner, Paul Tillich, Reinhold Niebuhr, and others would give theological voice to an older Kierkegaardian understanding of sin as rooted in our anxious finitude and misused freedom. A focus on the existential, personal, and intrapsychic dynamics of sin emerged. This perspective was reinforced by many destructive events in the twentieth century.

Gradually, however, this existential and personal focus on sin was charged with excessive individualism and even narcissism. This view, it was said, treated human beings as disembodied, ahistorical persons lacking social, gender, race, and class identities. In other words, this view of the person was too abstract and universal. The specific differences between people were overlooked. Worse still, the so-called essential human qualities of personhood were defined largely by white men in positions of power. Women and other minorities were overlooked. Their stories did not become a part of the master narrative of the human condition. Marginalized voices were not heard. Persons in power dictated the portrait of the human condition, a portrait flat in color because of its diversity-denying tendencies.

This "totalizing" discourse committed a form of intellectual genocide. Again, voices outside of the "norm" were simply not heard.

This new perspective identified oppression, the foul enemy of freedom, as the primary evil. And this evil was fundamentally systemic and social. A preoccupation with individual, private sin has kept us from seeing the big picture: we live in a world wrought with oppressive, dehumanizing, freedom-denying forces. These social structures represent the *real* root of sin and evil. Rather than focusing on individual, personal concerns, clergy need to be challenging the larger problems of sexism, racism, classism, and other forms of oppression. Liberation theologies gained more and more momentum as the notions of "freedom" and "salvation" were often equated. This new social and systemic perspective, along with its focus on oppression as the primary sin, has been called a "paradigm shift" in pastoral care and counseling.[1]

The question quickly emerged, "Which form of oppression is primary?" For early feminist theologians, the most basic sin was sexism and patriarchy. Surely this gender inequality and violence toward one-half of the population represents the root of sin. Yet others quickly suggested that not all women share the same plight. Audre Lorde put the issue directly: "If white American feminist theory need not deal with the differences between us, and the resulting difference in our oppressions, then how do you deal with the fact that the women who clean your houses and tend to your children while you attend conferences on feminist theory are, for the most part, poor women and women of Color? What is the theory behind racist feminism?"[2]

Thus a competition emerged as to which form of oppression is the most basic. Put another way, What is the central form of oppression from which other forms are derivative? Perhaps most theologians of liberation would agree with Eleazar Fernandez's statement, "I suggest that we view the four systemic forms of oppression [classism, sexism, racism, naturism] in dynamic interaction, and recognize that the predominance of one over the other shifts in different contexts along with the interaction of several factors."[3]

This controversy over individual versus social sin is very much still with us. While many understand the importance of both forms of sin, an emphasis is often placed on one form over the other. Before examining more fully some feminist and other liberation critiques of a theology of sin, let's examine the work of two prominent theologians, Langdon Gilkey and Reinhold Niebuhr, who represent a view of sin as excessive self-regard.

SIN REAFFIRMED: LANGDON GILKEY AND SHANTUNG COMPOUND

Langdon Gilkey, one of America's most prolific theologians in the second half of the twentieth century, witnessed a disturbing picture of the human condition *before* he later studied with his two mentors, Reinhold Niebuhr and Paul Tillich. For two-and-a-half years, Gilkey was a prisoner in a civilian internship in North China during America's war with Japan.[4] Life in this camp provided a unique and rare opportunity to observe others (and himself) in a crowded, highly insecure situation that often did not bring out the best in "civilized" people. At the time, Gilkey was a bachelor of twenty-four. He lived in three small eight-by-twelve-foot rooms with eleven other bachelors. There were almost two thousand people in the camp and many of the families were extremely pressed for space. Gilkey had the interesting opportunity to serve on the housing committee. As such, he dealt with many of the "space" problems. With everyone being so crowded, the physical closeness quickly led to a need for more psychological space as well. Privacy was nearly impossible.

At first, Gilkey was quite pleased with the progress of this microcivilization. Surely this reaffirmed the humanistic, progressive faith that had been deeply engrained in his upper-middle-class, educated life in America. As time continued, however, this view was severely challenged. Here's the way Gilkey describes it:

> By the end of the first month of camp, my view of life was being
> altered. I went back to the confident humanism so characteristic of
> the liberal academic circles in America I had recently quitted. As I
> looked around me during those early weeks, I felt convinced that man's
> ingenuity in dealing with difficult problems was unlimited, making
> irrelevant those so-called "deeper issues" of his spiritual life with which
> religion and philosophy pretended to deal. . . . Gradually, however,

as I encountered more and more unexpected problems in my work in housing, I began to realize that this confident attitude toward things simply did not fit the realities of camp life. It was not that our material crises seemed any less urgent, or that our minds were any less capable of dealing with them. Rather, new sorts of problems kept arising that improved know-how could not resolve. For over and over what we can only call "moral" or "spiritual" difficulties continually cropped up. Crises occurred that involved not a breakdown in techniques, but a breakdown in character, showing the need for more moral integrity and self-sacrifice. The trouble with my new humanism, I found myself deciding, was not its confidence in human science and technology. It was rather its naïve and unrealistic faith in the rationality and goodness of the men who wielded these instruments. If the courage and ingenuity of man were evidenced in every facet of camp life, equally apparent was the intense difficulty all of us experienced in being fair-minded, not to say just or generous, under the hard pressure of our rough and trying existence. . . . On a critical level equal to an outbreak of dysentery or a stoppage of our bread supply, these moral breakdowns were so serious that they threatened the very existence of our community.[5]

This crisis became so bad at times that Gilkey was glad there were armed Japanese guards available to dispel uncontrollable violence.

Gilkey describes how, in one situation, a group of eleven men occupied a small space while a group of nine men occupied the same amount of space. Surely it would make good sense to send one person from the group of eleven over to the group of nine, thus balancing it out fairly, ten and ten. Yet he never suspected that he would encounter such violent resistance to this switch. When he approached the group of nine men, the response he got was, "Sure we're sorry for those chaps over there. But what has that got to do with us? We're plenty crowded here as it is, and their worries are their tough luck. Listen, old boy, we're not crowding up for you or anyone!"[6] These men further reported that if he sent anyone over, they would throw him out.[7] If a change meant losing even an inch or two of space, regardless of how reasonable and just it was, these individuals fought it with all their being. As Gilkey puts it, "Self-interest seemed almost omnipotent to the weak claims of logic and fair play."[8] In fact, there was only one case in which a person was willing to make an unpleasant change because it was the fair and rational thing to do. From extreme justification to violent language to getting doors shut in his face, Gilkey found that compassion went out the door when it came to issues of "space."

> "Out of those forty-four families, everyone saw *only* the logic of his own case," I reflected. "If that is at all typical of human affairs, then what sort of reality *is* there to the concept of 'impartial reason?' For when it is needed most desperately, that is, when the stakes are high for both parties and they begin to be overwrought, then impartial reason is sadly conspicuous by its absence! Does it fly away every time it is needed, to return only when harmony reigns, when the conflict is over? If that is so, then surely reason is more a symptom or effect of social harmony that it is a cause—and if *that* is so, from whence can we expect social health to come?"[9]

Even a missionary rationalized to Gilkey that because he had to prepare a lot of sermons for others and wanted to do a good job *for them*, he clearly needed more space. Gilkey's view of human beings, and this included himself, was undergoing a major change. Self-interest overwhelmingly seemed to push issues of fairness, reason, and justice out of the way. Worse still, reason and appeals to fairness were used as instruments of self-interest. All sorts of moral reasons could be pitched for something that ultimately served the interests of the self. When life is calm and unthreatened, it is easy to be numb and unaware of this hounding voice of self-interest. It is camouflaged. But when life becomes uncomfortable, a hostile self-concern can easily take over. In fact, an important point can thus be stated: Gilkey found that a moral commitment was necessary in order to think rationally, rather than rationality leading naturally to moral commitment. Reason was all too easily employed for self-interest. Moral character allowed for the possibility of rationality, rather than the reverse.

On other occasions, this self-interest raised its head in a selfish preoccupation with food parcels that arrived. While there were enough for everyone, many claimed a monopoly on them and ended up causing a postponement of their delivery. If the food had simply been used for the good of the entire community, there would have been no problem. In fact, it would have been a welcomed blessing. But instead, greed and self-centeredness ruined the possibility of communal unity.

What is crucial here, particularly in light of our previous discussions of Milgram's experiments, is Gilkey's conviction that a marginal situation such as camp life does not "make" a person wicked, but instead reveals an intense self-regard that is already present. Gilkey had previously believed that in severe situations, the goodness of humanity would quickly come forward. These marginal situations would reveal our true character—helpful, compassionate, and even other-centered. Not true. Yet the marginal situation did not change human character for the better or worse. It simply intensified and exposed what is already there. Extreme situations thus *expose* rather than *create* natural inclinations. Here, then, Gilkey's perspective is at odds with Milgram's emphasis on the powers of the situation to change ordinary, decent folk into destructive people.

Also, Gilkey was well aware that many intellectuals would interpret this camp experience as the inheritance of our animal instincts that had not yet been brought under rational control. Yet, "the selfishness that had shown itself so widely among the internees was by no means merely 'instinctual.' Its roots lay in fears concerning the self's security which only a self-conscious and intelligent being could experience."[10]

> Man's mind thus adds dimensions to his instinctive "will to live" that quite change its character. Here the will to live, because now conscious and intelligent, becomes the much more dynamic will to power and will to possess an infinity of goods. Men and animals both want to survive, and in both this might be called "instinctual." But because he is made up of spirit as well as instinct, mind as well as organic drives, man is much more dangerous to his fellows in his effort, and much more rapacious in his demands for goods. To call this behavior "instinct" is to minimize the relative innocence of our animal cousins, and to exonerate the spiritual, mental, and conscious elements in our nature which are even more deeply involved. . . . [M]an's problem is

not just a matter of enlightened minds and devoted wills controlling a rebellious instinctive nature. Rather man is to be seen as a totality, a unified being made of body and of instincts, of consciousness and subconscious, of intelligence and will, all in baffling and complex interaction. And it is that total psychological organism, that total existing self in its unity, which determines whether the "higher" powers of mind and of will are going to be used creatively or destructively.[11]

This excessive self-interest seemed to imprison camp members even when they wanted to break free of it. The promotion of one's own interests outweighed a concern for others. "Though quite free to will whatever we wanted to in a given situation, we were not free to will to love others, because the will did not really want to. We were literally bound in our own sin."[12] Thus Gilkey found two primary truths about the human condition: (*a*) humanity desperately needs to be morally concerned about its neighbor's welfare for community to be possible, and (*b*) on their own, humans cannot seem to overcome their self-concern in order to accomplish this. Changing one's thinking is not enough. Instead, one needs to find a new center for security and health, a center that transcends the demanding voices of the self. Insecurity and anxiety are not healed by more intense self-preoccupation. In fact, that makes things worse.

In Shantung Compound, Gilkey's faith in the goodness of humanity was severely altered. Yet what is interesting to Gilkey is the fact that humanists so often stay committed to their credo in spite of so much evidence for excessive self-regard and a corresponding disregard for one's neighbor.

Liberal humanists often express amazement that their apparently intelligent Christian friends believe many things about God which cannot be proved. At least the Christian can answer that what he believes about God cannot be disproved. But the main article of faith of the humanist, namely the goodness of mankind and man's consequent capacity to be moral, is refuted by any careful study of human nature. If it is unreasonable to hold a religious faith that cannot be demonstrated, surely it is irrational to defend a humanistic faith that the evidence so universally contradicts.[13]

The way out of this dilemma is to find a true center of existence in the ultimate source of God's love. Without such a center, a series of idolatries will confound our lives and we will give ourselves over to gods unworthy of our ultimate concern. "Given an ultimate security in God's eternal love, and an ultimate meaning to his own small life in God's eternal purposes, a man can forget his own welfare and for the first time look at his neighbor free from the gnawings of self-concern."[14]

While Gilkey left Shantung Compound with some keen observations about the human condition, those observations found greater explication and analysis when he studied with Reinhold Niebuhr at Union Seminary. Niebuhr provided a vivid conceptual map that made Gilkey's experience much more understandable.

NIEBUHR, ANXIETY, AND SIN

Reinhold Niebuhr's theological anthropology, stated so eloquently in *The Nature and Destiny of Man*, is surely one of the twentieth century's most important theological reflections on the human condition.[15] Niebuhr breathed new life into the concept of original sin. While he deliteralized the Adamic story, he nevertheless showed the extreme relevance this myth has for our own time. This focus on sin pushed Niebuhr away from the optimistic liberalism he had learned from his father, as well as some of his earlier professors.

Niebuhr makes a very interesting case study for this chapter's focus on the conflicts between an individual and social emphasis on sin. On the one hand, Niebuhr was enormously influenced by the nineteenth-century existentialist Søren Kierkegaard. Kierkegaard, who was rediscovered by the neoorthodox theologians, emphasized the inevitable, internal dilemma of anxiety brought on by human existence. We are able to think about our own finitude, how our choices define us, and realize that we are going to die. This ontological anxiety, rather than merely a neurotic anxiety, provokes us to seek security in finite things that cannot possibly provide the assurance we need. Anxiety is therefore not sin, but the precondition or forerunner of sin. It is in this state of profound anxiety that we often make ourselves the center of life and act destructively toward others. As we saw from Gilkey's experience, individuals do some ugly things when they feel threatened.

On the other hand, Niebuhr was parented by the social-gospel movement, had great respect for its icon, Walter Rauschenbusch, and never lost his profound concern for social justice. In fact, Niebuhr very much disliked a preoccupation with personal piety, particularly when it was at the expense of social concerns. Clearly he is known primarily as a social ethicist, as one who kept an eye on social manifestations of sin.

For Niebuhr, the rub came with the view of humanity that accompanied the social gospel. As Niebuhr grew older, he began to identify this perspective on humanity as Pelagian because it indicated that humanity can resolve its own dilemmas apart from an appeal to the transcendent. As we have seen, nineteenth- and early twentieth-century Protestant liberalism largely held that human beings come into the world with an innate ability to be altruistic, to progress toward greater and greater spiritual growth, and with proper education, social and economic support, to usher in the kingdom of God.

But World War I, along with a pastorate in Detroit in which he regularly watched Henry Ford exploit autoworkers, began to change Niebuhr's thinking. He frequently said that when the war started he was an optimist trying not to fall into sentimentality. But by the time the war ended, he was a realist trying hard to not be a cynic. After the First World War, he could no longer believe there was a smooth continuity between Western civilization and the kingdom of God. In Detroit, he had seen deplorable working conditions, poor benefits, and exploitation everywhere. He saw Henry Ford's pretentious claims about offering humanitarian conditions as a disguise for greed and personal advancement. When Niebuhr became active in the labor movement, he found that most of the churches supported the status quo and didn't want to question management. The moral pretentiousness of the industrialists and the church's indifference toward injustice would be two major themes throughout the rest of Niebuhr's life.

Influenced by Marx, Niebuhr believed that religion often *is* the opiate of the people as it gives sanction to oppressive groups. Institutional religion, unfortunately, can be a tool of the status quo and an impediment to social change. Yet Niebuhr went beyond Marx's negative view of religion and found resources within prophetic faith to stand up against the prevailing injustice in the social order. He believed that prophetic religion has the seeds within it to challenge all social orders and push them toward greater justice. Also, Niebuhr was convinced that Marx did not look deeply enough into the human condition. Marx, according to Niebuhr, naïvely believed that once today's oppressed are liberated, there will not be any further oppression. This optimistic eschatology was unrealistic. History clearly reveals that those who are oppressed today, when they are released, often oppress others. Thus even Marx falls prey to a gullible optimism about the human condition as he exclusively locates "sin" in socioeconomic injustice. For Marx, all so-called individual problems are in reality social and economic problems. There is nothing "wrong" with our psyches. Thus, once the social and political demons are exorcised, the intrapsychic demons will disappear also. The problem is certainly not *within* us. Niebuhr could not accept the moral optimism of Protestant liberalism, Marxism, or any other utopian thinking. He further did not believe that clearing away all social and political problems would automatically lead to a "sinless" world.

For Niebuhr, we are clearly a "mixture" of nature and spirit. By this, Niebuhr means that while we are finite, limited, and contingent creatures, we are also capable of "stepping outside" this contingency and reflecting on the totality of our lives, a self-consciousness which realizes, among other things, that we are going to die. This capacity for self-transcendence is what it means to be created in the "image of God." Niebuhr states it this way: "In its purest form the Christian view of man regards man as a unity of God-likeness and creatureliness in which he remains a creature even in the highest spiritual dimensions of his existence and may reveal elements of the image of God even in the lowliest aspects of his natural life."[16] Thus, no matter how "lofty" and other-worldly our spirituality may seem, we are still embodied creatures, and this embodiment is not sin. Like Augustine, Niebuhr regularly fought against any form of Manicheism that presented our natural, physical lives as inherently evil. And at the same time, no matter how far we fling ourselves into a spirit-denying indulgence of the flesh, we cannot eradicate the capacity for self-transcendence. Put another way, we cannot "get rid of" the image of God within us.

Because we are both immersed in the contingencies of life and capable of reflecting on those contingencies, we experience anxiety. For Niebuhr, however, as for Tillich, this anxiety is not a neurotic anxiety that can be eliminated through psychotherapy or education. This anxiety is not pathological; instead, it is ontological. In other words, it is simply part of our existence, built into our human condition. Again, this anxiety is not itself sin. To call anxiety "sin" would be to condemn human beings for their very existence, since anxiety is a necessary component of human life. Yet anxiety tempts us to sin. Borrowing heavily on Kierkegaard, Niebuhr explains how anxiety is the precondition of sin.

> In short, man, being both free and bound, both limited and limitless, is anxious. Anxiety is the inevitable concomitant of the paradox of freedom and finiteness in which man is involved. Anxiety is the internal precondition of sin. It is the inevitable spiritual state of man, standing in the paradoxical situation of freedom and finiteness. Anxiety is the internal description of the state of temptation. It must not be identified with sin because there is always the ideal possibility that faith would purge anxiety of the tendency toward sinful self-assertion. The ideal possibility is that faith in the ultimate security of God's love would overcome all insecurities of nature and history. That is why Christian orthodoxy has consistently defined unbelief as the root of sin, or as the sin which precedes pride. It is significant that Jesus justifies his injunction, "Be not anxious," with the observation, "For your heavenly Father knoweth that ye have need of those things." The freedom from anxiety which he enjoins is a possibility only if perfect trust in divine security has been achieved. . . . no life, even the most saintly, conforms to the injunction not to be anxious.[17]

This comment is crucial for seeing Niebuhr's differences with various psychologists. As we saw in chapter 3, he differs with Freud in that he does *not* believe, as does Freud, that our natural instincts are innately destructive, out of control, or mechanistically determined by natural forces.[18] We are not so governed by our instincts that we are "biologically wired" to act in destructive, self-centered ways. Put simply, *thanatos* is not part of our created condition. It results instead from a mishandling of our freedom, an anxiety-based scramble to find security and escape our finitude. We are not fated to act in destructive ways. Evil is not "natural" in the sense of being part of our biological inheritance. Thus, while Niebuhr was deeply influenced by Augustine, he deliteralized Augustine's notion of original sin. Instead of sin being biologically inherited, Niebuhr believe that the Adamic story describes in vivid symbols our own experience with temptation.

While Niebuhr disagrees with Freud on the inherent, biological rootedness of human destructiveness, he also parts company with any neo-Freudian or humanistic psychology that locates destructive behavior completely *outside* of the internal state of anxiety. In other words, Niebuhr takes issue with the conviction that human beings engage in destructive behavior *only* because they have been "pushed into it" by external forces. Niebuhr does not think human sin can simply be attributed to the corrupting influences of family or society. This view emphasizes the innocence of the individual and the corrupting nature of society. It sees human destructiveness as an outside-in condition—we only act in unhealthy ways because we have been wounded, hurt, and abused by the family or the larger social system. Sin is not an outgrowth of our own existential anxiety; instead, it is the result of familial and social injustice. We act destructively because we have been treated unfairly.

It is crucial to grasp here a significant difference in the understanding of anxiety. For humanistic psychologists such as Carl Rogers, anxiety results from threats imposed from our relationships with others. If we could create a nonthreatening atmosphere of supportive relationships, our anxiety would not be a problem.[19] There is nothing *within us* that tempts us to act destructively. We are born only with an actualizing tendency that biologically unfolds when the right conditions are present. So the essential argument is this: clean up the psychological environment, and anxiety will not be a problem. Yet Niebuhr, following Kierkegaard, insists that anxiety is *not* simply the result of ineffective relationships; instead, anxiety is part of the human condition, built into our freedom as self-transcending people. We are quite capable of acting in destructive ways simply because of internal temptations born out of an anxious awareness. *Self-consciousness itself carries anxiety, and this tempts us to act in destructive ways.* It is this self-consciousness that can lead to greedy, aggressive, extremely competitive, selfish, and compulsive behavior. We are always tempted to erect forms of security that are not humanly available. Even if we grew up with very "functional" parents, and the healthiest of environments, we would still be tempted to act in destructive ways because of this ontological anxiety. Even if others did not "provoke us" to sin, we would still be tempted out of our internal state.

For humanistic psychology, the internal force toward actualization and growth has no competitor. We experience destructive anxiety only when something is done *to us*. Our experiences with conditional acceptance, the school system, and socioeconomic realities corrupt the self. The linkage with Rousseau is obvious: Our natural state is "corrupted" by social influence.

Niebuhr would no doubt respond that these schools, societies, and cultural trends are made up of *individuals* who perpetuate injustice and the distortions of the self. To be alive is to be anxious, and to be anxious creates the possibility of sin. Destructiveness is always a "live option" in our psyches because we cannot eliminate ontological anxiety. Thus, while Niebuhr was an avid critic of social injustice and group egoistic corruption, he never lost sight of the fact that sin is rooted in our own struggles with anxiety as well as the social transmission of oppression and inequality.

PRIDE AND SELF-OBSESSION

Niebuhr applauds Augustine's refusal to locate the source of sin in the rebellious *behavior* of the first couple. Augustine emphasized that the real source of sin came from the couple's gradual desire to be disconnected from their Creator and to be the Source of their own lives. This desire for God-replacement preceded any rebellious activity. It was the development of an unwarranted self-sufficiency, of pride, that prompted Adam and Eve to disobey God's command. Put differently, the "fall" began in Adam's mind long before he ate the fruit. Augustine states this as follows.

> We can see then that the Devil would not have entrapped man by the
> obvious and open sin of doing what God had forbidden, had not man
> already started to please himself. That is why he was delighted also

with the statement, "You will be like gods." In fact, they would have been better able to be like gods if they had in obedience adhered to the supreme and real ground of their being, if they had not in pride made themselves their own ground. For created goods are gods not in their own true nature but by participation in the true God. By aiming at more, a man is diminished, when he elects to be self-sufficient and defects from the one who is really sufficient to him. . . . This then, is the original evil: man regards himself as his own light, and turns away from that light which would make man himself a light if he would set his heart on it. This evil came first, in secret, and the result was the other evil, which was committed in the open.[20]

Thus, for Augustine, this external disobedience was a result of an internal process that had been gradually developing. The problem was not so much "rebellious" behavior as it was distrust and exaggerated self-sufficiency.

Niebuhr does *not* agree, however, with the extent of the damage done by original sin. For Augustine, we have been so negatively affected by Adam's sin that we do not even realize we are sinners. We can't even diagnose our own condition, much less do anything about it. For Niebuhr, however, we retain a sense of obligation, a need for forgiveness, and a sense that we are dependent on a Reality much larger than ourselves. We somehow know that things are not the way they are supposed to be. This uneasy conscience is a matter of general, and not special, revelation.

Niebuhr also disagrees with Augustine's move from original sin to original guilt. Augustine argued that because of Adam's sin, we do not merely have an inclination to sin; instead, we are already guilty. When Adam rebelled, we all mysteriously made this decision with him. Thus, while Adam was originally created with essential goodness (in fact, perfection), none of the rest of us has ever known this experience. In Augustine's historical-causal explanation, we are biologically "born in sin" and bear the taint of Adam's dreadful decision. While Adam's *essence* may have been good at one time, the essence into which we are born is already flawed and defective. Thus, Augustine, in his battle with the Pelagians, was forced by his own logic to the drastic conclusion that unbaptized babies will be damned. Why? Because they carry the mark of original sin. Embodied existence is sinful because we have inherited a corrupt disposition. Niebuhr offers some insightful comments on the legacy of this literalized account of Genesis.

> Unfortunately, Christian orthodoxy has usually bedeviled this doctrine by trying to construct a history of sin out of the concept of its inevitability. The vice of all mythical religion is that its interpreters try to reduce its suprahistory to actual history. Thus the myth of creation is constructed into an actual history of origins when it is really a description of the quality of existence. The myth of the Fall is made into an account of the origin of evil, when it is really a description of its nature. The orthodox doctrine of "original sin" is an effort to extend the history of sin from its origin through successive generations of mankind. It therefore becomes a doctrine of an "inherited corruption," the precise nature of which could never be found by theologians, but which they most frequently identified with the sexual lust, attendant upon the process of generation. If original sin is an inherited corruption, its inheritance destroys the freedom and therefore the responsibility which is basic to the conception of sin. The orthodox doctrine is therefore self-destructive. Augustine faced this problem, but it is an inevitable fact of human existence, the inevitability of which is given by the nature of man's spirituality. It is true every moment of existence, but is has no history.[21]

As a result of the anxious distortion of our freedom, our relational qualities of faith, hope, and love have been lost. We do not have faith in the ultimate providence of God, and therefore we continue to be overwhelmed with anxiety. We become obsessed with mastering our worlds and often try to control that which is clearly beyond our ability to control. Our anxiety is therefore *increased*, rather than decreased, and our attempts to manage our own lives become even more exaggerated. We often no longer see any creative possibilities in our lives, become entangled in despair, and experience our situation as hopeless. And finally, because of our anxious self-preoccupations, it is not possible for us to genuinely love and attend to the needs of others. As Niebuhr puts it, "Without freedom from anxiety man is so enmeshed in the vicious circle of egocentricity, so concerned, about himself, that he cannot release himself for the adventure of love."[22] We are instead trapped inside our own egocentricity, which is the antithesis of loving others. Thus our problem can be stated as follows: in order to calm our anxiety enough to move away from a frantic self-preoccupation and toward a love of others, we need to trust in the providence of God. Also, as we shall soon see in more detail, Niebuhr is saying that our problem is bigger than a prideful *egotism*; instead, it has to do with an anxious *egoism*. This will be important as we look at Niebuhr's critics who charge him with a narrow focus on self-assertive pride as the primary sin.

For Niebuhr, the condition of pride or excessive self-regard is the "flip side" of a distrust in God. Without this basic trust, our anxiety pushes us into excessive self-preoccupation. Writing, as he did, amidst the emergence of fascist leaders and arrogant power displays, Niebuhr emphasized the pride of self-exaltation and excessive self-assertion. This pride, for Niebuhr, always has a double dimension: "horizonically," it is a denial of our dependency on God, and vertically, it is an immoral oppression and subordination of our brothers and sisters. A distorted relationship with our Source inevitably leads to a distorted relationship with neighbors.

There are four types of empirically verifiable forms of pride. The first is the *pride of power*. In this form of pride, one clearly assumes a self-mastery that ignores the vicissitudes of one's life. This form of pride is insatiable as it seeks more and more power in its attempt to alleviate all threats of insecurity. This drive toward power refuses to look seriously at its own weaknesses. It is ignorantly arrogant as it boasts of its mastery. Its self-inflated opinion eliminates the possibility of dialogue with others.

At times, this form of pride doesn't view itself as having "arrived" yet, but it is nevertheless full of a self-preoccupied, excessive ambition. Whether we think we have arrived or are still on our way, the primary factor is an exaltation of the powerful self. It is important to recognize both forms of pride, because some of Niebuhr's critics argue that he fails to see the insecurity beneath pride. Niebuhr would in fact say that at some level *all* forms of pride contain insecurity buried beneath them because they claim a form of mastery not humanly possible. Thus we are ontologically insecure even if we appear, psychologically, to be secure. Whether one is drunk on the glory of who one *is* or who one *will be* is beside the point. The issue is an undue focus on the self. For instance, even a seemingly insecure person involved in psychotherapy may in fact be trying to reach a place of such complete confidence that he or she is no longer shaken by the vicissitudes of life. The craving for this type of ego fortification can be a form of pride, a desire to attain an unperturbable self.

Because others are perceived as a threat to one's total power and mastery, they must be conquered and subordinated to one's own control. Security necessitates the elimination of the competition. Yet no position of power can assure that others won't rise up as rivals and threaten one's position. And too, even the powerful must come to grips with their own mortality.

> The fact that human ambitions know no limits must therefore
> be attributed not merely to the infinite capacities of the human
> imagination but to an uneasy recognition of man's finiteness, weakness
> and dependence, which become the more apparent the more we
> seek to obscure them, and which generate ultimate perils, the more
> immediate insecurities are eliminated. Thus man seeks to make himself
> God because he is betrayed by both his greatness and his weakness; and
> there is no level of greatness and power which the lash of fear is not at
> least one strand in the whip of ambition.[23]

While insecurity is present in this quest for self-exaltation, Niebuhr highlights the undue focus on self that accompanies the attempt to escape anxiety.

The second type of pride Niebuhr explores is *intellectual pride*. While intellectual pride may be less crude than the will to power, it is nevertheless connected to it. Powerful groups need ideological justification. Intellectual insecurity, like all forms of insecurity, must be conquered in the name of an Absolute. Thus intellectual pride claims to have discovered a cognitive terrain free of ambiguity, a mental world that "owns" the Total Truth.

> All human knowledge is tainted with an "ideological" taint. It pretends
> to be more than it is. It is finite knowledge, gained from a particular
> perspective; but it pretends to be final and absolute knowledge. Exactly
> analogous to the cruder pride of power, the pride of intellect is derived

on the one hand from ignorance of the finiteness of the human
mind and on the other hand from an attempt to obscure the known
conditioned character of human knowledge and the taint of self-
interest in human truth.[24]

Thus intellectual pride claims a pure truth and final word that is
no longer subject to historical and social limitations. As Niebuhr rather
brilliantly put it, "Each great thinker makes the same mistake, in turn of
imagining himself the final thinker."[25] Reason all too easily thinks it has
risen above historical location and speaks for all eternity. It can easily see the
limits in other perspectives but is blind to its own limits. Yet for Niebuhr,
this blindness is not simply an innocent blindness of ignorance. Instead,
our reason often avoids the recognition of it own particularity because it
would rather speak from the standpoint of the Absolute. Thus the pride of
intellect is also driven by a deep anxiety which unconsciously knows that
it, too, is finite.

The next form of pride involves *a sense of moral superiority or self-
righteousness*. In this form of pride, all behavior is judgmentally brought
under the standards of our own group. In fact, the opinions of our own
group are thought to reflect God's ultimate standards: "Moral pride is
the pretension of finite man that his highly conditioned virtue is the final
righteousness and that his very relative moral standards are absolute. Moral
pride thus makes virtue the very vehicle of sin, a fact which explains why the
New Testament is so critical of the righteous in comparison with 'publicans
and sinners'."[26] Self-righteousness, for Niebuhr, is responsible for the most
hurtful injustices, cruelties, and dehumanizing actions in humanity's
history. As Niebuhr puts it, "The whole history of racial, national, religious
and other struggles is a commentary on the objective wickedness and social
miseries which result from self-righteousness."[27]

The last form of pride is *spiritual pride*, an attitude that moves beyond
moral pride by grounding its outlook in a religious framework. On the one
hand, we claim that God is our judge; on the other hand, God is *always* on
our side. This attitude, the ultimate form of pride, legitimates intolerance
toward others in the name of one's God. It smoothly identifies one's own
perspective with that of the Divine. One not only speaks "for God" but one

has the right to carry out God's justice toward those who are different.

Niebuhr's theological anthropology has had enormous influence. It emphasizes the relationship to God as pivotal for understanding human destructiveness. Without a transcendent Source who serves as the grounding, trustworthy center of our lives, we inevitably fall into the absolutizing of relative goods. In other words, we turn limited things into objects of devotion, thus falling into destructive forms of idolatry. This idolatry does not simply affect us. As we scramble to find a final source of security outside of God, we act unethically toward other human beings. Preoccupied with the elimination of our own anxiety, we are not free to see others as fellow travelers. Instead, they become sources of our own exploitation and instruments for our own self-advancement. This excessive self-regard, while taking many forms, always has the consequence of distorting both our individual lives and communities. In fact, these idolatries and egoistic corruptions accumulate into the social structures around us as they embed themselves in our history. Sin is "already present" when we arrive on the scene, waiting for our own participation in it. Evil is both "given" and personally promoted. It is universal.

Also, sin is often connected with an attempt to get rid of ambiguity. But to get rid of ambiguity is to get rid of life. We are ontologically insecure and at some level we know it. We strive relentlessly to change this situation but it persists. Some may argue that we only do destructive things when we feel threatened. But the problem is that, without a trust in God, we *always feel threatened*. Feeling threatened is part of the human package. Thus when psychologists, for instance, suggest that destructive behavior comes only from anxiety, this is like saying that human destructiveness comes only from being human. When anxiety is part of the very essence of being human, we cannot claim anxiety as the "foreign" element that pushes us over the edge.

In similar fashion, we have biologically inherited the capacity to be aggressive for our own defense. This obviously aids the process of survival. But anxiety-provoked aggression usually involves an unnecessary, destructive overreaction. As Edward Farley states very well, "When fear and anxiety lure the human being to absolutizing or to idolatrous relations, this constitutive or 'benign' aggressiveness is transformed into inclinations of malice, avarice, distrust, and cupidity which in turn predispose the person toward acts which violate others."[28] Destructive violence is not a *necessary* part of our being.

Niebuhr thus offers us an understanding of sin that refuses to reduce our human predicament to a series of psychological problems. Sin is not merely an outgrowth of psychopathology. However much we may therapize our inner demons, we are still stuck with the human predicament—namely, we are anxious creatures who often seek forms of security beyond our grasp. But sin is also not simply a result of social injustice. Niebuhr is very critical of any perspective, such as Marxism, that highlights the self-serving bias in the ideology of others, but then claims to bring in a utopian world free of oppression. As we shall see, this has led to plenty of conflict between Niebuhr and liberation theology. Niebuhr is profoundly anti-Pelagian, and he sees many psychotherapeutic and social attempts at liberation to be based on a model of utopian self-sufficiency.

In spite of Niebuhr's deep concern with social ethics and his important contributions to politics and religion, he has been criticized for holding a highly individualistic and masculine conception of sin. Notable feminist theologians have objected that he is too concerned with pride as self-exaltation and therefore misses the experience of many women, an experience in which self-loss, not self-assertion, is the dominant reality. Liberation theologians sometimes criticize Niebuhr for not adequately emphasizing oppressive social structures, rather than existential concerns, as the source of sin. An emphasis on liberation has become quite disenchanted with individualism and insists that if we are to understand evil we must think more systemically.[29] Let's examine these critiques of Niebuhr.

FROM THE ANXIOUS INDIVIDUAL TO THE CORRUPT SYSTEM

One of the milestones in the history of feminist theology was Valerie Saiving's 1960 article, "The Human Situation: A Feminine View."[30] In this pivotal article, Saiving questioned the appropriateness of the Augustinian/Niebuhrian pride thesis for women's experience. Saiving argued that Niebuhr's description of sin as self-exaltation is far more applicable to male, rather than female, experience. The exaltation and magnification of the self is not a common experience for women. In fact, the experience of self-loss or self-abnegation is far more prevalent. Rather than chastising women for excessive self-assertion, women need to be encouraged to "have" a self. Put another way, sin, for women, may involve a shrinking process rather than an expanding process. In other words, the failure to assert oneself is the primary problem.

In these early days of feminist liberation theory, Saiving tended to lump all women's experience together without adequately separating the various particulars of women's experience. This early tendency to include *all* women under a typical white, educated, middle-class, privileged position would later be corrected. But Saiving provided an extremely important insight concerning the identification of all sin as pride. While Niebuhr *did* discuss the experience of self-loss, he highlighted the notion of self-exaltation in such a way that little focus was placed on the failure to be a self. Therefore, Saiving's article triggered important contributions of other feminist theologians such as Daphne Hampson, Susan Nelson Dunfee, and especially Judith Plaskow.[31] Plaskow, who has written the most comprehensive critique, says that "theology, insofar as it focuses on the sin of pride, not only neglects women's experience, but adds to the pressures that keep women from being 'women and persons' by suggesting that self-assertion and the struggle for self-definition are sins."[32] In fact, throughout the history of Christian theology, a history dominated by male reflection, men have spent too much time focusing on their own experience without inviting women into the discussion. Because an expanded ego, domination of others, and extreme self-assertion have emerged in male experience, the assumption is that this must be true for women as well. But women, argues Plaskow, have a very different set of issues. Their primary temptation is to withdraw from being a self, to refuse the burden of freedom, and to live a "borrowed" existence rather than risk self-assertion. The last thing in the world many women need to hear is the admonition to be selfless, self-sacrificing, and to ignore their own needs while they give to others. Put simply, that's what many (but not all) *men* need to hear, and not *women*. Self-sacrificial love is an important message to exaggerated forms of pride, but it is not a healing message to women who have not even found themselves in the first place.

It is important to point out, however, that Plaskow does appreciate Niebuhr's insights into human pride and she thinks it does apply to some women. However, Niebuhr claims to be describing *all* of human experience, rather than powerful men and a few women. Plaskow also notes that some underprivileged males are also less inclined to pride and perhaps more inclined toward self-loss. Nevertheless, the common experiences of women are not adequately described by Niebuhr's portrayal of pride.

The major reason that women have not experienced self-assertion, of course, is that they have been caught in a highly sexist social matrix that has privileged men and treated women as second-class citizens. Thus systemic injustice has already affected us before we begin to make our own choices. Yet these early feminist theologians are not prepared to say that women are blameless, innocent victims of a sinful male system. Instead, they focus on reasons as to why some women have refused the path of self-assertion. One reason is simply material. Being selfless has sometimes had the benefit of being financially supported. Another reason is that selflessness avoids the burden of freedom and the struggles associated with becoming a self. Dependency is sometimes easier. Plaskow is quite direct on this issue: "Insofar as women accept this status for its rewards and welcome relief from the burden of freedom, they are guilty of complicity in their own oppression; they sin."[33] Sin is therefore refusing the journey of authentic personhood as we back away from the burdensome world of freedom. Susan Nelson Dunfee, who calls this tendency "the sin of hiding," puts it as follows:

> Most obviously, by making self-sacrificial love the ultimate Christian
> virtue, one makes the sin of hiding into a virtue as well, and thereby
> encourages those already committing the sin of hiding to stay in that
> state. One then becomes glorified for never truly seeking to become
> fully human. Furthermore, by uplifting hiding to a virtue, and by
> denying the sin of hiding as a possibility, Niebuhr's theology has no
> understanding of how the one guilty of the sin of hiding can be judged
> in his/her sin and called to actualize his/her freedom. There is no
> judgment upon the one who escapes; there is no call to emerge from

the state of hiddenness.[34]

Thus, when we make pride the *primary* sin, the sin of hiding often goes unnamed. Oppressed individuals remain oppressed because they are afraid of self-assertion. Theology thus serves the interests of a male-dominated system of oppression.

It is important to understand what these feminist theologians are *not* saying. They are not saying that men have a monopoly on evil and that the entire history of sin is simply a male problem. Men have perpetuated a highly unjust, dehumanizing, and oppressive system of social injustice, but they are not the embodiment of pure evil. A view of human history that locates all evil in male pride and privilege is naïve. Granted, because men have been in positions of power, they have had greater opportunities to engage in destructive behavior. But a "reading" of human history that completely exonerates women as pure, innocent victims of masculine evil is not helpful. Astute feminist theologian Rosemary Radford Ruether addresses this issue.

> This does not mean that women and subjugated men are not also capable of evil, but their opportunities to do evil have been generally limited to the subsystem relationships within this overall monopoly of power and privilege by the male ruling class. Women sin by cooperating in their own subjugation, by lateral violence to other women who seek emancipation, and by oppressing groups of people such as children and domestic servants under their control. Women can be racist, classist, self-hating, manipulative toward dominant males, dominating toward children.[35]

Ruether goes on to say, however, that while we are all capable of evil, we are not all *equally* responsible for it. Niebuhr essentially says the same thing when he discussed the "equality of sin and the inequality of guilt." Powerful, prideful oppressors have done more damage than persons who have been oppressed. The traditional power-hungry male who runs over people in a quest for self-expansion is more guilty than the self-abnegating oppressed. Indeed, while sin is universal, some are more guilty than others.

ORIGINAL VIOLENCE: MARJORIE SUCHOCKI'S OBJECTION TO NIEBUHR

Marjorie Hewitt Suchocki has offered a very provocative alternative to the Augustinian-Niebuhrian emphasis on pride and rebellion as the primary sin.[aj] Instead, she suggests that violence is the root of all sin. Suchocki defines sin as "participation through intent or act in unnecessary violence that contributes to the ill-being of any aspect of earth or its inhabitants."[37] Rather than locating the source of sin in a rebellion against God through human pride, she understands sin as violence against creation, a violence that also includes God since God is intricately involved with the world. In fact, because of her process-theology orientation, Suchocki argues that it is impossible for God *not* to be affected by violence toward creation. As she puts it, "I have reappropriated the ancient doctrine of original sin, albeit in a relational world where its fundamental nature is measured by the degree to which it contributes to unnecessary violence against creation."[38] Suchocki wants to move away from the imagery of sin as rebellion against God because that fosters an image of God primarily as law giver and judge: "To call sin a rebellion against God too easily translates into a social formula for keeping marginalized and oppressed peoples in places of poverty and/ or powerlessness, since it tends to interpret rebellion against any form of political, social, or personal power as a rebellion against God."[39]

Further, to lump all sin together as rebellion against God is to miss a crucial distinction between various types of sin. Destructive acts such as political torture, genocide, oppression of the poor, child abuse, and personal, idiosyncratic sin are too diverse to be put in one category of "rebellion against God." A preoccupation with sin as rebellion against God also promotes a hierarchical view of creation in which God inevitably becomes the authoritarian parent. And perhaps most importantly, this defiance of the deity image is completely remote from most people's experience. As one falls into various forms of sin, it is hardly with a deliberate defiance of the Almighty. The primary ingredient is not a conscious rebellion against one's creator or source. Further, the Kierkegaardian-Niebuhrian focus on anxiety as the breeding ground of sin has led us away from the real source of our problems—our own innate tendencies toward aggression and unnecessary violence. We have both biologically and socially inherited tendencies toward violence. Violence is both all around us, as well as a deep inclination within us.

Suchocki believes that Niebuhr's identification of sin as the striving to be our own God already assumes a position of power. For marginalized individuals, this temptation is not very real. We should include in our understanding of sin the situation of the powerless. Like other feminists, she argues that the resistance and obstacles to becoming a full self are the primary problems. Focusing on the rebellion against God as the primal sin keeps us submissive to authority. Because defiance is identified as the primary sin, obedience and submission become major virtues of the life of faith. Consequently, the social order remains unquestioned and intact. Oppression continues as individuals are prohibited from "rebellious" or revolutionary thinking. Self-abnegation becomes the tool by which the powerful stay in power. Whereas Niebuhr identified the primary problem as humanity's inability to *define* it own limits, Suchocki argues that for many, the problem is not *defying* our limits.[40]

Suchocki also argues that too much has been made of anxiety based on our own experience of finitude. For her, most individuals are not particularly concerned with their own death, as Ernest Becker suggested (chapter 3). Instead, violence triggers anxiety. The ever-present possibility of violence is the primary contributor to anxiety. As Suchocki puts it, "To live in a world where the most basic fact of existence is that life requires other life in order to live is to live in a world that is necessarily marked by violence."[41] Again, this violence is *both* all around us *and* within us: "I suggest that innate human aggressiveness and its corollary violence are the basis for sin, and that God's continuing creative call is toward a transcendence of unnecessary violence. We are called toward a spirituality that embraces the well being of all things. In such a process, aggressiveness itself may be dissociated from violence, and turned toward an instrument for the good."[42] Living in a world of constant violence, we often unconsciously internalize this pervasive threat. Thus, again, violence creates anxiety, rather than anxiety creating violence. Violence is the original sin against creation, the starting point of all sin.

THE SHIFT FROM THE INDIVIDUAL TO THE SOCIAL IN PASTORAL CARE

The movement away from a Kierkegaardian-Niebuhrian emphasis on the human condition is also obvious in current discussions of mainline pastoral theology, care, and counseling. In fact, pastoral theology's previous love affair with psychology is being rejected as more and more individuals are turning to a social focus on care. The previous concern with intrapsychic issues has been shifted to the social and political realities behind our so-called psychological problems. In a sense, Freud is out and Marx is in. Psychology has been entirely too apolitical, ahistorical, and asocial. As Nancy Ramsay, the editor of the major work announcing a paradigm shift has put it, "rather than focusing on the particular pain of individuals, attention shifts to naming dominant norms and practices such as patriarchy, racism, classism, and ethnocentrism as major barriers to human well-being."[43] This shift claims a move from a person-centered to a community-centered perspective. It opposes what pastoral counselor Larry Graham calls the "existential-anthropological" model that has previously dominated pastoral care.[44] According to Graham, almost every pastoral counselor has fallen victim to this previous trend. Reinhold Niebuhr, too, is indicted for his conviction that the morality of individuals often supercedes the morality of groups.[45] Further, Niebuhr's insistence on the capacity for self-transcendence, in Graham's view, does not adequately grasp our social and historical embeddedness. Pastoral counselors and psychotherapists are encouraged to move away from an individual focus and become competent political analysts, cultural critics, and public-policy specialists. The major fear in the older, client-centered framework was missing something in the client's inner world; the major fear in a culture-centered approach is missing something in the client's sociopolitical world.

Graham, Ramsay, and other pastoral theologians have made very important contributions concerning how pastoral care has excessively focused on the individual at the exclusion of the larger social context. In this sense, they are moving toward the argument of earlier thinkers such as Schur, Lasch, and others. They also wisely point toward how we as privileged Westerners easily universalize our own experience, thereby ignoring the particularities of personhood accociated with race, gender, class, social, and historical location. These are important realizations that are part of an increasingly postmodern consciousness. However, some movements within this "paradigm shift" in pastoral theology come dangerously close to a preoccupation with systemic issues that ignores the real psychological dilemmas of individuals. Put another way, the pendulum is swinging too far in the direction of identifying all evil as systemic. This was the very mistake that nineteenth-century Protestant liberalism made, a mistake corrected by many neoorthodox thinkers. Granted, theologians such as Bultmann excessively "individualized" the message of the gospel, which led to a personal, existential preoccupation with the decision of faith. Yet, neoorthodox conceptions of sin were a corrective to a previous generation's overemphasis on the systemic roots of all evil. Some contemporary pastoral theologians come very close to saying that the personal dimension of human destructiveness is an unfortunate fixation along the way to where the real problems are—namely, the social, political, and ecological dimensions. To state it bluntly: the repentance from psychology in mainline pastoral theology is moving toward an equally dangerous preoccupation with sociology. As surely as we do this, we will eventually see another generation rise up and say, as Kierkegaard said to the Hegelians, that we have lost the self in the system.

While psychotherapists need to be careful not to "blame the victim" as they attribute sociopolitical problems to personal pathology, it is also true that some clients are quite willing to attribute the source of all their personal problems to outside factors. If the fundamental attribution error is a problem, so is a self-serving bias that blames the external world for one's predicament. Any therapist knows that while some people enter therapy with a ready-made willingness to condemn themselves for every problem in their lives, there are other clients who desperately avoid responsibility by attributing all their problems to an unfair system or other external realities.

The problem in much of contemporary pastoral theology's reaction to the so-called existential-anthropological approach is that it sometimes acts as if absolutely nothing good has come from this movement. We are encouraged to take a sociohistorical and political view of all psychological theories, yet this courtesy is often not extended to the existential therapists who are being criticized. In other words, when they round up the usual suspects—Freud, Fromm, Rogers, Maslow, and others—they seem to easily forget the specific situations out of which those theories arose. For instance, is it any wonder, when we consider the way Fromm frantically fled the destructive obedience in Nazi Germany, that he focused most of his energies on the importance of existential freedom? Given the social pressures toward conformity, is it any wonder that Rogers emphasized the importance of "being your own person?" While I agree that many of these therapies fell prey to ethical egoism, it also true that many of their emphases on personal autonomy were a necessary part of their theory. There are, after all, important values connected with individuality and personal autonomy.

Leading family therapist Michael Nichols has voiced a deep concern about how our preoccupations with systemic thinking, which were initially helpful, are now leading us too far in the direction of self-loss.[46] For Nichols, we must recognize that we are *both* separate *and* embedded. As family therapists have stepped back to look at the larger system, they have often lost sight of the individual. Neither a psychology of embeddedness or separateness is able to account for the full range of human experience. The system easily becomes "determinative" rather than influential. Individuals are mechanistic pawns of a larger system.

> We are not just links in a circular chain of events; we are people with names who experience ourselves as centers of initiative. Our most basic impulse is to protect our integrity. What's more, we are hopelessly absorbed with ourselves. Certainly, we are linked to others. Much of what we do is with other people in mind, some of what we do is with others, and once in a while for others. But the "we" who are the authors of the doing are single organisms, with hearts and minds and bodies all encased within our skin. . . . Systemic thinking in the extreme dismisses selfhood as an illusion. The problem is when roles become reified and rigidified as prescribed determinants of behavior *and* as independent of personal agency on the one hand or wider family relations on the other. Systems thinkers have unfortunately implied that the role plays the person rather than the other way around. Whether they act in concert or separately, it is finally the selves in the system who must act to bring about change.[47]

For Nichols, this movement away from individual concerns has led to a "new wave of esoteric theorizing and a proliferation of mechanistic, highly technical interventions."[48] Following Howard A. Liddle and G. W. Saba, he refers to much of this theorizing as "systemic chic," as it seems to conjure up a lot of weighty thoughts and puffed-up "epistemologies" but in fact says very little.[49] Stanton Jones and Richard Butman also point toward the dangers of reducing the person to a manifestation of the system, a perspective they call the "collectivist view of persons."

> A collectivist view of persons is one that sees persons as largely
> or exclusively a product of social interaction. More specifically, it
> contends that our core identity is best seen as that of being part
> of a system, a collective of people, whether that be a class, familial
> or societal grouping. Individual personality is deemed trivial or
> insignificant. Because who we are and how we behave is a function of
> the interpersonal systems we exist in, what matters is the character and
> functioning of the system, not the person.[50]

There is a danger of seeing personhood as nothing more than an epiphenomenon of social forces. Regardless of the "excesses" in the existential-anthropological model, the reduction of pastoral care to structural analysis is surely a mistake. The cure for excessively individualized forms of therapy is not to eliminate therapy. The hazards of a self-absorbing individualism has needed to be exposed; but so do the pretenses that social change will eradicate the personal struggles of the individual psyche. At times, when there is such anti-individualistic thought in so much of postmodern pastoral theology, one wonders if pastoral theologian Donald Capps is not correct when he describes "expressive individualism" as the new scapegoat for all the world's woes.[51]

A NIEBUHRIAN RESPONSE TO FEMINIST AND LIBERATION CHARGES

Feminist critics of Niebuhr are quite right that Niebuhr focused primarily on the sin of self-exaltation almost at the exclusion of the sin of self-loss.

While Niebuhr clearly recognized other forms of sin, he said little about them. And he did, as feminists charge, lump other sins under that banner of pride. Considering the historical situation in which Niebuhr was a part, this is somewhat understandable, but nevertheless, as feminist theologians have said, Niebuhr claims to speak for the entire human condition.

When Niebuhr does speak of self-abandonment, he emphasizes the idea that as we refuse to be a self, we always focus on something that helps us avoid selfhood. That something on which we fixate is a God replacement. It offers an avoidance and sanctuary from the burden of being a self in relation to God. Yet Plaskow and others would insist that this God replacement does not always involve "pride." Self-abandonment, for her, is a problem in its own right and has nothing to do with "pride."

It is here that Niebuhr seems to be using a more expansive definition of pride than his feminist critics. For Niebuhr, pride does not simply mean an arrogant, puffed-up quality. Pride is instead the experience of trying to find one's own solutions to the problem of finitude *without* a reliance on our Source. Pride, for Niebuhr, means *both* self-exaltation *and* self-preoccupation. Because of anxiety, Niebuhr would argue that any attempt to live one's life without a dependence on God will inevitably involve excessive self-regard. That self-regard may not take on an inflated, arrogant version, but it will nevertheless involve an undue focus on one's own security. One may seem to focus on others, but the focus will have a relationship-distorting quality as one seeks one's sense of security through another. As we seek to solve our own anxiety problem through others, we often need them too badly to "let them be." As our own source of security, we manipulate them in subtle ways to meet our own needs. Lacking a relationship with our Source, our own relationships become our gods, and we attempt to resolve a self-preoccupying anxiety through them. This is a form of God replacement because it is up to us, and not God, to provide our final security. In so far as this God replacement occurs, at least for Niebuhr, it is an act of pride.

Also, for Niebuhr, pride is *always* the outgrowth of distrust. It is our distrust in our Creator that sets up a frantic attempt at a self-remedy for our security problem. A distrust in God places our own solutions to anxiety at the center of our lives. It is up to us, not God, to deliver a sense of ultimate security. For Niebuhr, the minute we cease to trust God, we fall into pride. We may tremble with insecurity, feel frightened, and have underlying self-doubts. Yet we are now seeking our own ultimate solution. We are attempting to outmaneuver life and console ourselves with our own self-soothing. In our attempt to find our own security, we are rejecting the security offered by God. Even the self-abnegating, worshipful attitude toward another does not eliminate the reality that it is *my* solution and *my* attempt to find security that creates a problem. Again, the whole time I am doing this, my self may seem fragile and undeveloped. Nevertheless, as I rely on my own strategies to defeat finitude and its accompanying anxiety, I engage in pride. The desire for more and more security is a kind of greed that places the needs of the self at the center of one's life.

It is also important to understand that when Niebuhr writes about pride, he is writing from a *theological*, rather than a *psychological*, angle. We are accustomed to thinking about pride in strictly psychological categories. Thus we think of someone who is arrogant and conceited. Yet when Niebuhr uses the word *pride* he is already assuming a distrust and break with God as the Source of our security. It does not matter if pride manifests itself in grandiosity or not; the point is that it involves excessive preoccupation with the self's security. Psychologically, it seems strange for us to connect the word *pride* with a soft-spoken, insecure, and self-avoidant person. But for Niebuhr, one can have a theological problem with pride while one has a psychological problem with low self-esteem.

Given the common usage of the word *pride*, and the manner in which Niebuhr's use of it leads to so much misunderstanding, I believe that he would alter his wording if he were alive today. The central point he is making, however, is that the problem of *egoism*, or self-preoccupation, is much larger than the issue of *egotism*, or self-inflated arrogance. For Niebuhr, anxiety can easily push us toward a frantic attempt to solve our own problem with finitude. In so far as we seek ultimate security on our own, whether we do it through what seems like arrogance or low self-esteem, we fall into sin, a sin that distorts our relationship with God, others, and ourselves.

Niebuhr was quite aware that beneath this prideful self-assertion lurks a fragile, insecure ego trying desperately hard to find a source of absolute security outside of a trust in God. This underlying anxiety and insecurity is part of both prideful self-assertion and self-abnegation. It is far easier to see it in self-loss, but it is also present in self-assertion. Rosemary Radford Ruether points this out:

> Sin, therefore, has to be seen both in the capacity to set up prideful, antagonistic relations to others and in the passivity of men and women who acquiesce to the group ego. This passivity has been primary for women, but the hostility of the male ego toward inferiors is also based on the insecurity of lacking a grounded self. One's "superiority" is based on a passive identification with the group ego, so one is always afraid that if one appears different, the male group ego will repudiate you as a member of that group.[52]

Insecurity lingers beneath both arrogant self-assertion and timid self-avoidance.

Niebuhr, I believe, would have both theological and psychological objections to Suchocki's argument that violence is the primary sin. He might well agree with her that a straightforward, Promethean-like rebellion against the heavens is *not* the way in which most individuals experience sin. But he would quickly add that Augustine, too, did not think along those lines. As we have seen, for Augustine, sin involves a gradual process of placing oneself at the center, and not sudden rebellious and defiant behavior. Sin is much too subtle for that. The "fall" occurred long before the eating of the forbidden fruit. In fact, the fall is associated with distrust in God and an acceptance of the serpent's interpretation of the human condition. Both Augustine and Niebuhr are far more nuanced and sophisticated in their portrayal of sin's beginning than a simple "Let's defy the authority" adolescent revolt.

Niebuhr, along with most psychologists, would want to know what *precedes* the act of violence. What triggers it? What motivates it? Violence is a *behavior*, not an *explanation*. What underlies this behavior? Suchocki argues that the realization that life is violent makes us anxious. So it is violence, and not finitude or death, that promotes our anxiety. But again, we should ask the deeper question: Why does violence scare us? Surely it is because it points to our shaky, precarious, life-threatening condition of finitude. Violence threatens life. The threat of life is the anxiety of nonbeing or death. Put simply, there is something deeper at work than a mere fear of being on the receiving end of violence. Violence threatens life because it may *end* life. It is this precarious, insecure position of life's fragility that is deeper than the anxiety generated by violence. Violence may be the means by which life is eliminated; but it is the elimination of life that is the deeper concern.

Again, it is not very psychologically satisfying to simply posit a behavior such as violence to account for or explain the underlying psychological motivations for such behavior. As we saw in Aaron Beck, reactive violence is based on anxious self-concern. Few psychologists or psychiatrists would say of a patient, "He or she is simply violent," without inquiring into the motivational apparatus beneath the violent tendencies. Whether it is understood as painful childhood experience, distorted thinking, incongruence, or whatever, the point is that something is *beneath* the behavior.

Also, many within both the scientific and theological community would disagree with Suchocki's emphasis on innate violence. Biologically, many scientists believe that humans, as well as other animals, act in violent ways primarily out of a defensive, self-protective reaction. Konrad Lorenz's thesis concerning the innate, explosive, irrational aggression of human beings has hardly been canonized in the scientific community. Further, most psychoanalysts, as we have seen, have moved away from Freud's death instinct as a basic biological tendency. And theologically, Suchocki runs into problems when she identifies the source of sin in our biological makeup. She comes dangerously close to saying that we are "hard-wired" to sin, a kind of Manichean view of creation that identifies sin with the human body rather than distorted freedom. This shortchanges human responsibility as it blames biological impulses toward violence as our fundamental problem. Thus, while Suchocki has written a provocative and insightful book, I suspect Niebuhr would say that her "violence thesis" is not psychologically or theologically satisfying.

Another problem with Suchocki and some other liberation and feminist perspectives is that they tend to completely identify sin as "oppression," and therefore equate salvation with "liberation." While it is imperative to emphasize the sin of oppression and to work hard toward social justice, this hardly means that oppression is the *only* form of sin, or even the *root* of all sin. Similarly, liberation, or the establishment of freedom, does not guarantee a healthy and constructive use of that freedom.

Langdon Gilkey is instructive here. Gilkey is critical of any equation of sociopolitical liberation with the Christian understanding of salvation.[53] The more basic problem of the human condition is not the loss of freedom, but the misuse of freedom. While social and political freedom is an important goal, it does not represent the ultimate redemption of humanity. It helps heal the consequences of sin, but it does not get rid of sin. The establishment of greater freedom also brings with it the possibility of sin. Redemption requires a new relation with God, self, and neighbor, something which a political platform, however worthy, can never provide.

> [N]o level of political achievement, no "freeing of freedom," could prevent the reappearance of the injustice, the domination and the oppression which follow from it, because the latter follow precisely from freedom, albeit a freedom misused. In the long run, warped social structures are *consequences* not causes of human greed, pride, insecurity and self-concern which in turn flow from the exercise of freedom, not its oppression. We all sin in history with our freedom, not without it; thus the freeing of freedom frees us for sin as well as good works, for the creation of injustice as well as the creation of justice.[54]

Political action, Gilkey goes on to say, is crucial because it can help empower individuals and decrease human suffering. But the establishment of greater freedom hardly guarantees an eradication of freedom. Greater self-determination does not make us immune from sin. In fact, those of us who have been recently liberated can oppress others in the next breath. Human freedom is ambiguous and carries no guarantee that our choices will be just. Critiquing social inequality, racism, classism, sexism, and other deadly patterns is important. But correcting them is no guarantee that the same thing will not happen all over again. Sin is not simply a matter of social reform, as many of the nineteenth-century Protestant liberals believed. It is deeper than that, rooted in the mishandling of our anxiety and the misuse of our freedom. It is here that we can see many Marxists and psychotherapists making the same error. They both assume that once liberation has occurred the ethical struggles of a liberated life will largely fade away. Marx's utopianism sees the end of class conflict and the establishment of peaceful relations. Psychotherapists often argue that "therapized" individuals will automatically act in ethical ways. Both of these views neglect the reality that postliberated life is also ambiguous. We may have gained more freedom but we have hardly eliminated sin. Marx, for instance, vividly points out the tainting ideology and bias of the ruling classes. He is not so effective, however, at examining his own assumptions. His razor-sharp criticisms indict the self-serving ideology of those in power. We need his critique and diagnosis. Yet his own conviction that the revolution of the proletariat will completely change this injustice, and that we will find healing from our alienation, is, at least to me, very naïve. Becoming the masters of our society by controlling the economic factors that have alienated us will not deliver a sinless world. For Marx, all individual problems are simply a by-product of socioeconomic problems. Once the social demons are exorcised, the internal demons will be cast out as well. The problem is never *within* us. One wonders how Marx can combine such brilliant diagnosis and such inadequate prognosis. And one also wonders how Marx cannot see the limitations of his own perspective. As Niebuhr puts it, "The proud achievement of Marxism in discovering the intellectual pride and pretension of previous cultures therefore ends in a pitiful display of the same sin."[55]

SUMMARY

In this chapter, we have explored the debate concerning whether to privilege an individual or a social understanding of sin. We reviewed the experience of Langdon Gilkey at Shantung Compound and investigated the work of his mentor, Reinhold Niebuhr. While Niebuhr was a crusader against social injustice, he believed that cleaning up systemic issues alone would never resolve our "sin problem," because this problem grew out of the misuse, and not just the denial, of our freedom. We examined important feminist correctives to Niebuhr's historically understandable emphasis on sin as aggressive assertiveness and pride. We also examined the work of Marjorie Suchocki, in her challenge of Niebuhr. For Suchocki, our "fall" results from violence, yet I suggested that while her work is important, her understanding of violence as the "primary" or "root" sin is neither psychologically nor theologically compelling. I then examined how liberation themes have provided a paradigm shift in much of contemporary pastoral theology and counseling within mainline denominations. While this new emphasis is helpful in moving us away from those extreme forms of individualism that ignore our social, racial, gender, and political orientations, this new perspective is moving too far in the direction of a social and political reduction of personhood. If our previous problem was that the self ignored the system, our current problem is that the self may be lost in the system. And finally, I offered, with the help of Langdon Gilkey, a Niebuhrian response to his critics.

Indeed, an added emphasis on social injustice, oppression, and the particular inequalities of specific individuals needs to be employed. But the answer is not to swing the pendulum so far in the opposite direction that we lose all the deep insights into personhood offered by Niebuhr and other midcentury "existential-anthropological" voices. Granted, we must be careful not to make generalizations from our own limited and privileged position. But the answer is not rejecting all attempts to describe common factors in the human condition. The attempt to remedy all systemic evils in our world will not deliver us from the personal temptations arising from our own ontological anxiety and desire for security. Of course we should attempt to change the world, and any understanding of "original sin" which suggests that such an attempt is hopeless should be rejected. Being cynical about all our efforts is not the same as realistically recognizing that oppression may well emerge in new forms tomorrow, and that today's victims can easily become tomorrow's perpetrators. But this realism does *not* have to lead to passivity and inaction; instead, it can offer a kind of sober recognition that our own forms of temptation will emerge as we strive toward greater social justice. Sin is never simply "the other group's problem." This is not to say that some are not far more guilty than others in their levels of abuse, violence, and destruction. But it is to say that freedom is never the "end of the story" when it comes to eliminating sin. Out of newfound freedom will come new possibilities, and these new possibilities will tempt us to act in self-serving ways. Such is the human condition.

CHAPTER SEVEN

CONCLUDING THOUGHTS

Throughout this book, I have attempted to describe three overlapping dimensions of destructiveness—the natural, the personal, and the social or systemic. In the introduction, I suggested that I did not want to collapse one dimension into the other, but instead, respectfully acknowledge the power of all three forms. Consistent with this has been the belief that a multidisciplinary approach is necessary for the study of evil. As the reader can no doubt tell, most of these investigations have been brought back to the doorstep of theological commentary. I would now like to emphasize twelve major convictions derived from this exploration.

TWELVE MAJOR CONVICTIONS

First, no view of evil should be taken seriously that does not fully acknowledge the enormous waste, destructiveness, and brutality which has accompanied evolution. Any view of God's providence that does not *seriously wrestle* with Darwin's findings is a reality-denying, rose-colored view of reality. It is way past time to realize that evolutionary findings are not going to go away. Darwinism has permanently damaged the smooth continuity between nature's design and God's existence. It is no longer possible to say that nature unambiguously reflects God. We must face and theologically incorporate nature's cold, detached principle of natural selection. Further, any plausible view of providence must work on the basis of a very large picture of time and the ultimate purposes of God. The surest way in the world to make religion obsolete is to say that we live in a world only a few thousand years old, that nature conveyed a pure harmony before humanity arrived to foul things up, and that because a literal and specific man and woman ate a piece of fruit, everything has gone downhill ever since. Bad science makes for bad theology. And any theology that claims to offer hope for the future must fully embrace the struggles of a very long past—a past full of much waste and extinction as well as hope for renewal. Put another way, *any believable theodicy must address the evil and destructiveness in the natural world.* If it does not do this, then its hope is cheap and its promises are unrealistic. For too long, perhaps out of a sense of timidity or charity, Christians have remained silent as scientific nonsense is promoted beneath their banner. It is past time for Christians to caringly, but firmly, challenge both bad science and bad theology.

As we have seen, however, part of this antiscientific reaction has been brought on by the smugness of philosophical materialists who set forth their metaphysical views as science. This is another form of fundamentalism— one that has decided in advance that all truth can be discovered through the method of experimental investigation, and that it has a monopoly on reality. If it's not empirical, it cannot be real. If science cannot verify it, it does not exist. The ease with which many scientists move into the role of metaphysicians is staggering. Again, they have every right to make philosophical claims; however, they should not pretend to do so in the name of science.

Enormously exciting things are happening in the theology of evolution. As I have indicated, John Haught's work, along with many others, holds particular promise for a post-Darwinian providence. The God of classical metaphysics is not a good candidate for this new view of providence. A much more relational God, a God willing to grant freedom and autonomy to both humanity and nature, is a far better fit for the realities of evolution. Plus, this God is much more congruent with the God most people actually encounter in religious experience. A dominating, detached, controlling God belonged to a previous age. It cannot be reconciled with the world's evil, unless of course one wants to make God the author of that evil.

Second, while offering interesting and helpful insights into some aspects of human behavior, evolutionary psychology does not tell the whole story of human destructiveness. As we have seen, for most evolutionary psychologists, gene perpetuation is the all-inclusive, master motive that determines human behavior. Granted, the perpetuation of our genes may be a significant factor in life, but it is *speculation*, and not *science*, to argue that this is the singular, ultimate story behind human behavior. Indeed, this is a most interesting conceptual map, but it is a leap of faith—not unlike that in religion—to suggest that it is the master narrative of the human condition. While evolutionary psychologists sometimes acknowledge both proximate and ultimate causes, the proximate causes are employed in the service of the ultimate cause, gene replication. Proximate causes include environmental factors, personal motivation, or prior experience, but again, these are all under the governing control of our selfish genes. For instance, we love our children because we want to nurture something cute (proximate cause), but the much deeper reason is that the "one with the most genes wins." Yet the problem with any master or ultimate instinct—whether it is gene perpetuation, self-actualization, or a host of others—is that it fails to acknowledge the plurality of instincts which seek expression. Following William James and Don Browning, I suggest that single-, or even dual-instinct theories such as Freud's, do not do justice to the multiple inclinations within us. Thus, while we may have an inclination to reproduce, we may also experience an inclination to be free of this responsibility. A master motive driving the entire course of our lives does not adequately address our diverse instinctual tendencies.

One can, of course, say that beneath all these "other" inclinations is the much deeper, unconscious motivation of gene perpetuation. But this is a *huge* assumption to make, an assumption that collapses psychological explanations into an all-encompassing biological one. Quite understandably, many have a hard time swallowing this argument hook, line, and sinker. Does it have some explanatory power? Yes. Does it offer an adequate account of the full range of human behavior? No.

Evolutionary psychologists believe we engage in destructive behavior because it is advantageous for us to do so. For David Buss, as we have seen, aggression is driven primarily by sexual and reproductive competition. He pinpoints the twenties as the time in the life cycle in which most killing occurs. This is the time of greatest reproductive competition. He minimizes pathological and sociological explanations of violence in favor of his survival explanation. Yet while Buss is an extremely bright and provocative thinker, he asks us to put all of our theoretical eggs in one basket. Survival and gene perpetuation explain everything, including aggression and violence. But without reducing the significance of Buss's work, I must question the universal applicability of his claims. Put another way, I simply believe that there are *other* psychological reasons for destructiveness which are not subservient to this survival impulse. While he offers highly interesting speculation, it is not, in the view of many, genuine science.

This leap from speculation to science is also very obvious in evolutionary psychology's "scientific" account of religion. The idea that all forms of religion—even forms that encourage celibacy—are the unwitting pawns of our gene's desire for self-perpetuation seems extremely reductionistic. This is a "reification" of our genes as a behind-the-scenes master of human puppets. To take the desire for transcendence, the deep conviction that we've encountered the sacred, or the life-changing quality of discipleship and say that it is an "illusion pushed on us by selfish genes," is way too much of a leap. Again, it's an interesting idea, and one that I'd be happy to entertain in a religious-studies course, but it should *not* be taught as science. Most evolutionary theories of religion begin with a rigid atheistic materialism, then make sure they "find" what they are looking for—namely, a Godless world full of religious illusions. This "scientific" explanation of religion is as religious as the religion it indicts. Faith, not evidence, is its primary foundation. When many of us hear outstanding intellectuals such as Richard Dawkins or Daniel Dennett start talking about religion, we feel much like they must feel when they hear creation scientists talking about science. In both cases, they are out of their fields of expertise. While many evolutionary psychologists are very leery of hearing theologians talk about science, they have no qualms about offering pronouncements on religion.

Does evolutionary theory eliminate the traditional notion of original sin? I have argued that this depends on what we mean by "original sin." If we mean the literal and historical fall of the first couple from a perfect paradise, yes, it does. The literal, historical, and scientific reading of the poetic book of Genesis can no longer be taken seriously. Christian theology needs to cut the umbilical cord to this prescientific way of thinking and read the story as the allegory it is.

Many, in response to evolutionary theory, have been prompted to reclaim Irenaeus for purposes of theological anthropology. As we have seen, this view is certainly more evolution friendly. Yet the Augustinian perspective can still speak powerfully to our experience when it is deliteralized. Few do this as well as Reinhold Niebuhr and Langdon Gilkey. Their careful analysis of excessive self-concern in the face of anxiety raises devastating problems for an optimistic view of evolutionary progress and moral superiority.

Third, while the neo-Freudians are probably right when they say that Freud's death instinct or biological tendency toward aggression is not an ongoing, inherent part of the human condition, they are overly optimistic in thinking that humanity can cure its own condition of estrangement. As we saw, Freud only gradually arrived at the notion that the death instinct, or the aggressive drive, has a separate line of development from libido. Certainly the bloodshed of the twentieth century brought some of this awareness into view, but Peter Gay makes a strong case that psychoanalysis was already moving toward that conclusion. For Freud, this psychological division between eros and thanatos reflects a larger, cosmic portrait of life against death. While many of Freud's sobering thoughts about the human condition seem penetratingly insightful, Paul Tillich, as we have seen, argued that Freud confused our *estranged* condition with our *essential* nature. For Tillich, our essential nature is not estranged, neurotic, or hopelessly self-destructive. Nothing essentially within our nature demands that we act in distorted ways. Put another way, our sin cannot be blamed on our biology. While Tillich greatly prizes Freud for helping us grasp a *dynamic*, rather than *static*, view of sin, he thinks Freud is much better at describing our alienated condition than he is at locating its source. Freud provides a vivid diagnosis but a poor etiology. Our destructive behavior is not *necessitated* by the very structure of our being. Put theologically, we don't "have" to sin. Also, the battle is not simply between our "higher" and "lower" natures. Instead, the battle occurs at both levels. Our so-called higher nature can produce its own form of sin. The drives of sex, aggression, and survival are never raw, mechanical inclinations completely determined by natural forces. They are always accompanied by a certain degree of freedom and imagination. Therefore, *evil never simply results from our essential nature.*

Thus neo-Freudians are right to question the idea that human destructiveness is a biologically inherited problem. Yet for Tillich, as we have seen, this neo-Freudian correction goes too far in its optimistic understanding of human possibility. As noted, Freud ended up with a rather gloomy portrait of the human condition, a predicament with which we are stuck. While we can eliminate some of our misery, any hint of a utopian world in which we are neurosis-free is out of the question. Yet for some neo-Freudians, there is a possibility of healing our estrangement problem through confidence in our own reason and human potential. For Erich Fromm, the destructive forces within us are strong, but they are not *primary*, nor are they necessarily *permanent*. By achieving more and more self-consciousness, humanity can eventually overcome them, thus ushering in an eventual utopia. Fromm believes that Freud's death instinct represents *psychopathology*, rather than normal biological development. It is a frustration of the life instinct that is primary. Thus it is the social conditions of the child, rather than biological drives, that represent the problem. These damaging social conditions, with enough labor and self-consciousness, can be fixed. Dr. Jekyll can heal Mr. Hyde. This clearly goes beyond Freud. Whereas Freud might suggest that, through a great deal of effort, we can *manage* Mr. Hyde, we will never completely *eradicate* him.

Another psychoanalytic thinker, Ernest Becker, identifies evil with our attempt to outmaneuver our biggest fear—the fear of death. For Becker, we humans spend our lives denying our own mortality as we narcissistically attempt to be heroic. This heroism denies our finitude and vulnerability, thus providing an illusion of immortality. We want to stand out, to fulfill the ache of cosmic specialness. In fact, sibling rivalry is a concrete example of this more general drama: we yearn to be special in a world that guarantees our own demise. Thus all forms of heroism are unconscious attempts to deny reality. Evil, then, is a by-product of our fear of death. We are quite capable of doing destructive things to each other in an attempt to establish our own sense of immortality. By trying to escape this great evil (death), we actually create more evil. In fact, the anxiety about death is the backdrop for all other forms of anxiety. It is here that Becker definitely disagrees with the position of Marjorie Suchocki, who argues that the primary anxiety concerns violence, but not death.

As we saw, Donald Evans calls into question this entire understanding of evil. He says that we do *not* need to rely on biological explanations of narcissism. There are plenty of good psychological explanations. Narcissism, contrary to Becker, is not built into us. Also, our desire to relate to others is as strong as our desire to stand out. In fact, Evans argues that narcissism is derivative of a frustrated desire to connect, love, and be loved. And the extent of one's denial of death depends on this level of narcissism. It is clearly much stronger in some than in others. For Evans, Becker universalizes and exaggerates narcissism, which then escalates the denial of death. Put simply, the more special one feels, the more "awful" death seems. While Becker offers a brilliant analysis, I suspect that Evans may be somewhat right that he overextends the condition of narcissism.

Fifth, the central problem with many neo-Freudian views of evil is essentially the same as the problems with Aaron Beck's cognitive view—namely, the conviction that unaided human reason, in the face of ontological anxiety, can resolve its own problems. In agreement with Tillich and Niebuhr, I would suggest that without a deeper sense of ontological acceptance and grace, accompanied by an anxiety-reducing trust in our Source, this Pelagian self-salvation scheme will run out of steam.

Beck's explanation of destructive thinking is a rich resource for recognizing how so much destructive thinking results from anxious, threatened, and distorted thinking. Indeed, Beck provides a vivid account of how our egocentric thinking, in the face of a challenge, reverts back to a primal mode of us-and-them thinking. This black-and-white mentality promotes destructive violence. Even when there is not a physical threat, our minds can easily move into survival thinking as we respond to a psychological challenge as if our entire lives were at stake. Beck believes that we manifest two basic tendencies: one toward self-indulgence and selfishness, and another toward altruism, humility, and generosity. Our prosocial tendencies are as strong as our antisocial tendencies. Beck therefore backs away from the claim of some evolutionary psychologists that altruism is always a disguised form of self-interest.

But the primary problem, again, is Beck's reduction of the sometimes overwhelming experience of ontological anxiety to a simple fear. As we have seen, Beck refuses to acknowledge objectless anxiety, and instead argues that human reason is capable of smoking out the objects of all our fears. We simply do not have this form of existential anxiety so frequently discussed in the twentieth century. In reality, we have only manageable fears. Thus Beck believes that we can tame all of our fears on the basis of conscious reasoning. In my mind, this both minimizes the significance of the unconscious and exaggerates the significance of reason to guide our lives in an unruffled manner. Can a cognitive therapy approach be helpful with everyday disturbances? Of course. Can it quiet the existential anxiety that comes from raising ultimate questions about meaning, purpose, and significance? I don't think so. Reason cannot sedate existential anxiety because anxiety is more than a "psychological" condition; instead, it is an ontological one. Beck's naturalistic metaphysic appears to leave us with only one option—a trust in our own reason, rather than a trust in a Source greater than ourselves.

Also, Beck seems convinced that an egocentric bias strongly influences us only when we are severely threatened. But as we saw with Reinhold Niebuhr and Langdon Gilkey, there is a mountain of evidence to support the view that "sophisticated" forms of thinking can also have an egocentric bias. Beck's conviction that calm thinking will automatically lead to the flourishing of morality seems suspicious. Put bluntly, people can sin while thinking out of their neocortex as well as their "reptilian" brain.

Fifth, while Carl Jung and John Sanford equip us with an extremely insightful understanding of how evil results from the projection of our shadow, they come dangerously close to turning all *interpersonal* issues into strictly *intrapsychic* ones. I agree with Sanford when he says that many of us want to turn our own personal evils into social and political demons that are external to us. Yet his solution seems to reduce genuine issues between oneself and another to internal battles. Put another way, sometimes the alienation is not simply within ourselves. My "enemy" may tell me a lot about my own projected shadow; however, it may also tell me something about the "other."

Sanford believes there are two fundamentally different views of evil in the New Testament. The first view, represented by Jesus, and later reflected in the theologian Origen, encourages us to integrate our shadows through a nonrepressive acceptance of the dark side. In fact, says Sanford, Jesus became the most confrontational and angry primarily with the shadow-denying religious leaders of his day. But if we strictly follow Sanford's own theory, why wouldn't we say that in reality Jesus was simply reacting to his own shadow? In other words, the legalistic demeanor of the religious leaders somehow triggered his own battle with his condemning shadow and he projected this self-condemnation onto these leaders. The real battle was within his own mind, a battle between a gentle and a condemning voice. If such a battle had not been going on, he would not have reacted so extremely to the religious leaders. Granted, most of us completely understand what Sanford means here, and granted, I'm pushing the point a little too far. Yet while a lot of our anger or reaction to others may be shadow projection, there are other times when it is not.

Further, Sanford's highly interesting division between Jesus and Paul ends up condemning the Pauline tradition for nearly everything "wrong" with Christianity. This is an interesting thesis—namely, that Paul encouraged repression rather than genuine healing. Yet as I indicated, this thesis is in profound need of greater confirmation. If Sanford is right, then Christians need to treat the bulk of the New Testament with deep suspicion because it encourages that which is psychologically damaging. Saying that Paul did not understand depth psychology is one thing; but saying that his teaching has psychologically damaged millions of people in the history of Christendom is quite another. Further, it seems a little too convenient how much of a Jungian that Jesus turns out to be. Put differently, it seems a stretch to say that his primary message had to do with embracing our shadow.

Nevertheless, there is much to be gained in Sanford's extensive analysis of evil. As a very skilled Jungian analyst, he masterfully unpacks the Jekyll and Hyde tale as a description of all of us. Indeed, the confrontation of our own shadow is a central aspect of a healthy life.

Sixth, David Augsburger's argument that the goal in life is learning to hate injustice rather than people is most helpful. Augsburger has gifted us with what may very well be the most comprehensive treatment of hatred in print. His description and developmental scheme concerning various forms of hatred, his use of a multiple-theory approach, and his conviction that the goal in life is to learn to hate injustice itself are all richly informative.

Seventh, while social psychology has helped us understand the significance of situational factors in the emerge of evil, this does not eradicate dispositional factors. As we saw, the work of Stanley Milgram and Philip Zimbardo, especially, offers significant understanding as to how ordinary individuals can do some very destructive things when under the pressure of situational factors. Their work greatly helps us move away from an "us-and-them" view of evil in which we cannot even "imagine ourselves" doing the kinds of destructive behavior we see in others. Instinctivist or dispositional views of evil, by themselves, are not adequate. I concur. We must not decontextualize individuals and attribute *all* evil behavior to internal sources. Internal psychological states do not tell the whole story as to why people do destructive things. Yet neither does the situational approach. I have suggested that Zimbardo seems to move back and forth from a deterministic to a nondeterministic framework. He makes a strong case for environmental influences, then turns around and uses the language of determinism. He says that we must not look at dispositional factors if we want to understand how people succumb to pressuring social contexts. Yet when examining people who do *not* succumb, the "heroic" individuals, he reintroduces dispositional factors. We can't have it both ways. If dispositional factors were not instrumental in a refusal to be socially destructive, how can they be instrumental in a *refusal* to be socially destructive? Zimbardo overstates the social context in such a way that internal forces are ignored and freedom is nearly lost. Yet he then wants to smuggle freedom back into his framework when he examines the ability to resist social pressure. While he is an outstanding social scientist, his philosophical conclusions about his findings seem, at least to me, inconsistent.

Further, can a study such as Milgram's shock experiments provide a definitive explanation of the destructive obedience characteristic of Nazi officers in the Holocaust? I don't believe it can. It is helpful, but not adequate as a fully explanatory theory. Milgram's subjects expressed great distress over inflicting pain for the "greater good" of learning. This was not the case with many Nazi officers. The dehumanization of the Jewish population seems to be the key factor. The idea of understanding Nazi officers as "well-intentioned people" who got swept away by evil circumstances does not do justice to the horrors of the Holocaust.

Eighth, though it may be politically unwise to say so, Roy Baumeister is probably right that if we are to understand *most* destructiveness, we must move away from the "myth of pure evil." Notice that I said "most" destructiveness, rather than "all" destructiveness. Baumeister wants to temporarily suspend the issue of morality in an effort to gain understanding from the perspective of the perpetrator, as well as the victim. He believes that we normally understand evil only from the standpoint of the victim, a standpoint that is usually black and white, involving radical evil vs. total innocence. For Baumeister, we can be sympathetic to the victim without necessarily taking the victim's perspective as the total, objective description of the destructiveness done to him or her. As a general rule for understanding everyday destructiveness from a social-scientific perspective, I think Baumeister's approach is useful. However, I also reserve the possibility that evil, in some situations, may indeed be "pure" in its dark and vile nature.

Ninth, as Gilkey has pointed out, in contrast to Milgram and Zimbardo, marginal situations may not cause people to act in highly self-centered ways so much as bring out a self-centeredness that is already there. Also, for Gilkey, the selfish and destructive tendencies he witnessed at Shantung Compound were not simply a carryover of animal instincts or a relapse back to "primitive" ways of being. Instead, highly sophisticated rationalizations were used to justify self-centeredness. Our "higher" powers can be used creatively or destructively.

I am further in agreement with Gilkey that overcoming of this self-concern, on one's own, does not appear possible. Contrary to Aaron Beck, changing our thinking is not enough. Instead, we need a new center for security and health, a center that transcends the demanding voices of the self. In short, we need a trust in God to help quiet the self-preoccupying voice of existential anxiety. Following Niebuhr, Gilkey believes that self-consciousness itself leads to anxiety. Anxiety cannot always be attributed to external factors affecting us. It is not always an "outside/in" phenomenon. Anxiety is not simply a matter of something being done "to us." Instead, it is built into our existence, an ontological fact and not merely a psychological disturbance.

Tenth, the identification of violence as the primary sin of the human condition offers insight and understanding, but it is ultimately neither psychologically nor theologically satisfying. Marjorie Suchocki is a creative, intelligent, and excellent theologian whose work is clearly rewarding to read. However, her thesis, in my opinion, goes too far. Her suggestion that violence is itself the primary problem of life misses the deeper psychological question as to what motivates this violence. Further, she comes very close to theologically identifying sin as something fundamentally intrinsic to our essential condition—namely, our built-in tendency to be violent. While her work is instructive, I do not think it adequately explains destructiveness and evil.

Suchocki's concern, along with others, is that Niebuhr's strong emphasis on the notion of original sin will have the negative side effect of reinforcing the status quo by encouraging individuals to do nothing. In other words, any assertiveness will be seen as born out of sinful rebelliousness and therefore snuffed out. The notion of original sin encourages us to simply accept things the way they are. But my question is a simple one: Did it do this to Niebuhr? Quite the contrary. One would be hard pressed to find anyone in the twentieth century more involved in social justice than Niebuhr. In fact, his political involvements often left him little time for quiet and reflective theological thinking. Indeed, he was a man who "thought on the move."

Eleventh, while feminist theologians have made an important point that Niebuhr's description of the sin of pride overshadowed the development of a notion of sin as self-loss, Niebuhr used a wider understanding of pride than many of his critics. When Niebuhr used the word *pride*, it meant both *egotistic* and *egoistic* tendencies. Granted, given his historical time frame, Niebuhr focused primarily on the sin of egotism, or the self-assertive and puffed-up pride typical of males. Yet egoism, the excessive preoccupation with security in the face of anxiety, was also considered a part of pride, though it was not adequately developed. For Niebuhr, the minute we cease to trust God, we fall into pride. We may tremble with anxiety and feel self-conscious. We may seek a "god" in someone else to whom we totally devote ourselves, someone who will deliver us from the burden of freedom. This is theological pride, which may or may not look like psychological arrogance, conceit, and self-mastery. But it is our own attempt to resolve our finitude problem, an attempt that does not rely on a trust in God, and hence, for Niebuhr, involves pride. I believe that if Niebuhr were alive today he would alter his language for clarification and address in far more detail the sin of self-loss or self-abnegation.

And twelfth, while feminist and other liberation theologians have helped us move away from a limited existential-anthropological model, the current danger is reducing all individual sin into social and systemic destructiveness. Warped, oppressive, dehumanizing social structures are very real. Of course we need to "think socially" in our understanding of sin. But this is only part of the picture. Further, I am in agreement with Gilkey: while we should work hard for the establishment of freedom, freedom must not be equated with salvation. Sin is not simply the denial of freedom; instead, it is the misuse of freedom. Working for greater freedom, more social justice, and less oppression is a wonderful thing. But this will not eliminate our sin problem. The establishment of freedom brings with it both the opportunity to help others as well as the opportunity to exploit them. Have we so soon forgotten the lessons we learned from the optimistic promises of classical liberalism, promises which asserted that if we clean up our social institutions we will have no "sin" problem? Do we really want to ignore the rich understanding of the relationship between existential anxiety and sin so well developed in the neoorthodox thinkers while we turn back the clock to an exclusive focus on social and political sin?

This social and political emphasis in current mainline pastoral care and counseling sometimes makes one wonder if there are any more "individual" problems at all. This movement has emphasized an important corrective to the radical individualism often associated with traditional psychotherapy, but it often seems to come equipped with an excessive disdain for psychotherapy. It tends to collapse genuine psychological issues, wounds, and hurts into public-policy concerns. Psychology is out; sociology is in. But a fixation on the social structures surrounding individuals can sometimes lead to an ignoring of the flesh-and-blood person sitting in front of us. Not all problems are systemic in nature. Challenging systemic injustice is important; but so is the careful and tedious care for the inner life of others.

AN OPEN-ENDED ISSUE

The philosopher Richard Bernstein, in the conclusion to his *Radical Evil: A Philosophical Interrogation*, asserts that the investigation of evil is an open-ended, ongoing process.[1] This is especially the case because new forms of evil can always emerge. Bernstein refers to evil as an "excess" that resists total comprehension. He states this as follows:

> [W]e find ourselves in a paradoxical situation in interrogating evil. We seek to understand it, to find the concepts that are adequate to describe and comprehend it. Yet the more rigorously we interrogate it, the more we realize that there is something about the most extreme and radical forms of evil that eludes us. We ineluctably come up against the limits of comprehension. . . . We seek to comprehend the meaning of evil, its varieties and vicissitudes. We want to know why it is that some individuals choose evil and others resist it. We want to know why some individuals adopt good maxims and others adopt evil maxims. There is much we can say about someone's background, training, education, character, circumstances, etc. The social disciplines and psychology all contribute this understanding. But it never adds up to a *complete* explanation of why individuals make the choices they do. There is always a gap, a "black hole," in our accounts.[2]

While the realization of evil's evasiveness is important, it should not lead us to an indifference concerning its investigation. The answer is not throwing up our hands and saying that this "impenetrable mystery" no longer requires our careful attention and best thinking. One can simultaneously employ reason while recognizing its limitations. And one can also realize that evil can often be so cunning that reason itself can be used as its instrument.

My hope is that this survey of destructiveness—natural, personal, and social—a survey that is by no means exhaustive, will prove helpful as we continue both to understand and combat the evil around us and within us. Theologian David Tracy has said, "The most basic anthropological principle of Christianity is this: one may have as radical an understanding of evil and sin as necessary as long as one's understanding of grace and salvation are equally radical."[3] I agree. My hope is that with God's help, evil will never have the final word.

ACKNOWLEDGMENTS

There are several people I would like especially to thank for their encouragement in making this book possible. John Haught, David Augsburger, Ron Stone, and Don Browning supported this project and read parts or all of this manuscript. Their affirmation of my effort is greatly appreciated. Cindy Epperson has offered very valuable discussions about the topic of evil as we have developed an interdisciplinary course together, "Evil and the Human Condition." I also want to thank Matt Becker and Steve May for deeply valued conversation. Michael West and Josh Messner from Fortress Press both have been encouraging, receptive, and insightful. Josh has done outstanding editorial work.

As I began writing this book, I did not know that the late Langdon Gilkey would be as influential for me as he has been. Time and time again, I found myself going back to Gilkey's work for guidance and wisdom. Although I never had an opportunity to study with Professor Gilkey, I wish to honor his memory by expressing my appreciation for his life-time achievement. Indeed, he is missed by many in the theological community.

I would like to thank my family—including my wife Linda, my parents Don and Barbara Cooper, and my two step-daughters, Lori and Michelle—for their ongoing support and love.

And finally, I am dedicating this book to some wonderful friends. Robert Asa, Dan Reynolds, David Johnson, Marty Maddox, James Willis, Rick Wilson, and Hazel and Mike Jackson have been, for over three decades, excellent companions on this journey of life. I thank them for their friendship and I greatly appreciate them.

NOTES

INTRODUCTION

1. M. Scott Peck, *People of the Lie* (New York: Simon & Schuster, 1983), 43.
2. Arthur G. Miller, ed., *The Social Psychology of Good and Evil* (New York: Guilford, 2004).
3. Carl E. Braaten, "Powers in Conflict: Christ and the Devil," in Carl E. Braaten and Robert W. Jenson, eds., *Sin, Death, and the Devil* (Grand Rapids: Eerdmans, 2000), 96–97.
4. Walter Wink, *Unmasking the Powers: The Invisible Forces That Determine Human Existence* (Philadelphia: Fortress Press, 1986), 11, author's emphasis.
5. Peter C. Hodgson, *Christian Faith: A Brief Introduction* (Louisville: Westminster John Knox Press, 2001), 90.
6. Rosemary Radford Ruether, *Sexism and God-Talk: Toward a Feminist Theology* (Boston: Beacon, 1983; rev. ed., 1993), 181–82.
7. Peter L. Berger, *Question of Faith: A Skeptical Affirmation of Christianity* (Oxford: Blackwell, 2004), 38.
8. Ibid., 21.
9. Jeffrey Burton Russell, *Satan: The Early Christian Tradition* (Ithaca, N.Y.: Cornell University Press, 1981), 222.

CHAPTER I
EVIL AND EVOLUTION

1. Harold Y. Vanderpool, "Charles Darwin and Darwinism: A Naturalized World and a Brutalized Man?" in R. Johnson, E. Wallwork, C. Green, and H. Vanderpool, *Critical Issues in Modern Religion* (Englewood Cliffs, N.J.: Prentice-Hall, 1973), 78.
2. Ibid., 85.
3. Stephen Jay Gould, "Darwin's Revolution of Thought: An Illustrated Lecture for the Classroom," videocassette, directed by Robert DiNozzi (Northampton, Mass.: Into the Classroom, 1995).
4. For an excellent discussion of this, see James C. Livingston, *Modern Christian Thought, Vol. 1,* 2nd ed. (Upper Saddle River, N.J.: Prentice-Hall, 1997), chap. 10.
5. Aubrey L. Moore, *Science and the Faith: Essays on Apologetic Subjects* (London: Kegan, Paul, Trench, Trubner, & Co., 1889).
6. Ibid., 184–85, author's emphasis.
7. Livingston, *Modern Christian Thought,* 261.
8. Ibid., 262–66.
9. Quoted in ibid., 263.
10. John F. Haught, *Responses to 101 Questions on God and Evolution* (Mahwah: Paulist, 2001), 99–100.

11. Charles Darwin, *The Autobiography of Charles Darwin,* ed. Nora Barlow (New York: Collins, 1958), 86.

12. Ibid., 86–87.

13. For a much fuller account of Annie's death, see Randal Keynes, *Darwin, His Daughter, and Human Evolution* (New York: Penguin Putnam, 2002). Darwin's reflection on his daughter's life, written one week after her death, is quite moving.

14. Quoted in Vanderpool, "Charles Darwin and Darwinism," 105.

15. Livingston, *Modern Christian Thought,* 255.

16. John Polkinghorne, *Serious Talk: Science and Religion in Dialogue* (Harrisburg: Trinity International, 1995), 61–62.

17. Haught, *Responses to 101 Questions,* 60–61.

18. Langdon Gilkey, *Creationism on Trial: Evolution and God at Little Rock* (Minneapolis: Winston, 1985), 33.

19. Ibid., 115.

20. Ibid., 179.

21. John F. Haught, *Deeper Than Darwin: The Prospect for Religion in the Age of Evolution* (Boulder: Westview, 2003), 16.

22. Ibid., 3.

23. Alister McGrath, *Dawkins' God: Genes, Memes, and the Meaning of Life* (Oxford: Blackwell, 2005).

24. Ibid., 9.

25. Ibid., 10.

26. Richard Dawkins, *River Out of Eden: A Darwinian View of Life* (London: Phoenix, 1995), 133.

27. Quoted in McGrath, *Dawkins' God,* 54.

28. Stephen Jay Gould, "Impeaching a Self-Appointed Judge," *Scientific American* 267, no. 1 (1992): 119.

29. McGrath, *Dawkins' God,* 50.

30. Stephen Jay Gould, "Stephen Jay Gould in Conversation with Win Kayzen," *A Glorious Accident: Our Place in the Cosmic Puzzle,* videotape, (Princeton: Films for the Humanities and Sciences, 1994).

31. McGrath, *Dawkins' God,* 55.

32. Ibid., 71.

33. John F. Haught, *God After Darwin: A Theology of Evolution* (Boulder: Westview, 2000), 41.

34. Actually there are some interesting parallels here between Calvinistic determinism and the radical behaviorism of B. F. Skinner. Substitute Calvin's "God" with the notion of Skinner's "environment" and it's possible to see that Skinner, who grew up as a Calvinist, is still remaining loyal to his determinist roots.

35. Clark Pinnock, "Systematic Theology," in C. Pinnock, R. Rice, J. Sanders, W. Hasker, and D. Basinger, *The Openness of God: A Biblical Challenge to the Traditional Understanding of God* (Downers Grove: InterVarsity, 1994), 103.

36. William Hasker, "A Philosophical Perspective," in Pinnock, et al., *The Openness of God,* 151.

37. Sallie McFague, *Models of God: Theology for an Ecological, Nuclear Age* (Minneapolis: Fortress Press, 1987).

38. Sallie McFague, "Is God in Charge: Creation and Providence," in William C. Placher, ed., *Essentials of Christian Theology* (Louisville: Westminster John Knox, 2003), 102.

39. Daniel Migliore, *Faith Seeking Understanding: An Introduction to Christian Theology* (Grand Rapids: Eerdmans, 1991).

40. Pinnock, "Systematic Theology," in Pinnock, et al., *The Openness of God,* 123.

41. Haught, *Responses to 101 Questions,* 5.

42. Ibid., 23.

43. Haught, *God After Darwin,* 2.

44. John Macquarrie, *Principles of Christian Theology,* 2nd ed. (New York: Scribner's 1977), 257.

45. Haught, *God After Darwin,* 36.

46. Haught, *Responses to 101 Questions,* 49–50.

47. John Polkinghorne, *Serious Talk: Science and Religion in Dialogue* (Harrisburg: Trinity International, 1995), 74.

48. Haught, *Responses to 101 Questions,* 51.

49. Ted Peters, *Playing God: Genetic Determinism and Human Freedom* (New York: Routledge, 1997), 60.

50. Haught, *Responses to 101 Questions,* 61.

51. Ibid., 103.

52. Ibid., 104.

53. Haught, *Deeper Than Darwin,* 24.

54. Ibid., 45.

55. Ibid., 53.

56. Ibid., 80.

57. Haught, *God After Darwin,* 112.

58. Jerry D. Korsmeyer, *Evolution and Eden: Balancing Original Sin and Contemporary Science* (Mahwah: Paulist, 1998), 106.

CHAPTER 2
EVIL, ETHICS, AND EVOLUTIONARY PSYCHOLOGY

1.   John F. Haught, *Deeper Than Darwin: The Prospect for Religion in the Age of Evolution* (Boulder: Westview, 2003), 103.

2.   Mikael Stenmark, *Scientism: Science, Ethics, and Religion* (Burlington, Vt.: Ashgate, 2001), viii.

3.   This interview with Dawkins can be found on the Web site for "The Evolutionist," http://www.lse.ac.uk/collections/darwin/evolutionist/dawkins.htm.

4. Edward O. Wilson, *Sociobiology: The New Synthesis* (Cambridge, Mass.: Harvard University Press, 1975), 4.

5. Harold Y. Vanderpool, "Charles Darwin and Darwinism: A Naturalized World and a Brutalized Man?" in R. Johnson, E. Wallwork, C. Green, and H. Vanderpool, *Critical Issues in Modern Religion* (Englewood Cliffs, N.J.: Prentice-Hall, 1973). 104.

6. Charles Darwin, *The Descent of Man and Selection in Relation to Sex* (New York: D. Appleton, 1986), 124–25.

7. Ibid., 100.

8. Vanderpool, "Charles Darwin and Darwinism," 102.

9. Richard Dawkins, *The Selfish Gene* (New York: Oxford University Press, 1976; 2nd ed., 1989).

10. B. R. Hergenahn and Matthew Olson, *An Introduction to Theories of Personality,* 6th ed. (Upper Saddle River, N.J: Prentice-Hall, 2003), 384.

11. David Barash, *The Whisperings Within: Evolution and the Origin of Human Nature* (New York: Penguin, 1979), 25.

12. David M. Buss, *The Murderer Next Door: Why the Mind Is Designed to Kill* (New York: Penguin, 2005), 35.

13. Barash, *Whisperings Within,* 4–5.

14. Hergenhahn and Olson, *Introduction to Theories of Personality,* 387.

15. Ibid.

16. Ibid., 390.

17. Barash, *Whisperings Within,* 225.

18. Ted Peters and Martinez Hewlett, *Evolution from Creation to New Creation* (Nashville: Abingdon, 2003), 65.

19. Don Browning, *Marriage and Modernization: How Globalization Threatens Marriage and What to Do about It,* Religion, Marriage, and Family series (Grand Rapids, Mich.: Wm. B. Eerdmans, 2003); Browning, et. al., *From Culture Wars to Common Ground: Religion and the American Family Debate,* Family, Religion, and Culture series (Louisville: Westminster John Knox, 1997).

20. Thomas Aquinas, *Summa Contra Gentiles* (London: Burns, Oates, and Washbourne, 1928), III, ii, 118.

21. Browning, *Marriage and Modernization,* 87–88.

22. Philip Hefner, *The Human Factor: Evolution, Culture, and Religion,* Theology and the Sciences series (Minneapolis: Fortress Press, 1993), chap. 12; Hefner, "The Evolution of the Created Co-Creator," in Ted Peters, ed., *Cosmos as Creation: Theology and Science in Consonance* (Nashville: Abingdon, 1989), 211–33.

23. Hefner, "The Evolution of the Created Co-Creator," 215.

24. Ibid., 230.

25. Hefner, *The Human Factor,* 32.

26. Ibid., 44; John Hick, "An Irenaen Theodicy," in Stephen Davis, ed., *Encountering Evil* (Atlanta: John Knox, 1981), 39–68.

27. Hergenhahn and Olson, *Introduction to Theories of Personality*, 412.

28. Buss, *The Murderer Next Door*, p. 23.

29. Ibid., 25.

30. Ibid., 26.

31. Ibid., 36.

32. Ibid., 37.

33. Ibid., 51.

34. Ibid., 58.

35. Ibid., 63.

36. Haught, *Deeper Than Darwin*, 105.

37. Ibid., 108.

38. William Burkett, *Creation of the Sacred: Tracks of Biology in Early Religions* (Cambridge, Mass.: Harvard University Press, 1996); Pascal Boyer, *Religion Explained: The Evolutionary Origins of Religious Thought* (New York: Basic, 2001).

39. Loyal Rue, *By the Grace of Guile: The Role of Deception in Natural History and Human Affairs* (New York: Oxford University Press, 1994), 125–26.

40. Haught, *Deeper Than Darwin*, 111.

41. Ibid., 114–15.

42. Ted Peters, *Playing God: Genetic Determinism and Human Freedom* (New York: Routledge, 1997).

43. Ibid., 7.

44. Ibid., 25.

45. Richard Lewontin, Steven Rose, and Leon Kamin, *Not in Our Genes: Biology, Ideology, and Human Nature* (New York: Pantheon, 1984), 75.

46. Peters, Playing God, 28–29.

47. Edward O. Wilson, *On Human Nature* (Cambridge, Mass.: Harvard University Press, 1978), 71.

48. Peters, *Playing God*, 44.

49. Ibid., 45.

50. Langdon Gilkey, *Through the Tempest*, ed. Jeff Pool (Minneapolis: Fortress Press, 1991), chap. 13.

51. Peters, *Playing God*, 45–46.

52. Holmes Rolston III, *Genes, Genesis, and God* (Cambridge, UK: Cambridge University Press, 1999), 367.

53. Peters and Hewlett, *Evolution from Creation to New Creation*, 63.

54. Langdon Gilkey, "Biology and Theology of Human Nature," in Holmes Rolston III, ed., *Biology, Ethics, and the Origins of Life* (Boston: Jones and Bartlett, 1955); Gilkey, *Through the Tempest*.

55. Gilkey, *Through the Tempest*, 201 n.8.

56. Ibid., 211.

57. Ibid., 213.

58. Peters and Hewitt, *Evolution from Creation to New Creation,* 69.

59. Paul Ricoeur, *Symbolism of Evil* (Boston: Beacon, 1967), 239.

60. Friedrich Schleiermacher, *The Christian Faith,* ed. H. R. Mackintosh and J. S. Stewart (Edinburgh; T&T Clark, 1928); John Hick, *Evil and the God of Love* (London: Macmillan, 1966); Matthew Fox, *Original Blessing* (Santa Fe: Bear and Co., 1983).

61. Irenaeus, "Against Heresies," in *Theological Anthropology,* trans. and ed. J. Patout Burns, *Sources of Early Christian Thought* (Minneapolis: Fortress Press, 1981), 23.

62. Stephen J. Duffy, *The Dynamics of Grace: Perspectives in Theological Anthropology* (Collegeville, Minn.: Michael Glazier, 1993), 47–48.

63. Augustine, *The City of God,* Book XIV, chap. 13, trans. Henry Bettenson (New York: Penguin, 1972), 571.

64. Irenaeus, "Against Heresies," in Burns, ed., *Theological Anthropology,* 25.

65. Hefner, *The Human Factor,* 138.

66. Ibid., 139.

67. Ian G. Barbour, *Nature, Human Nature, and God,* Theology and the Sciences series (Minneapolis: Fortress Press, 2002), 52.

68. Peters, *Playing God,* 88.

69. Gilkey, *Through the Tempest,* 207.

70. Ibid.

71. Ibid., 209.

72. Ibid., 209–10.

73. Ibid., 198.

74. Ibid., 199.

75. Ibid.

76. Robert R. Williams, "Sin and Evil," in Peter C. Hodgson and Robert H. King, ed., *Christian Theology: An Introduction to Its Traditions and Tasks* (Minneapolis: Fortress Press, 1994), 197.

CHAPTER 3
EVIL AND THE PSYCHOANALYTIC TRADITION

1. Sigmund Freud, *Civilization and Its Discontents,* trans. James Strachey (New York: Norton, 1961), 67.

2. Stephen A. Mitchell and Margaret J. Black, *Freud and Beyond: A History of Modern Psychoanalytic Thought* (New York: Basic, 1995), 19.

3. Thomas Hobbes, *Leviathan,* ed. Richard Tuck (Cambridge, UK: Cambridge University Press, 1991).

4. Freud, *Civilization and Its Discontents,* 67.

5. Ibid., 66.

6. Erich Fromm, *The Anatomy of Human Destructiveness* (New York: Henry Holt, 1973), 486–87.

7. Peter Gay, *Freud: A Life for Our Times* (New York: Norton, 1988), 395.

8. Quoted in Fromm, *Anatomy of Destructiveness,* 492.

9. Gay, Freud, 395–403.

10. Ibid.. 400.

11. Ibid., 400–01.

12. Sigmund Freud, *Beyond the Pleasure Principle,* trans. James Strachey (New York: Bantam, 1963), 71.

13. Freud, *Civilization and Its Discontents,* 70

14. Ibid., 70–71.

15. Ibid., 69.

16. Ibid.

17. For a fuller development of Freud's quasi-religion, see Don S. Browning and Terry D. Cooper, *Religious Thought and the Modern Psychologies,* 2nd ed. (Minneapolis: Fortress Press, 2004).

18. Ludwig Feuerbach, *The Essence of Christianity,* trans. George Elliot (Buffalo: Prometheus, 1989).

19. Armand M. Nicholi Jr., *The Question of God: C. S. Lewis and Sigmund Freud Debate God, Love, Sex, and the Meaning of Life* (New York: Free, 2002), 20.

20. Sigmund Freud, *The Standard Edition of the Complete Psychological Works of Sigmund Freud,* trans. James Strachley in collaboration with Anna Freud, 24 vols. (London: Hogarth, 1962), 22:159.

21. Nicholi, *The Question of God,* esp. chap. 2.

22. Paul Tillich, "The Theological Significance of Existentialism and Psychoanalysis," in Perry LeFevre, ed., *The Meaning of Health* (Chicago: Exploration, 1984).

23. Ibid., 88–89.

24. Ibid., 89–91.

25. For a fuller development of this theme, see Terry D. Cooper, *Paul Tillich and Psychology: Historic and Contemporary Explorations in Theology, Psychotherapy, and Ethics* (Macon, Ga.: Mercer University Press, 2005), esp. chap. 1.

26. Tillich, "The Theological Significance of Existentialism and Psychoanalysis," 89–90.

27. Ibid., 88–89.

28. Reinhold Niebuhr, "Human Creativity and Self-Concern in Freud's Thought," in Benjamin Nelson, ed., *Freud and the Twentieth Century* (Gloucester, Mass.: Peter Smith, 1974).

29. Reinhold Niebuhr, *The Nature and Destiny of Man,* 2 vols. (New York: Scribners, 1964).

30. Browning and Cooper, *Religious Thought and the Modern Psychologies,* 25–26.

31. Erich Fromm, *The Heart of Man: Its Genius for Good and Evil* (New York: Harper & Row, 1964).

32. Ibid., 20–21.

33. Ibid., 20.

34. Ibid., 21.

35. Ibid., 27.

36. Ibid., 29.

37. Ibid., 30.

38. Ibid., 32.

39. Ibid., 33.

40. Quoted in Fromm, *The Heart of Man,* 49.

41. Fromm, *The Heart of Man,* 50–51.

42. See Browning and Cooper, *Religious Thought and the Modern Psychologies;* also, Terry D. Cooper, *Sin, Pride, and Self-Acceptance: The Problem of Identity in Psychology and Theology* (Downers Grove: InterVarsity, 2003).

43. Fromm, *The Heart of Man,* 77.

44. Ibid., 82.

45. Ibid., 95.

46. Ibid., 106–08.

47. For an excellent study of Fromm's differences with Tillich, see Guy Hammond, *Man in Estrangment: A Comparison of the Thought of Paul Tillich and Erich Fromm* (Nashville: Vanderbilt University Press, 1965); see also, Cooper, *Paul Tillich and Psychology,* esp. chap. 3.

48. Hammond, *Man in Estrangement,* 76.

49. Tillich, "Erich Fromm's The Sane Society" in LeFevre, ed., *The Meaning of Health,* 96–99.

50. Ibid., 96

51. Hammond, *Man in Estrangment,* 63.

52. Ernest Becker, *The Denial of Death* (New York: Free, 1973).

53. Ernest Becker, *Escape from Evil* (New York: Free, 1975).

54. Becker, *Escape From Evil,* xvii.

55. Becker, *The Denial of Death,* 4.

56. Ibid., 4–6.

57. Ibid., 16.

58. Paul Tillich, *The Courage to Be* (New Haven: Yale University Press, 1952), 43.

59. Becker, *The Denial of Death,* 26.

60. Ibid., 31.

61. Ibid., 66.

62. Ibid., 60, author's emphasis.

63. Becker, *Escape from Evil,* 64.

64. Ibid., 96.

65. Ibid., 111.

66. Ibid., 136, author's emphasis.

67. Ibid., 158.

68. Donald Evans, "Ernest Becker's Denial of Death and Escape From Evil," *Religious Studies Review 5,* no. 1 (Jan. 1979): 25–34.

69. Ibid., 27.

70. Ibid., 28.

71. Ibid.

72. Ibid.

73. Ibid., 29.

CHAPTER 4
HUMAN POTENTIAL AND HUMAN DESTRUCTIVENESS

1. Aaron Beck, *Prisoners of Hate: The Cognitive Basis of Anger, Hostility, and Violence* (New York: HarperCollins, 1999).

2. John Sanford, *Evil: The Shadow Side of Reality* (New York: Crossroad, 1981; 2d ed., 1989); *The Strange Trial of Mr. Hyde: A New Look at the Nature of Human Evil* (San Francisco: Harper & Row, 1987).

3. David W. Augsburger, *Hate-Work: Working Through the Pain and Pleasures of Hate* (Louisville: Westminster John Knox, 2004).

4. Beck, *Prisoners of Hate.*

5. David D. Burns, *Feeling Good: The New Mood Therapy* (New York: New American, 1980), 46.

6. Beck, *Prisoners of Hate,* 42.

7. Ibid., 43.

8. Ibid., 48.

9. Ibid., 44.

10. Ibid., 27.

11. Ibid., 144.

12. Ibid., 151.

13. Ibid., 161.

14. Ibid., 73.

15. Ibid., 6.

16. Ibid., 15.

17. Ibid., 26.

18. Ibid., 125.

19. Ibid., 126.

20. Ibid., 126.

21. Sam Keen, *Faces of the Enemy: Reflections of the Hostile Imagination* (San Francisco: HarperSanFrancisco, 1986).

22. Beck, *Prisoners of Hate,* 204.

23. Ibid., 227.

24. Ibid., 231–32.

25. Ibid., 34–35.

26. Sanford, *Evil.*

27. Sanford, *The Strange Trial of Mr. Hyde.*

28. Sanford, *Evil,* 1.

29. Ibid., 7.

30. Ibid., 15.

31. Carl Jung, *Collected Works,* vol. 2 (Princeton: Princeton University Press, 1969).

32. Sanford, *Evil,* 69.

33. Ibid.

34. Ibid., 71.

35. Ibid.

36. Ibid., 72.

37. Ibid., 74.

38. Ibid., 75.

39. Ibid., 81.

40. Robert Louis Stevenson, *Dr. Jekyll and Mr. Hyde* (1886; New York: Bantam, 1981).

41. Sheldon Kopp, *Mirror, Mask, and Shadow: The Risks and Rewards of Self-Acceptance* (New York: Bantam, 1980), 16.

42. Sanford, *Evil,* 103.

43. Carl G. Jung, *The Visions Seminars,* Book One (Zurich: Spring, 1976), 213.

44. See esp. Karen Horney, *Neurosis and Human Growth* (New York:Norton, 1950).

45. Augsburger, *Hate-Work.*

46. Ibid., 3.

47. Ibid.

48. Ibid., 131.

49. Ibid., 10.

50. Ibid., 11–12.

51. Ibid., 12.

52. Ibid., 21.

53. Ibid., 33.

54. Melanie Klein, "Love, Guilt, and Reparation," in R. E. Money-Kyrle, ed., *The Writings of Melanie Klein,* vol. 1 (1937; New York: Macmillan, 1975).

55. Christopher F. Monte, *Behind the Masks: An Introduction to Theories of Personality,* 6th ed. (Fort Worth: Harcourt Brace, 1999), 263.

56. Klein, "Love, Guilt, and Reparation," 306.

57. Augsburger, *Hate-Work,* 57.

58. Ibid., 62.

59. Richard Galston, "The Longest Pleasure: A Psychoanalytic Study of Hatred," *International Journal of Psychoanalysis* 68 (1987): 371–78.

60. The word resentment is being used somewhat differently here than it is in Alcoholics Anonymous literature. A.A. has consistently held that resentments are a "luxury" alcoholics cannot afford. By this they refer to ruminating, score-keeping preoccupations that threaten sobriety. I am in full agreement with this wisdom. I refer instead to resentment as simply the capacity to recognize and not like that an injustice has been done. This differs from the toxic experience of resentment insightfully discussed in twelve-step groups.

61. James W. McClendon, Jr., *Ethics: Systematic Theology,* vol. 1 (Nashville: Abingdon, 1986), 225.

62. Augsburger, *Hate-Work,* 72.

63. Ibid., 78.

64. Ibid., 99.

65. Ibid., 116.

66. Paul Tillich, *Systematic Theology,* vol. 3 (Chicago: University of Chicago Press, 1963), 102–06.

67. H. Richard Niebuhr, *The Meaning of Revelation* (New York: Macmillan, 1941).

68. Ibid., x.

69. Augsburger, *Hate-Work,* 132.

70. Ibid., 135.

71. Keen, *Faces of the Enemy,* 21.

72. Augsburger, *Hate-Work,* 214.

73. Rollo May, *The Meaning of Anxiety* (New York: Norton, 1950); Paul Tillich, *The Courage to Be* (New Haven: Yale University Press, 1952).

74. Ernest Becker, *The Denial of Death* (New York: Free, 1973).

75. Albert Ellis, *The Case against Religiosity* (Austin: American Atheist, 1980).

76. See esp. Peter Berger, *The Sacred Canopy: Elements of a Sociological Theory of Religion* (New York: Doubleday, 1967); Terry D. Cooper, "The Plausibility of a New Self: Self-Esteem from a Sociology of Knowledge Perspective," *Counseling and Values 35,* no. 1 (October 1990), 31–38.

77. Keen, *Faces of the Enemy.*

78. Alfred Adler, *Understanding Human Nature,* trans. W. Beran Wolfe (1927; Greenwich, Ct.: Fawcett, 1954).

79. Edwin Schur, *The Awareness Trap: Self-Absorption Instead of Social Change* (New York: McGraw-Hill, 1976).

CHAPTER 5
ORDINARY PEOPLE AND MALEVOLENT CIRCUMSTANCES

1. Roy Baumeister, *Evil: Inside Human Violence and Cruelty* (New York: Freeman, 1997), 322.

2. Stanley Milgram, *Obedience and Authority* (New York: Harper & Row, 1974), 6.

3. Quoted in David Myers, *Social Psychology,* 5th ed. (New York: McGraw-Hill, 1996), 243.

4. Quoted in ibid., 251.

5. Philip G. Zimbardo, "A Situationist Perspective on the Psychology of Evil: Understanding How Good People are Transformed into Perpetrators," in Arthur G. Miller, ed., *The Social Psychology of Good and Evil* (New York: Guilford, 2004), 21.

6. Ibid., 25.

7. Ibid., 26.

8. Ibid., 47.

9. Ibid.

10. Ibid.

11. Hannah Arendt, *Eichmann in Jerusalem: A Report on the Banality of Evil* (New York: Viking, 1963), 276.

12. Stanley Milgram, "Behavioral Study of Obedience," *Journal of Abnormal and Social Psychology* 67 (1963): 375–77.

13. Allan Fenigstein, "Were Obedience Pressures a Factor in the Holocaust?" *Analyze and Kritik* 20 (1998): 68, 71.

14. D. R. Mandel, "Instigators of Genocide," in L. Newman and R. Erber, ed., *Understanding Genocide: The Social Psychology of the Holocaust* (New York: Oxford University Press, 2002), 91.

15. J. P. Sabini, M. Siepmann, and J. Stein, "Author's Response to Commentaries," *Psychological Inquiry* 12 (2001): 46.

16. L. Berkowitz, "Evil Is More than Banal: Situationism and the Concept of Evil," *Personality and Social Psychology Review* 3 (1999): 250.

17. Mandel, "Instigators of Genocide," 279.

18. Quoted in Miller, *The Social Psychology of Good and Evil*, 232.

19. Arthur Miller, "What Can the Milgram Obedience Experiments Tell Us about the Holocaust?" in Miller, ed., *The Social Psychology of Good and Evil*, 193–239.

20. Ibid., 201.

21. Ibid.

22. Baumeister, *Evil: Inside Human Violence and Cruelty*, 17.

23. Ibid., 20.

24. Ibid., 38–39.

25. Ibid., 47.

26. Ibid., 54.

27. Ibid., 54–55.

28. Ibid., 90.

29. Ibid., 135–36.

30. Ibid., 141.

31. Michael H. Kernis, "The Roles of Stability and Level of Self-Esteem in Psychological Functioning," in Roy Baumeister, ed., *Self-Esteem: The Puzzle of Low Self-Regard* (New York: Plenum, 1993), 167–82.

32. Baumeister, *Evil: Inside Human Violence and Cruelty*, 149.

33. Ibid., 150.

34. Ibid., 152.

35. Dan Olweus, "Bullying at School: Long-term Outcomes for the Victims and an Effective School-Based Intervention Program" in L. R. Huesmann, ed., *Aggressive Behavior: Current Perspectives* (New York: Plenum, 1994), 97–130.

36. Baumeister, *Evil: Inside Human Violence and Cruelty*, 154.

37. Ibid., 181.

38. Ibid., 205.

39. Edwin Schur, *The Awareness Trap: Self-Absorption Instead of Social Change* (New York: McGraw-Hill, 1977); Christopher Lasch, *The Culture of Narcissism: American Life in an Age of Diminishing Expectations* (New York: Norton, 1978); Paul Vitz, *Psychology as Religion: The Cult of Self-Worship* (Grand Rapids: Eerdmans, 1977); Martin L. Gross, *The Psychological Society* (New York: Simon & Schuster, 1978); Michael Wallach and Lise Wallach, *Psychology's Sanction for Selfishness* (San Francisco: Freeman, 1983); Robert Bellah, Richard Madsen, William H. Sullivan, Ann Swindler, and Steven M. Tipton, *Habits of the Heart: Individualism and Commitment in American Life* (Berkeley: University of California Press, 1985); Phillip Cushman, *Constructing the Self, Constructing America: A Cultural History of Psychotherapy* (Cambridge, Mass.: Perseus, 1995); and Kenneth J. Gergen, *The Saturated Self: Dilemmas of Identity in Contemporary Life* (New York: Basic, 1991).

40. See Terry D. Cooper, "Karl Marx and Group Therapy: An Old Warning About a New Phenomena," *Counseling and Values* 29, no. 1 (1984): 22–26.

41. Christopher Lasch, "Sacrificing Freud," *New York Times* Magazine, Feb. 22, 1976, 11.

42. Don Browning and I have argued that most of these therapies are actually "quasi-religious" rather than "antireligious." They each carry assumptions about the ultimate context of our lives, even if that context places the self at the center. See Browning and Cooper, *Religious Thought and the Modern Psychologies,* 2nd ed. (Minneapolis: Fortress Press, 2004).

43. Lasch, *The Culture of Narcissism,* 26–27.

44. Vitz, *Psychology as Religion.*

45. Vitz has been heavily influenced here by Donald Campbell, "On the Conflict Between Biological and Social Evolution and Between Psychology and Moral Tradition," *American Psychologist* 30 (Dec. 1974): 1103–126.

46. Gross, *The Psychological Society,* 44.

47. Ibid?

48. See Jerome Frank, *Persuasion and Healing,* rev. ed. (New York: Schocken, 1974).

49. Browning and Cooper, *Religious Thought and the Modern Psychologies,* chap. 4.

50. Don S. Browning, *The Moral Context of Pastoral Care* (Philadelphia: Westminster, 1976).

51. Ibid., 27.

52. William J. Doherty, *Soul Searching: Why Psychotherapy Must Promote Moral Responsibility* (New York: Basic, 1995).

53. Ibid., 7–8.

54. Ibid., 11–12.

55. Ibid., 27.

CHAPTER 6
INDIVIDUAL AND SYSTEMIC EVIL

1. Nancy Ramsay, ed., *Pastoral Care and Counseling: Redefining the Paradigms* (Nashville: Abingdon, 2004).

2. Audre Lorde, *Sister Outsider: Essays and Speeches* (Freedom, Calif.: Crossing, 1984), 112.

3. Eleazar S. Fernandez, *Reimagining the Human: Theological Anthropology in Response to Systemic Evil* (St. Louis: Chalice, 2004), 37.

4. Langdon Gilkey, *Shantung Compound* (New York: Harper & Row, 1966).

5. Ibid., 75–76.

6. Ibid., 77.

7. Ibid., 78.

8. Ibid., 79.

9. Ibid., 84.

10. Ibid., 114.

11. Ibid., 114–15.

12. Ibid., 116.

13. Ibid., 230.

14. Ibid., 234.

15. Reinhold Niebuhr, *The Nature and Destiny of Man,* 2 vols. (New York: Scribners, 1964).

16. Ibid., 1:150.

17. Ibid., 1:182–83.

18. For a fuller account of this, see Donald S. Browning and Terry D. Cooper, *Religious Thought and the Modern Psychologies,* 2d. ed. (Minneapolis: Fortress Press, 2004), chap. 3.

19. For a more detailed account, see Terry D. Cooper, *Sin, Pride, and Self-Acceptance: The Problem of Identity in Theology and Psychology* (Downers Grove: InterVarsity, 2003).

20. Augustine, *City of God,* Book XIV, trans. Henry Bettenson (New York: Penguin, 1972), 573.

21. Niebuhr, *The Nature and Destiny of Man,* 1:55.

22. Ibid., 1:162.

23. Ibid., 1:194.

24. Ibid., 1:194–95.

25. Ibid., 1:195.

26. Ibid., 1:199.

27. Ibid., 1:200.

28. Edward Farley, "Sin/Sins," in Rodney Hunter, ed., *A Dictionary of Pastoral Care and Counseling,* exp. ed. (Nashville: Abingdon, 2005), 1173–176.

29. Ramsay, ed., *Pastoral Care and Counseling: Redefining the Paradigms.*

30. Valerie Saiving, "The Human Situation: A Feminist View," in Carol P. Christ and Judith Plaskow, ed., *Womanspirit Rising: A Feminist Reader in Religion* (San Francisco: Harper & Row, 1979).

31. Daphne Hampson, "Reinhold Niebuhr on Sin: A Critique," in R. Harries, ed., *Reinhold Niebuhr and the Issues of Our Time* (Grand Rapids: Eerdmans, 1986); Susan Nelson Dunfee, "The Sin of Hiding: A Feminist Critique of Reinhold Niebuhr's Account of the Sin of Pride," *Soundings* 65, no. 3 (1982): 316–26; Judith Plaskow, *Sex, Sin, and Grace: Women's Experience and the Theologies of Reinhold Niebuhr and Paul Tillich* (Lanham, Md.: University Press of America, 1980).

32. Plaskow, *Sex, Sin, and Grace*, 68.

33. Ibid., 64–65.

34. Dunfee, "The Sin of Hiding," 321.

35. Rosemary Radford Ruether, *Sexism and God-Talk: Toward a Feminist Theology* (Boston: Beacon, 1983; rev. ed., 1993), 180–81.

36. Marjorie Hewitt Suchocki, *The Fall to Violence: Original Sin in Relational Theology* (New York: Continuum, 1995).

37. Ibid., 12.

38. Ibid., 14.

39. Ibid., 17.

40. Ibid., 32.

41. Ibid., 107–08.

42. Ibid., 87.

43. Nancy Ramsay, "A Time of Ferment and Redefinition," in Ramsay, ed., *Pastoral Care and Counseling: Redefining the Paradigms*, 16.

44. Larry Kent Graham, *Care of Persons, Care of Worlds* (Nashville: Abingdon, 1992).

45. Ibid., 71.

46. Michael Nichols, *The Self in the System: Exploring the Links of Family Therapy* (New York: Brunner/Mazel, 1987).

47. Ibid., 35–36.

48. Ibid., 9.

49. H. Liddle and G. Saba, "Systemic Chic: Family Therapy's New Wave," *Family Therapy News* 9 (July 1981): 12.

50. Stanton L. Jones and Richard E. Butman, *Modern Psychotherapies: A Christian Appraisal* (Downers Grove: Intervarsity, 1991), 361.

51. Donald Capps, *The Depleted Self: Sin in a Narcissistic Age* (Minneapolis: Fortress Press, 1993), chap. 5.

52. Ruether, *Sexism and God-Talk*, 164.

53 Langdon Gilkey, *Reaping the Whirlwind: A Christian Interpretation of History* (Eugene: Wipf & Stock, 2000), 236–38.

54. Ibid., 236–37.

55. Niebuhr, *The Nature and Destiny of Man*, 1:197.

CHAPTER 7
CONCLUDING THOUGHTS

1. Richard J. Bernstein, *Radical Evil: A Philosophical Investigation* (Cambridge, UK: Polity, 2002), 225.

2. Ibid., 228–35.

3. David Tracy, "Saving from Evil: Salvation and Evil Today," in David Tracy and Herman Haring, ed., *The Fascination of Evil* (London: SCM, 1998), 107.

INDEX